ORIGINS OF MASS COMMUNICATIONS RESEARCH DURING THE AMERICAN COLD WAR: EDUCATIONAL EFFECTS AND CONTEMPORARY IMPLICATIONS

D1477367

Sociocultural, Political, and Historical Studies in Education
Joel Spring, Editor

Spring • The Cultural Transformation of a Native American Family and Its Tribe 1763–1995

Reagan • Non-Western Educational Traditions: Alternative Approaches to Educational Thought and Practice

Peshkin • Places of Memory: Whitman's Schools and Native American Communities

Spring • Political Agendas for Education: From the Christian Coalition to the Green Party

Nespor • Tangled Up in School: Politics, Space, Bodies, and Signs in the Educational Process

Weinberg • Asian-American Education: Historical Background and Current Realities

Books (Ed.) • Invisible Children in the Society and Its Schools

Shapiro/Purpel (Eds.) • Critical Social Issues in American Education: Transformation in a Postmodern World, Second Edition

Lipka/Mohatt/The Cuilistet Group • Transforming the Culture of Schools: Yup'ik Eskimo Examples

Benham/Heck • Culture and Educational Policy in Hawai'i: The Silencing of Native Voices

Spring • Education and the Rise of the Global Economy

Pugach • On the Border of Opportunity: Education, Community, and Language at the U.S.–Mexico Line

Hones/Cha • Educating New Americans: Immigrant Lives and Learning

Gabbard (Ed.) • Knowledge and Power in the Global Economy: Politics and the Rhetoric of School Reform

Glander • Origins of Mass Communications Research During the American Cold War: Educational Effects and Contemporary Implications

Nieto (Ed.) • Puerto Rican Students in U.S. Schools

Benham/Cooper (Eds.) • Indigenous Educational Models for Contemporary Practice: In Our Mother's Voice

Spring • The Universal Right to Education: Justification, Definition, and Guidelines

Reagan • Non-Western Educational Traditions: Alternative Approaches to Educational Thought and Practice, Second Edition

Peshkin • Permissable Advantage? The Moral Consequences of Elite Schooling

ORIGINS OF MASS COMMUNICATIONS RESEARCH DURING THE AMERICAN COLD WAR: EDUCATIONAL EFFECTS AND CONTEMPORARY IMPLICATIONS

Timothy Glander
Nazareth College of Rochester

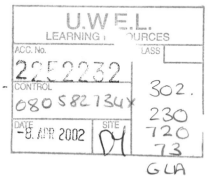

2000

LAWRENCE ERLBAUM ASSOCIATES, PUBLISHERS
Mahwah, New Jersey   London

Lawrence Erlbaum Associates, Inc., Publishers
10 Industrial Avenue
Mahwah, NJ 07430

Cover design by Kathryn Houghtaling Lacey

Library of Congress Cataloging-in-Publication Data

Glander, Timothy Richard, 1960–   .
Origins of mass communications research during the American Cold
    War : educational effects and contemporary implications / Timo-
    thy Glander.
        p. cm.
    Includes bibliographical references and index.
ISBN 0-8058-2734-X — ISBN 0-8058-2735-8(pbk.)
1. Mass media—Research—United States—History. 2. Mass media
    in education—United States. I. Title.
P91.5.U5G57 1999
302.23'07'2073—dc21   99-38568
                                                          CIP

Books published by Lawrence Erlbaum Associates are printed on
acid-free paper, and their bindings are chosen for strength and dura-
bility.

Printed in the United States of America
10   9   8   7   6   5   4   3   2   1

To my parents

Contents

Preface

The use of history is to rescue from oblivion the lost causes of the past.
—Benjamin Nelson, cited in Goodman, 1960

This book is a critical examination of the origins of mass communications research from the perspective of an educational historian. It is not a comprehensive and exhaustive treatment of the history of communication study, nor could it be, given the vast and varied nature of this relatively new field. Nevertheless, the book does attempt to document, contextualize, and interpret the dominant expressions of this field during the time in which it became rooted in U.S. academic life, and tries to give articulation to the larger historical forces that gave the field of communications research its fundamental purposes. Future historians, equipped with greater historical distance and record, will be able to flesh out details and provide a more complete overview; still, they will need to confront the roots of the field and look squarely at the legacy of those roots in order to develop any kind of adequate and honest understanding. I contend that it is now possible to get a bearing on those roots, and to see the major directions of their growth. This book aims to be a small contribution to that understanding.

The history of communications research has been written almost entirely from within the field of communication studies and, as a result, tends to refrain from asking troubling foundational questions about the origins of the field. I think there are some fairly obvious reasons for this, having to do with the natural tendency of people to simply accept the dominant values and practices that guided their own education and eventual assimilation into a field. When one becomes acclimated to the governing worldview, it becomes difficult to ask about fundamental purposes, or even to see such questions as meaningful and important. However, I think there is something far more intentional at work in many standard histories of communications research, which suggests a more deliberate obfuscation about the origins of the field. I argue that deception of various kinds was at the heart of much early communication research, and continues to be reflected in many "in-house" historical interpretations of this research. As a work in the history of education, this book endeavors to examine the origins of the field from a vantage point that allows such foundational questions to be raised.

There should be no doubt about why the origins of communications research should be of interest to historians of education, despite the continued tendency of much scholarship in the history of education to focus narrowly on schools. Common sense should indicate the necessity of attending to other institutions that serve an educative function, and that in various ways redefine traditional notions of schooling and learning in light of their activities. Of course, the mass media represent the dominant force in this regard. Inquiring into how earlier educators responded to the emerging mass media, how their hopes and fears about these mass media were translated into particular research approaches, how powerful political and economic interests influenced the direction and legitimization of that research, as well as many other related questions, should be of central interest to historians of education. It is precisely because the educational meaning of the mass media remains so problematic that a study of this past should be of relevance to contemporary educators. Such a study might reveal not only why certain views of the mass media dominate, but also why alternative perspectives were pushed to the periphery. It is hoped, then, that this book has something to say to teachers, teacher educators, and others involved in educational matters, as well as to students of communication and sociology who are interested in the history of their fields.

But there is another, perhaps even more basic, reason that educators should focus their inquiry in this direction. Education and communication are fundamentally linked, inescapably affiliated in theory and in practice. Educational philosophers from Socrates to Dewey to Freire have recognized this and have sought to make this relationship clear. Education and communication can not be separated, although our present academic arrangements make believe that they can be so partitioned. Contemporary organization of knowledge suggests that education and communication are distinct phenomena that can be studied and practiced in isolation from one another. This book tells part of the story of how and why this division occurred, what occasioned this divorce, and how the emergence and ascendance of the new field of communication affected educational matters in the 20th century. The ultimate objective of this book is to recover an understanding that posits the essential connection between education and communication, and is able to do so cognizant of the interests that have benefited from this cleavage.

The primary approach in this text is to examine the intersection between the individual biographies of significant leaders in the communications field and the larger historical context in which they lived and worked. Individuals are clearly influenced by the dominant historical forces of their time; some individuals, by dint of their particular place in the social order, are able to exert significant influence on the nature of that order. This much is a truism, but it seems necessary to restate it during a time of general retreat from even this simple proposition. The goal is to get a measure of how one's life experiences during an historical period shape the kind of person one becomes, without losing sight of the actual human agency and freedom that one possesses. For this study, it means recognizing that key figures in the origins of communication study, although in part shaped by their experiences, acted in ways that reflected their intentionality. Such an approach should result in neither simple glorification nor condemnation of their actions, but rather make clear that the kind of world they helped to create was neither accidental or entirely beyond the realm of deliberate human action. Such an historical approach, it seems to me, is also a necessary precondition for any view that values and demands freedom and responsibility in the present context.

The factors giving rise to communication study and research on university campuses are as complicated and pervasive as those factors shaping the United States in the 20th century—the advent of new communication technologies, the rise of the behavioral sciences, the demands of two world wars, and so on—and there are no easy ways to account for these factors or to evaluate their significance. Nevertheless, certain general themes and tendencies come to light as the story behind the origins of communication study begins to unfold. It is clear that circumstances surrounding World War II were highly significant both in the institutionalization of communications study and in shaping the field's dominant paradigm. The particular shape that communications research held during the war was, in large part, the result of forces alive in the culture prior to the war. Therefore, we begin with an analysis of those forces at work prior to World War II that prompted people to look closely at the role of the mass media in society.

Central among these forces was the concern with the growing use of propaganda that seemed to develop as a consequence of World War I. In the aftermath of World War I, many people became worried about the social uses of propaganda, while others saw in the techniques of propaganda the opportunity by which greater social order, conformity, and efficiency could be achieved. Thus, a debate emerged, which raised fundamental questions about the role of propaganda in a democratic society and the proper educational response to the new mass media. Chapter 1, "Education and Propaganda: The Propaganda Debate Between the Wars," reviews the contours of this debate and argues that the debate was resolved not by the cogency of the arguments brought to bear on the issue but because of the exigencies relating to World War II. Those individuals interested in utilizing propaganda in the conduct of the war orchestrated a semantic shift away from the term *propaganda*, which had come to possess negative connotations, to a series of more neutral-sounding terms, the most common being *mass communications*. By the onset of World War II, then, *mass communications research* was the new term to describe what were previously regarded as attempts to develop effective propaganda techniques.

Chapter 2, "Communications Research Comes of Age," looks at the development of this research during World War II, and its extension into the Cold War period that followed. The construction of wartime government propaganda and intelligence agencies, which required this mass communications research, is reviewed. The war against fascism legitimized the work of mass communications researchers, and it helped to facilitate important personal connections among these researchers. During the period of the Cold War, these mass communications researchers profited from the personal and institutional contacts they made. The end of the war forced these researchers back into the university fold, yet they continued to engage in the same variety of research, supported predominantly by the large national security-related contracts awarded to universities during this period.

Chapter 3, "The Social Ideas of American Mass Communication Experts," borrows and reworks the title from a 1935 book by Merle Curti, and offers a preliminary analysis of the work of five central figures in this growing army of mass communications research: Bernard Berelson, Frank Stanton, Hadley Cantril, Carl Hovland, and Stuart Dodd. By nearly all accounts, these five researchers were major figures in establishing communications research on university campuses during the postwar years, and they have had enduring influence on the field. Chapter 3 outlines the contributions of these individuals to the field. Although other individuals could have been chosen in this analysis, these five were selected both because of the breadth of their involvement in the field and because of the disciplinary diversity they represent. These short professional biographies might serve as a basis from which a more extensive treatment of the influence of these individuals on the origins of mass communications research could be developed.

Chapters 4 and 5 undertake an analysis of the two most important early mass communications researchers and the research bureaus they directed. Paul F. Lazarsfeld was an undisputed leader in the field, although most reviews of his work have been written by his former students and colleagues and, as a consequence, are not very probing or critical. Lazerfeld's Bureau of Applied Social Research at Columbia University was in many ways a prototype for the other mass communications units that were established after World War II. The influences on his research in mass communications are discussed in chapter 4, as is some of the significant work conducted with the Bureau. As a mathematician, an Austrian émigré, and former socialist, Lazarsfeld's background stands in sharp contrast to that of Wilbur Schramm, who is discussed in chapter 5. "Wilbur Schramm and the Founding of Communication Study" examines the early work of the major figure in establishing the field of communications. In the words of Everett Rogers (1994), Schramm "was *the* founder of the field, the first individual to identify himself as a communication scholar; he created the first academic degree-granting programs with *communication* in their name; and he trained the first generation of communication scholars. . . At Illinois, Wilbur Schramm set in motion the patterns of scholarly work in communication study that continue to this day" (p. 29). Schramm was educated in the neo-humanist tradition of Irving Babbitt, Paul Elmer More, and Norman Foerster, and in many ways inherited its aristocratic orientation and emphasis on persuasion. The neo-humanist influences on Schramm are discussed in chapter 5, and an overview of some his research projects within the Institute of Communications Research at the University of Illinois is provided.

Despite the great differences in backgrounds among certain key leaders in communications research, important commonalities existed among them. Most important, these researchers shared a common vision about the need to develop techniques by which the mass media could be used to most effectively shape the opinions of an emerging mass society. This, it is argued, was their raison d'être, and was the major defining feature of communications research at mid-century. Chapter 6, "The Universe of Discourse in Which We Grew Up," juxtaposes this research with the work of those who were critical of the new mass media, and who theorized about the emergence of a mass society. C. Wright Mills's conceptualization of the mass society is explored here, as is the educational response to the mass society created by William Biddle at Earlham College in the late 1940s and 1950s. The concluding chapter discusses the way mass communications research was utilized to deny the social impact of the mass media and to refute the potentially transformative concept of the mass society. A few preliminary questions are also asked here, regarding what relevance such a theory of a mass society might have for an understanding of contemporary educational and social problems.

Conceived in the turbulent years before World War II, put into operation during that war, and institutionalized as a legitimate field of study during the Cold War, mass communications research was the by-product of an increasingly precarious and insecure world. Now that the Cold War is over, however, the social climate that created and sustained this research would also appear to be over. It is now time to examine the origins of this research and to see how it has influenced our thinking about education and the mass media.

ACKNOWLEDGMENTS

I wish to thank the many people who have assisted me in various ways on this project. The work began as a dissertation under the advisorship of Professor Clarence J. Karier, and I am indebted to him for his skillful guidance throughout the process. James Anderson, Ralph Page, and Philip Zodhiates also served on that dissertation committee and provided key insight during the early stages of this work. Many people read portions of the manuscript in its numerous stages and have offered invaluable criticism. Thanks especially to: Sally DeCarolis, Sean Delthony, John Marciano, Leigh O'Brien, Walter Price, and Christine Shea. Sally DeCarolis deserves a special note of thanks for her assistance in formatting the footnotes and bibliography. Various parts of the manuscript were given at the annual conferences of the American Educational Studies Association, American Educational Research Association, History of Education Society, and New York State Foundations of Education Association; the manuscript is stronger due to the critical responses received at these conferences. I would like to give a special acknowledgment to my colleagues with the New York State Foundations of Education Association, who have kept alive a culture conducive to critical inquiry and open dialogue that is sadly too rare today. Nazareth College of Rochester—especially Kay Marshman, Mary Palamar, and Dennis Silva—has been supportive of this project from the start, providing me with research assistance and release time. The staff of the Nazareth College Lorette Wilmot Library has been particularly helpful in tracking down my requests for obscure materials. I am very appreciative of the strong encouragement, wise advice, and patience I've received from Naomi Silverman at Lawrence Erlbaum Associates, and Joel Spring, the editor of the Sociocultural, Political, and Historical Studies in Education series. I would also like to thank Debbie Ruel and the production staff at Lawrence Erlbaum Associates for their fine work in producing the book. Of course, I am solely responsible for the contents of this book.

Portions of this text have been adapted from previously published material. Part of chapter 5 originally appeared as "Wilbur Schramm and the Founding of Communication Study," in *Educational Theory* 46 (Summer 1996): 373-393. Part of chapter 6 originally appeared as "C. Wright Mills and the Rise of Psychological Illiteracy," in *Educational Change* (Spring 1996): 51–62. I thank the editors and publishers of these journals for permission to adapt and reprint this material.

Finally, my deepest expression of gratitude must go to my wife, Suzanne Kolodziej, and our daughter, Maria-Lian. They have made many sacrifices so that I could complete the work. They have been a constant source of hope.

REFERENCES

Goodman, P. (1960). *Growing up absurd*. New York: Vintage Books.
Rogers, E. M. (1994). *A history of communication study: A biographical approach*. New York: The Free Press.

CHAPTER ONE

Education and Propaganda: The Propaganda Debate Between the Wars

Educators can be controlled simply by controlling their reading matter.
—Sir Gilbert Parker, 1918[1]

WORLD WAR II was the watershed; it is here that one can observe the forces demarcating what could have been from what actually came to be in so many aspects of U.S. life. Certainly this is the case with the study of communications. Communication was seldom conceptualized as a distinct area of study prior to World War II; after that, the field grew rapidly on U.S. campuses, shaped largely by the perceived exigencies of the war. Yet even before the German fascists invaded Poland in 1939, the technologies of mass communications and the uses to which they were being put became a prominent interest inside and outside of academic circles. The expansion of radio, like the expansion of motion pictures, had been swift on the North American continent. In 1922, there were only approximately 400,000 radio sets in use in the United States. Just 18 years later, in 1940, there were almost 51 million radios in operation.[2] This kind of technological expansion alone would warrant serious reflection on the kinds of social changes radio affected. However, a host of additional concerns also prompted people to turn their attention to the mass media and communications in general. The massive and largely effective propaganda campaigns in the early radio and film days of World War I, the increasingly refined advertising techniques, the birth and expansion of fascist societies, the growth of the use of public opinion polls, and the ascendance of the public relations (PR) expert in major organizational and institutional activities were among the forces that caused people to look at propaganda and the mass media more closely. By 1935, Harold D. Lasswell, Ralph D. Casey, and Bruce Lannes Smith listed more than 3,000 citations in their bibliography of articles relating to propaganda and communications.[3]

This intense interest in the mass media during the years between the two world wars was manifested in a wide variety of ideological perspectives, and many people expressed their ideas in popular and academic journals concerning the role, legitimacy, and likely impact of the phenomena of propaganda and the growth of the new mass communication technologies. Because these perspectives were not of one piece, a significant debate ensued that raised fundamental questions about the very nature of society and the individual, and the proper relationship of the new mass media to both. This debate, largely anchored around the issue of propaganda, existed in a lively and open fashion throughout the interwar years and it represents, arguably, the last comprehensive attempt to question the role of the mass media in a democratic society. Its resolution, more the consequence of the historical circumstances surrounding World War II than the force of the various theoretical perspectives provided, became an important component of the ideological foundation of communications study at mid-century.[4]

Many of the social and cultural changes experienced by the participants in the propaganda debate are largely imperceptible to us today, and this makes it difficult to understand the urgency with which this debate was conducted. It is hard for us to imagine just what a genuine community life might entail, let alone the experience of actually losing one's rootedness in a localized community. For instance, we take for granted a highly centralized and powerful national government; a ubiquitous, celebrity-rife electronic media; and an equally ubiquitous consumer culture. We take for granted the view of selfhood, the psychological characteristics, and the values that follow from these circumstances. Nevertheless, to the people of the early part of this century—people who witnessed the enormous social and cultural changes that conditioned the emergence of a mass society—these things were by no means certain, and from many perspectives they were by no means desirable. The new communication technologies, as well as the propaganda techniques associated with them, were seen as powerful causative agents in society, and discussions concerning their proper use and control were of monumental importance.[5] As such, the propaganda debate provided the arena where these concerns were aired. It is important to analyze this debate to understand the fears of this newly discovered phenomena, as well as the hopes for its positive transformation of society.[6]

The propaganda debate was not simply drawn across the dichotomous lines typically associated with the left-wing/right-wing political spectrum, because propaganda advocates and detractors could be found on both sides. Individuals were not permanently wedded to particular views on propaganda, but seemed to alter their views to meet perceived historical needs. Nor was the propaganda debate primarily waged over definitional issues regarding the constitutive elements of propaganda—there was a general agreement on what constituted propaganda during the interwar period. Furthermore, to call it a "debate" is somewhat misleading; with few exceptions, the major discussants did not speak directly to each other's positions as one would expect to find in a debate. Nevertheless, there were two largely divergent positions held on the legitimacy of propaganda during this period, and these divergent positions were particularly manifest on such questions of legitimacy as: Could a democratic government legitimately engage in propaganda programs to influence its populace and still retain its status as a democracy? What happens to local meaning and initiative when new communication technologies make it difficult or impossible to effectively answer back, and what are the sociological and psychological implications of this development? Should propaganda replace education as the function of the school, or should the school aim to develop the critical capacities by which this propaganda might be exposed? To what extent does propaganda upset the ideal of equality of opinion by giving the monied classes who control the communication networks an unfair advantage in having their views heard and, ultimately, their conception of reality enforced? These and similar questions of legitimacy were at the heart of the propaganda debate.

This chapter considers some of the central aspects of the propaganda debate. It is necessary first to point to some of the major features of the historical context in which the debate was located, primarily reactions to World War I and the emergence of fascism as an important and viable political ideology, as well as reactions to the larger structural changes occurring in the mass media at that time. In addition, the central aspects of the debate representing two basic yet polemical positions on the legitimacy of propaganda are discussed—one in favor of the use of propaganda, and hopeful for the positive and efficient transformation of society; and one against the use of propaganda, and fearful of the social and cultural consequences of such a system of social control. Not surprisingly, educators were often at the center of the controversy, because from various perspectives they were seen as both agents of propaganda and as important forces in teaching students to resist propaganda.

An exhaustive treatment of this debate cannot be provided here. The topic is a vast and extensive one, and it demands a volume in its own right. This chapter serves its purpose, however, by adequately demonstrating that the issues surrounding the development of the new mass communication technologies, and the propaganda phenomena associated with them, were not at all settled on during the years preceding World War II. That these issues could be muted and dismissed with the institutionalization of mass communications study after World War II suggests compelling historical questions concerning the social construction of knowledge during this most important historical juncture.

PROPAGANDA AS A SOCIAL PROBLEM

Prior to the outbreak of World War I, the term *propaganda* possessed neither pejorative connotations nor, apparently, the kind of inherent interest that would prompt scholars to take it up as an important object of study. The Latin root of the term refers benignly to the verb meaning to "sow," and the Roman Catholic Church had used the term *Propaganda Fidei* to refer to an official body of missionary cardinals at least as early as the 17th century.[7] The pre-20th-century propagandist was merely a spokesperson or a persuader of a particular cause. The techniques and tools of his or her craft—including the printing press, the soap box, and other localized means of oration—were, for the most part, no different from those available to other individuals and groups. Certainly the propagandist could deceive and manipulate the public through the careful control and shaping of information, but the largely local character of his or her work kept the propagandist under close scrutiny by the public. However, the development of large, centrally administered, governmental propaganda organizations during the war changed the very nature of the way in which propaganda was conceived, and it was seen in quite unfavorable terms by many people in the United States. Psychologist Raymond Dodge of Wesleyan University in Connecticut noted in 1920: "Propaganda antedates the War but its previous existence seems relatively mild and inoffensive. Only occasionally did it appear in the open. All that is changed now. Propaganda as the great art of influencing public opinion, seems to be a permanent addition to our social and political liabilities."[8]

Dodge was not alone in recognizing that the notion of propaganda had undergone a tremendous transformation in the United States during the war years. In 1927, University of Chicago political science professor Harold D. Lasswell emphasized the very threatening sound the term seemed to possess to many people: "A word has appeared, which has come to have an ominous clang in many minds—Propaganda. We live among more people than ever, who are puzzled, uneasy, or vexed at the unknown cunning which seems to have duped and degraded them."[9] Yale University Sociologist Leonard Doob noted in 1935 that the term propaganda had come to possess a "bad odor." "It is associated with the war and other evil practices," wrote Doob.[10]

Yet the transformation of the connotation of the term *propaganda* cannot be adequately understood as simply "A Good Word Gone Wrong," as one observer suggested in 1921;[11] nor can it be seen merely as a reflection of a "propaganda bogey" that haunted the culture, as a later observer maintained.[12] Rather, the transformation of the term represented a significant reaction by a large number of people in the United States to a complicated web of cultural, social, technological, and economic changes occurring at this time, as well as key historical events that thrust the phenomena of propaganda into widespread use: the increasing monopolization and centralization of important communication outlets, the major changes in communication technology, and the birth and growth of fascism and the central focus this ideology placed on the use of propaganda and the control of the mass media. Most significant was the way in which the centralized U.S. propaganda organization, the Committee on Public Information (CPI), had conducted its activities during the war, which first led to the great reevaluation of the term *propaganda* in the United States. In addition, the CPI represents perhaps the first, albeit extreme, example of some of these larger structural changes in the mass media occurring at that time, and the techniques employed by the CPI became increasingly commonplace in the years following the war. Some of the criticism of the CPI, then, can be understood to extend beyond the workings of the committee to entail those very structural changes that the CPI seemed to foreshadow.

The tasks faced by the CPI during the war were formidable, and the initiatives taken by the leadership of the CPI in attempting to meet these tasks were far-reaching. During the 3 years before the United States' entrance into the war, the Wilson administration had preached the value of neutrality, and there were large segments of the U.S. population who were pro-German, or who opposed the war on moral or political grounds.[13] That there was a need to create consensus, stifle opposition, and generally manufacture enthusiasm for the war when it was declared on April 6, 1917, was obvious to many who sat in the upper echelons of power. They knew that total mobilization for a modern technological war required not only a generation of young men who would willingly risk their lives for the stated war objectives, but also a population on the home front who would staff the industrial war machine and accept great personal and economic hardship. The Wilson administration knew that it was not about to garner such support for its war aims by remaining idle. Indeed, 6 weeks after the declaration of war, only 73,000 men volunteered for military service, although 1 million were needed.[14] The years preceding the war had witnessed a marked increase in political dissent in a number of different guises, including socialism, anarchism, and labor unionism.[15] If congressional action to establish military conscription could solve the problem of labor shortages, the problem of dissent remained more threatening and ominous to those in power.

It was in this atmosphere that Woodrow Wilson created the CPI on April 13, 1917, just 1 week after the declaration of war. Also known as the Creel Committee after its director, George Creel, the CPI became the nation's first "propaganda ministry" and grew into a massive bureaucratic organization in a very short time. Receiving a budget of almost $10 million in 1917, the CPI was divided into 3 foreign divisions and 15 domestic divisions (including the

Division of News, the Division of Civic and Educational Cooperation, the Film Division, the Labor Publications Division, the Division of Pictorial Publicity, the Bureau of Cartoons, the Speaking Division, the Division of Women's War Work, the Division of Work with the Foreign Born, and others).[16] From these various divisions flowed a continuous barrage of pro-American/prowar propaganda, much of which was racist in character, and nearly all of which reduced the complexities surrounding the war to a simplistic, black-and-white formula.

The CPI fed carefully prepared news stories to the various media outlets and closely monitored these media to determine if they were in fact adhering to the governmental line. To ensure that the government's position was enforced, and to decrease the likelihood of dissent, Congress disregarded the First Amendment of the Constitution and passed the Espionage Act of 1917. To increase the scope of the power of the federal government to extinguish dissent, Congress amended the Espionage Act with the Sedition Act in 1918, which set the maximum term of imprisonment to 20 years for any "wilful writing, utterance, or publication of any 'disloyal, profane, scurrilous, or abusive language about the form of government of the United States, or the Constitution of the United States, or the military or naval forces of the United States, or the uniform of the army or navy of the United States, or any language intended to bring the form of government of the United States . . . into contempt, scorn, contumely, or disrepute."[17] No doubt many people who disagreed with U.S. policy during this period withheld their dissent because of their fear of government reprisal through the Espionage Act. Nevertheless, approximately 900 people went to prison under the Espionage Act during World War I.[18] Either way, the Espionage Act was effective in ensuring that the CPI remained the dominant organ of news and opinion during the war.[19]

The CPI came into existence while the modern means of communication were still in their infancy. Television, of course, was a decade away from being invented and a full three decades away from being utilized widely. Radio as a mass medium was still in its rudimentary stages; broadcasting stations and receivers existed, although they were few and far between, and they did not represent the means by which most people received their news of the world. Film, too, was attracting much interest during this period, and several short-subject films with such titles as *Labor's Part in Democracy's War, Woman's Part in the War,* and *The American Indian Gets into the War Game,* as well as a few longer films such as *Pershing's Crusaders, America's Answer,* and *Our Colored Fighters,* were produced by the CPI and released to movie houses throughout the country.[20] However, the techniques of film making remained very underdeveloped during this period, and consequently films were used only marginally in the CPI's propaganda campaign. It should also be noted that the CPI's activities during World War I came a short time before the advent of modern opinion-polling techniques, and the propagandists were at a loss to determine the precise effectiveness of their messages. Still, the CPI foreshadowed the effects of these developing media, and the sophisticated techniques of measuring their effects, by saturating the communications market to ensure that their messages would not go unnoticed.

In the absence of these modern communication channels and techniques of persuasion, the CPI relied largely on existing but greatly expanded communication vehicles to promote the government's policy objectives. Most important to their efforts remained the press and other forms of print media, an organization of public speakers, and the nation's public educational system at all levels of instruction. The establishment press largely accepted the government's position and, for the most part, no threats of reprisal were necessary. Nevertheless, George Creel, the CPI's director and himself a former newspaper employee, reminded his journalism colleagues that "in this day of high emotionalism and mental confusion, the printed word has immeasurable power, and the term traitor is not too harsh in application to the publisher, editor, or writer who wields this power without full and solemn recognition of responsibilities."[21] In addition, the CPI asked readers to clip out news articles and editorials that appeared to be seditious or treasonable, and to mail these articles to the CPI, which in turn would take appropriate action.[22] The CPI thus had nearly full control of the nation's publishing organs during the war, and the press and print media in general became the predominant instruments by which the CPI effectively shaped the public's image of the circumstances surrounding the war.

The CPI also made full use of a highly organized group of public speakers known as the "Four-Minute Men." The Four-Minute Men consisted of 75,000 volunteers who gave official pronouncements concerning the war during intermissions at movie houses, theaters, and other public gatherings throughout the United States.[23] These speeches, lasting literally 4 minutes, covered a range of topics relating to the war, including "What Our Enemy Really Is," "Unmasking German Propaganda," "Why We Are Fighting," and "Carrying the Message."[24] Anticipating later days when radio and television would carry simultaneous messages to various parts of the country, the speeches of the Four-Minute Men were orchestrated so that their messages were heard on, or near, the same day in all parts of the country.

The Four-Minute Men, as well as the CPI's extensive control of the print media, represented a massive program of reaching deeply into U.S. communication networks to shape public opinion concerning particular policy objectives relating to the war. Yet this massive program of propaganda did not end there. In addition, the program spread widely across all levels of educational instruction. As historian of education Joel Spring explained, the CPI "was the first major attempt to bring the goals of locally controlled schools into line with the policy objectives of the federal government."[25]

The schools were conceived to be important socializing institutions and important links in the communication chain. With the increasing number of students attending educational institutions at all levels, schools represented important contact points by which government information could be spread to people who might not otherwise be exposed to such information. Through the careful construction and dissemination of curricular and other materials directed at both teachers and students, the CPI utilized the system of public education as a vehicle by which consensus could be engineered on particular governmental policy objectives relating to the war.

The individuals responsible for the preparation and distribution of curricular materials for school instruction came from the Division of Civic and Educational Cooperation of the CPI. The Division of Civic and Educational Cooperation (hereafter cited as the Educational Division) was headed by University of Minnesota historian Guy Stanton Ford. Ford, who had been Frederick Jackson Turner's student at Wisconsin during the early 1890s and who later served as President of the University of Minnesota during the 1930s, came to the attention of George Creel when he wrote an open letter to school principals in the early spring of 1917, urging the principals to utilize high school commencement addresses to promote the government's position on the war.[26] As a historian, Ford knew well how, through the effective use of propaganda and symbol manipulation, people could be persuaded to adopt opinions and behaviors that they might not ordinarily adopt. As a scholar of some notoriety, Ford's position lent legitimacy to the propaganda functions of the Educational Division. Finally, as a dean at the University of Minnesota, Ford developed the administrative skills that made him particularly well suited for the job of director of the Educational Division. All of these attributes contributed to Ford's ability to solicit the assistance of some of the nation's top scholars to the war effort. Coupled with the widespread threat of governmental reprisal for dissidence or noncompliance, Ford created an impressive list of scholars who wrote pamphlets and other school materials for the governmental propaganda campaign.[27]

During the 2-year span of its official existence, the Educational Division published, printed, and distributed more than 75 million pieces of literature, much of which was directly aimed at grammar and secondary students and their teachers. The Educational Division of the CPI made particular use of already-existing periodicals that were oriented toward the teaching profession, often demonstrating ways in which teachers could use CPI-created and -endorsed materials in their lessons. The Educational Division also published and distributed the *National School Service,* a newspaper that continued to be published even after the war was over. Official chroniclers of CPI's activities, James Mock and Cedric Larson, noted that schoolchildren at typical township schools, "saw war photographs issued by the Committee, recited war verse from a Committee brochure, learned current events from a

Committee newspaper, studied war maps with a teacher who had acquired her knowledge of international politics through the Committee's pamphlets, and when they came home at night bore more literature for their parents."[28] Furthermore, Mock and Larson argued that "through cooperating private and government agencies he (Guy Stanton Ford) brought about a veritable mobilization of the country's scholarly resources, and made schools, colleges, and various non-educational groups among the strongest of 'strong points' in the inner lines" (of domestic propaganda).[29]

It is clear from several of his public statements that Guy Stanton Ford aimed to move the Educational Division of the CPI deeply into the very fabric of U.S. education, and as an intended consequence CPI propaganda would be distributed to the homes that schoolchildren returned to at night. In a 1918 public address to the National Educational Association (NEA) entitled "A New Educational Agency," Ford boasted of the Educational Division's, as well as other CPI divisions', accomplishments in this respect, and spoke of the need to create an "Americanized, nationalized" country:

> The Committee has enlisted every modern agency of publicity and education. Pictures, posters, films, the press, pamphlets, the schools, and the public platform have served it in a work that has now become world wide. For it has cast aside the old American indifference to foreign opinion and is now making the fight for public opinion in every neutral land. . . . Over 25,000,000 of its pamphlets have been read by our own people and made texts in schools and in teacher reading circles. . . . During the coming year it will put itself even more at the service of the schools, for the schools and the teachers have as never before become parts of our national life. The teacher is enlisted in this war, and more and more the morale of the nation and the thinking in its homes will be determined by what she knows and teaches in this supreme crisis. . . . The Committee on Public Information and the schools have a great common war task to make an Americanized nationalized American nation. If we, working with all the agencies, fail, then America will fail.[30]

From Ford's perspective, as well as from the perspectives of others who sat in leadership positions in the United States' first propaganda ministry, the United States did not fail. Indeed, the CPI had successfully stoked the fires of U.S. nationalism, and large segments of the population came to regard U.S. involvement in the war as both morally just and politically correct. The CPI was so effective in persuading people to fear and hate the "Hun" that a near-hysterical mood was created in the United States. People were told to be on the lookout for Central Power spies, and individuals who were of German, Irish, or Scandinavian descent, as well as individuals who opposed the war or who held opposing political ideologies, were the victims of particularly strong suspicion and harassment. Books written by German authors were burned, and teaching the German language was forbidden by many state legislatures. Organizations such as the National Security League, National Protective Association, and other patriotic groups assisted the CPI in its program of propaganda and coercion.[31] Teachers who chose classroom discussion topics such as pacifism, Bolshevism, or the League of Nations could find themselves facing disciplinary actions.[32]

To Ford, it was the very character of U.S. schooling—a type of schooling that did not engender a critical perspective—that made possible the ease with which the CPI was able to mold U.S. opinions about the war. In a speech to the NEA in the aftermath of war in 1919, Ford maintained that U.S. victory was in large part due to the schools' success in creating a nation of people who—because of their limited understanding of their society, history, and government—could be easily manipulated when their leaders envisioned a "crisis." With surprising candor, although expressing his views in seemingly benign terms, the Dean of the Graduate School at the University of Minnesota told the NEA:

> The critics may be right when they say that we have an educational system which produces few if any educated men, fewer still who love books for life or do persistent thinking. But with all their shortcomings, it is the schools which supply the answer to the question: What was the most amazing thing about America's participation in the war, the one thing which conditioned and made possible all government activities in its prosecution? . . . It [the nation] was the product of an education which taught all the people a few simple things in history, reading and writing, and the elements of government, thus giving to all Americans the common denominator into which they could translate the appeal of the nation's leaders in a great crisis.[33]

To be sure, the position Ford offered here was not new to the history of U.S. educational thought, and one can locate suggestions of this sentiment from the very beginning of the establishment of public schools in the United States.[34] Nevertheless, the position that Ford endorsed is one that would become a hallmark of individuals who argued in support of propaganda in the postwar period. As the 20th century moved on and the notion of crisis became a permanent feature of both domestic and international relations, the need for a populace who "could translate the appeal" of those in power also became an increasing necessity.

POST-WORLD WAR I REACTIONS

As the war came to a close in November 1918, and as the United States counted its 119,956 dead and its 182,674 wounded, a period of great disillusionment, which intensified throughout the postwar period, swept through the nation.[35] Many people came to believe that the war had been waged primarily for the benefit of rich industrialists and bankers who had profited greatly from it. This notion received its most complete articulation in Englebrecht and Hanighen's 1934 book, *Merchants of Death,* in which they argued that U.S. involvement in the war was precipitated to serve the interests of bankers and munitions makers, including the Dupont Company and J. P. Morgan.[36] At least part of the disillusionment in the postwar period was spurred on by the belief among many people that they had been deceived by the CPI or that they had been coerced into becoming propagandists for it.

By the 1930s, several strong attacks had been written detailing the deceptive techniques employed by the CPI, and raising questions about the legitimacy of its propaganda. E. T. Saintsbury, a superintendent for a rural midwestern school district and a former Four-Minute Man, wrote about how only 1 day after the signing of the Armistice he first became suspicious that he "had been serving a cause other than his country" during the war.[37] In an article appearing in *The American Mercury,* Saintsbury confessed that in addition to giving his six prowar lectures per week, he also carried out all other actions that were expected of him as a patriotic citizen: He gave academic credit to students who were engaged in nonacademic, war-related work; he saw to it that the students were given the appropriate patriotic pamphlets and that "they were diligently instructed in hating the Hun"; he banned particular school texts alleged to endorse Kaiserism; and he cajoled people, many of whom were old and poor, to support the war by buying Liberty Bonds. When the war ended, Saintsbury came to the conclusion that it was the bankers, having played such an instrumental role in the perpetuation of the wartime propaganda machine, who had profited most from the sale of these Liberty Bonds.

In the postwar period, many other people also attacked the CPI and its propaganda activities. One observer, noting the magnitude of the CPI's various activities to induce hate, called the CPI "the greatest fraud ever sold to the public in the name of patriotism and religion."[38] Another observer, Arthur Ponsonby, who examined the atrocity stories and fabrications employed by all belligerents in his 1928 book *Falsehoods in Wartime,* concluded that "there must have been more deliberate lying in the world from 1914 to 1918 than in any other period of the world's history."[39] Ponsonby argued that although there were many reasons to object to the war—including its immorality, cruelty, and barbarism—nothing seemed more objectionable than the propaganda associated with the war: "There is not a living soul in any country who does not deeply resent having his passions roused, his indignation inflamed, his patriotism exploited, and his highest ideals desecrated by concealment, subterfuge, fraud, falsehood, trickery, and deliberate lying on the part of those in whom he is taught to repose confidence and to whom he is enjoined to pay respect."[40]

As the CPI's activities unleashed a series of criticisms on itself, it also led to some interest in defining the nature of propaganda. Most of the definitions of propaganda offered during the post-World War I period shared some important commonalities, as Jacques Ellul noted in his seminal 1962 treatment of propaganda. From 1920 through at least 1933, Ellul maintained, most definitions of propaganda in the United States emphasized its psychological aspects, as opposed to rational or cognitive aspects; propaganda was generally defined during this period as "a manipulation of psychological symbols having goals which *the listener is not conscious.*"[41] Most definitions of propaganda proposed during this time did in fact share the characteristics Ellul described. CPI propagandist George Sylvester Viereck defined propaganda as "a campaign camouflaging its origins, its motive, or both, conducted for the purpose of obtaining a specific objective by manipulating public opinion."[42] In 1922, Edward K. Strong, Jr., from the Carnegie Institute of Technology defined propaganda thus: "The word 'propaganda' means essentially the spread of a particular doctrine or a system of principles, especially when there is an organization or general plan back of the movement."[43]

Harold Lasswell discriminated propaganda from other forms of social control, stipulating that propaganda is concerned exclusively with the manipulation of symbols. "It [propaganda] refers solely to the control of opinion by significant symbols, or, to speak more concretely and less accurately, by stories, rumours, reports, pictures and other forms of social communication," Lasswell wrote in 1927. He continued, "Propaganda is concerned with the management of opinions and attitudes by the direct manipulation of social suggestion rather than by altering other conditions in the environment or in the organism."[44] And Leonard Doob defined propaganda in 1935 as "a systematic attempt by an interested individual (or individuals) to control the attitudes of groups or individuals through the use of suggestion and, consequently, to control their actions."[45] The definitions of propaganda proposed during this period varied somewhat; yet the notion of propaganda as a conscious and deliberate attempt to manipulate the thoughts and attitudes of people, and that the person doing the manipulating was often hidden and largely unaccountable, was fairly static. Likewise, the notion that propaganda operated in the symbolic realm was also a constant defining feature. Despite the fact that Ellul had a difficult time arriving at a concise definition in his 1962 text, *Propaganda,* the people living through the interwar years, having experienced some stark social changes firsthand, seemed to carry with them very similar notions as to what constituted propaganda.[46]

The war both accelerated and magnified the structural changes in the mass media that were occurring in the early part of the century, and several critics eyed these changes and voiced their concerns about the likely results of these changes. John Dewey, in "The New Paternalism," an article appearing in *The New Republic* in December of 1918, noted that there existed strong social forces that wished to continue into peacetime the mechanisms established for the formation of public opinion during the war. Dewey realized that the harsher elements of this form of social control would be dismantled: Censorship would be lessened, and he predicted a relaxation of other invasions of privacy and restrictions of freedom of expression. Nevertheless, Dewey thought that the developments in the means of opinion control that occurred during the war would not be readily dismissed. He wrote:

> There has been a remarkable demonstration of the possibilities of guidance of the news upon which the formation of public opinion depends. There has been an equally convincing demonstration of the effect upon collective action of opinion when directed systematically along certain channels. One almost wonders whether the word "news" is not destined to be replaced by the word "propaganda"—though of course words linger after things have been transformed.[47]

Dewey saw this new "intellectual paternalism" as resulting from two war-related developments. First, giving the communication controllers the benefit of the doubt, Dewey argued that the war itself created in leadership a profound fear with respect to what is appropriate knowledge for the masses. "The fact which stands out is that the war has generated an atmosphere of safety first regarding all facts knowledge of which stimulates social change."[48] Second, the war "increased the prior centralization" of the developing communication technologies, and this created the physical apparatus by which intellectual paternalism could operate. Doubtlessly speaking to the issues surrounding the growth of the two major news agencies, Associated Press (AP) and United Press International (UPI), Dewey wrote:

> The world has come to a curious juncture of events. The development of political democracy has made necessary the semblance at least of consultation of public opinion. The beliefs of the masses cannot be openly ignored. The immense size of a democracy like our own would make the development of community of sentiment and persuasion impossible unless there were definite and centralized agencies for communication and propagation of facts and ideas. Consequently just at the time when shaping public opinion has become an essential industry, there also exist the instrumentalities for news gathering and distribution on a large scale.[49]

Dewey did not express in 1918 what he thought would be the likely outcome of this "curious juncture of events," this recognized reliance on a politics of consensus and the creation of the physical apparatus by which consensus could be manufactured. But his intimated comparison between this new intellectual paternalism and the Roman emperors who attempted to stop the spread of Christianity through oppressive means suggests that Dewey was not altogether hopeful. "It must be admitted," Dewey wrote about the attempt to stop the spread of ideas, "that the means formerly at command were clumsy and brutal in comparison with those now available."[50]

In 1920, Raymond Dodge of Wesleyan University in Connecticut recognized two great dangers of propaganda to society. The first concerned the possibility of the concentration of the power to propagandize in "irresponsible hands." Dodge did not state whether or not he believed that this kind of concentration had already occurred or if it were likely to occur, and he did not offer suggestions by which the growth and concentration of propaganda might be limited. "We have some legal safeguards against careless use of high-powered physical explosives," he wrote, but "against the greater danger of destructive propaganda there seems to be little protection without imperiling the sacred principles of free speech."[51] Dodge's recognition of a second danger of propaganda to the social sphere was linked to the addition of motion pictures to the communication networks. "I believe there may well be grave penalties in store for the reckless commercialized exploitation of human emotions in the cheap sentimentalism of our moving pictures," he wrote while the medium was still in its infancy. "One of our social desiderata, it seems to me, is the protection of the great springs of human action from destructive exploitation for selfish, commercial, or other trivial ends."[52] Regardless of what one thinks of Dodge's hypothesis about the effect of motion pictures on U.S. society, Dodge was prophetic to attend seriously to this new mass medium that was making such deep inroads into U.S. life, and rapidly leading to replacement of the printed word with the moving image as the dominant means of discourse. The weekly movie audience in the United States would increase from 40 million people in 1922 to 90 million in 1930.[53]

Another structural change in U.S. mass media in the post-World War I period that prompted people to consider the issue of propaganda concerned the growth of the press agent or PR expert in corporate and other major organizational activities. One writer, Roscoe C. E. Brown, documented this development in a 1921 article entitled "The Menace to Journalism."[54] In this article, Brown argued that a significant number of former journalists and others with similar talents had gone into the employ of large corporations for the purpose of "circulating propaganda disguised as news" for the corporate bodies. The salaries commanded by these press agents were considerably higher than those earned by newspaper writers; therefore, Brown wrote, "trained writers that are ready to forego the journalists ideal and give their pens to the service not of society but of a patron's ends tend in increasing numbers to forsake the editorial room for the publicity office, to the impoverishment of newspaper staffs."[55] This, argued Brown, altered the traditional function of the newspaper as a watchdog agency to that of the newspaper as a vehicle for advertising. Brown wrote that the press agents, through "their systematic and extensive preparation of news," were:

> changing the condition of news gathering. They stand guard at many sources
> of news, fending off the too keen inquirer and leaving the newspaper the

choice of letting itself be spoon-fed or going empty. The inevitable result must be the decay of reporting in its more difficult and for public purposes most important aspects, the growth of a race of mere retailers of ready-made intelligence, and the turning of the newspapers more and more to distribution, less of news than of what somebody wishes to be considered news.[56]

Brown's remedy to this structural change in the gathering and reporting of news was "nothing but the absolute refusal to recognize the press agent, or to publish news that is not prepared by the editorial staff itself and its disinterested agents."[57] For Brown, the very essence of journalism was its capacity to serve as an "autonomous expression of itself as an interpreter of society," and only by rejecting the offerings of the press agent would the U.S. press be able to retain this essential characteristic.[58]

Finally, the birth of fascism—with its often open declaration of the need to mold public opinions through the mass media and other coercive measures—also caused people to take seriously the issues surrounding the growth of propaganda and mass communications. Some of the early figures in the invention and distribution of radio had become adherents of fascism, including RCA's Chairman of the Board David Sarnoff, who was an admirer of Benito Mussolini's dictatorship, and radio inventor Gugleilmo Marconi, who served as a member of the Grand Council of Fascism.[59] By the early 1920s, Adolf Hitler was attributing Germany's defeat in the war, in part, to its leadership's inability to create and administer effective propaganda on both the domestic and foreign fronts. In the program Hitler devised for Germany and the world, propaganda was to play a central role in regimenting all behavior and thought.[60] Ivy Lee, one of the first PR experts and the chief architect for the PR activities of John D. Rockefeller, was hired by the Nazi government to help bolster its worldwide image.[61] In 1933, Joseph Goebbels, the Nazi Minister of Propaganda and Public Enlightenment, announced to the world the Nazis' plans to make all of Germany's communication outlets subservient to the state: "The National Press Law is the most modern journalistic statute in the world. I predict its principles will be adopted by the other nations of the world within the next seven years. It's the absolute right of the state to supervise the formation of opinions."[62] Whether Goebbels was mad or prophetic was difficult to determine in 1933. Nevertheless, the growth of fascism in Europe and Japan, as well as the fascist movement in the United States, which one observer in 1939 estimated to consist of some 800 groups, created yet another dimension to those individuals who were concerned with the role of propaganda and the mass media in society.[63]

It is within the framework of these historical circumstances—the precedent-setting activities of the CPI, the larger structural changes occurring in communications, and the rise of fascism—that we interpret the significant antipropaganda movement that began to take shape in the United States between wars. By the late 1930s, there were several organizations, including the Institute for Propaganda Analysis and the National Council for Social Studies, that were actively involved in developing antipropaganda curricular materials. Although this antipropaganda movement became greatly diminished with the onset of World War II, this early critical-thinking movement remains an important response to the changes that mass communications effected in the United States.

THE ANTIPROPAGANDA MOVEMENT

The antipropaganda movement, although short-lived, reflected the interests of many practicing teachers, because the activity of propaganda seemed to run contrary to many widely held notions about the nature of education. In 1929, the NEA published its "Report of the Committee on Propaganda in the Schools," calling for greater scholarly attention to the problem of propaganda in all its guises.[64] One survey conducted in August 1937 by Teachers College and New York University revealed that:

> Ninety-eight per cent (of 500 teachers surveyed) advocated a critical study in the schools of propaganda which would help prepare young people to function as intelligent citizens in discussing and voting on controversial issues; they said that in treating such issues in the school, teaching pupils how to think is more important than teaching them what to think.[65]

This interest among teachers in teaching students to analyze and resist propaganda was in turn reflected in both the kinds of issues and concerns expressed in their journals, as well as those issues and concerns considered by their professional organizations.[66] By the spring of 1939, *Newsweek* magazine called critical propaganda analysis "one of the newest and fastest growing ideas in American education."[67]

There were several prominent people throughout the 1920s who envisioned a clear distinction between propaganda and education, and who rejected the popular conceptualization of propaganda but accepted a common conceptualization of education. Lucy Maynard Salmon, a New York historian, was quite explicit on this point. In her extensive 1923 treatment of the relationship between ruling power and the press, entitled *The Newspaper and Authority,* she expressed a progressive educational philosophy that was widely held among her contemporaries:

> Education by propaganda was the equivalent of education by injunction and to speak of education by either means was precisely the same as speaking of a square circle. To assume that education could be accomplished by passing information, either genuine or spurious, from above to those below was ignorantly to confuse information with education; to disregard the inherent desire of men, as well as children, to find out things for themselves; to fail to recog-

nize the exhilaration that comes from discovery; to misunderstand entirely
the meaning and the function of education.[68]

Everett Dean Martin, a lecturer at the New School for Social Research,
was equally adamant with respect to discriminating between propaganda
and education. In his 1926 text *The Meaning of a Liberal Education,* Martin
recognized that the methods and the goals of the propagandist were entirely
antithetical to the ideal of a liberal education. When an educator begins to
adopt the methods and goals of the propagandist, argued Martin, he or she
ceases to be an educator. What are these methods and goals of the propagandist that ran so contrary to the notion of a liberal education? Martin
wrote:

> The propagandist is interested in *what* people think; the educator in *how* they
> think. The propagandist has a definite aim. He strives to convert, to sell, to se-
> cure assent, to prove a case, to support one side of an issue. He is striving for
> an *effect.* He wishes people to come to a conclusion; to accept his case and close
> their minds and act. The educator strives for the open mind. He has no case to
> prove, which may not later be reversed. He is willing to reconsider, to be ex-
> perimental, to hold his conclusions tentatively. The result for which he strives
> is a type of student who will not jump at the propagandist's hasty conclusions
> or be taken in by his catch-words.[69]

Three years later, Martin extended his criticism of propaganda by arguing that the social existence of propaganda actually causes grievous harm to
the activity of education. First, those people most interested in promoting
the methods and aims associated with the propagandist have "seriously men-
aced the sanctuary of the disinterested pursuit of knowledge" by entering
the educational institutions through curricular and other materials, a topic
taken up extensively by Ohio State University professor Frederick Lumley
in his 1933 text *The Propaganda Menace.*[70] Second, Martin maintained that
propaganda harms the efforts of the educator because it causes "the public
to think that education and propaganda are the same thing, and thus to
make an ignorant multitude believe it is being educated when it is only being manipulated."[71]

Even Calvin Coolidge, who is hardly remembered for possessing a broad
and liberal outlook, could recognize the differences between the activities
of the propagandist and the educator. In a speech to the Association of
Newspaper Editors while he was still president, he said: "Propaganda seeks
to present part of the facts, to distort their relations, and to force conclusions which could not be drawn from a complete and candid survey of all the
facts. Of real education and of real information we cannot get too much; but
of propaganda—we cannot have too little."[72] Whether Coolidge expressed
what he really believed or what he believed others wanted to hear him say is
really beside the point. The fact that he expressed this view of the distinction

between propaganda and education suggests that this view was widely held in the culture at the time, and it helps us understand the context in which the antipropaganda movement evolved.

John Dewey explored the individual and social implications of the emergence of the propaganda problem in his 1930 book *Individualism Old and New,* a part of which was published in essay form in *The New Republic* before the October 1929 stock market crash.[73] Although not using the term *mass society* per se, his short book anticipated many of the concerns about the emerging mass society that would find fuller expression in the 1950s and early 1960s. Dewey placed significant emphasis on the role played by the mass media and propaganda in constricting individual thought and expression, and in creating a kind of masslike conformity. Observing this phenomenon starkly, he wrote:

> We live exposed to the greatest flood of mass suggestion that any people has ever experienced. The need for united action, and the supposed need of integrated opinion and sentiment, are met by organized propaganda and advertising. The publicity agent is perhaps the most significant symbol of our present social life. There are individuals who resist; but, for a time at least, sentiment can be manufactured by mass methods for almost any person or any cause.[74]

Dewey generally agreed with those critics of U.S. life who observed that "homogeneity of thought and emotion has become an ideal."[75] At the root of the U.S. movement toward "quantification, mechanization, and standardization" in nearly all aspects of life was what Dewey regarded as a pervasive "money culture" that subordinated humane values to pecuniary interests. Technology and an antiquated notion of "individualism" had been put in the service of these pecuniary interests, resulting in a social order that was not attuned to meeting genuine human needs. The older notion of the rugged, pioneering individual was now grafted on to the ideology of corporate capitalism, the activities of which (i.e., mass production and mass consumption) essentially contradicted the full development of the individual. The individual was now submerged, or "lost," to techniques promoting an "external" conformity, despite that fact that most Americans continued to express faith in the creed of individualism, and despite the fact that the development of scientific technique had the potential to serve an emancipatory role. "The problem of constructing a new individuality consonant with the objective conditions under which we live is the deepest problem of our times," Dewey wrote.[76]

Dewey was not prepared to depict the form this new individualism should take, although he maintained that any reasonable manifestation of this new individualism would necessarily be tied to a heightened understanding of the political, cultural, and economic realities of the time. Indeed, it was precisely the inability to see the relationship between individual experience and larger social structure that precipitated the confusion, apathy, and lethargy that Dewey noted. "Political apathy such as has marked our thought for many years past is due fundamentally to mental confusion arising from lack of consciousness of any vital connection between politics and daily affairs," he wrote. "To know where things are going and why they are is to have the material out of which stable objects of purpose and loyalty may be formed. To perceive clearly the actual movement of events is to be on the road to intellectual clarity and order."[77] Of course, for Dewey, educational institutions might be utilized to promote this kind of understanding if they were purposefully directed to this end. Educational institutions might, under different circumstances, provide opportunities for students to bring the activity of science to bear on relevant personal and social problems and questions. For Dewey, the very notion of knowledge and learning depended on this opportunity. He wrote:

> Since knowing is inquiring, perplexities and difficulties are the meat on which it thrives. The disparities and conflicts that give rise to problems are not something to be dreaded, something to be endured with whatever hardihood one can command; they are the things to be grappled with. Each of us experiences these difficulties in the sphere of his personal relations, whether in his more immediate contacts or in the wider associations conventionally called "society." At present, personal frictions are one of the chief causes of suffering. I do not say all suffering would disappear with the incorporation of scientific method into individual disposition; but I do say that it is now immensely increased by our disinclination to treat these frictions as problems to be dealt with intellectually. The distress that comes from being driven in upon ourselves would be largely relieved; it would in part be converted into the enjoyment that attends the free working of mind, if we took them as occasions for the exercise of thought, as problems having an objective direction and outlet.[78]

Clearly, in 1930, Dewey did not believe that educational institutions were providing for this opportunity for the "free working of mind." "The distinguishing trait of the American student body in our higher schools is a kind of intellectual immaturity," he wrote. "This immaturity is mainly due to their enforced mental seclusion; there is, in their schooling, little free and disinterested concern with the underlying social problems of our civilization."[79] Moreover, for Dewey, the forces that were impinging on the school's ability to encourage analysis of these problems were the same forces that were submerging the individual and encouraging the quantification, standardization, and mechanization of the culture. "That which prevents the schools from doing their educational work freely is precisely the pressure—for the most part indirect, to be sure—of domination by the money-motif of our economic regime."[80]

One of the strongest critics of propaganda as a means of social control and its apparent effects on individual consciousness was William W. Biddle.

In the 1930s, Biddle was a Case Western Reserve University Professor; in the 1950s (as seen in chap. 6) Biddle became the director of the Program of Community Dynamics at Earlham College.[81] In his 1932 text entitled *Propaganda and Education* Biddle placed the blame for the rise of propaganda on a prevalent value that seeks to "regiment the behavior of the masses" and that regards conformity "as more important than independence."[82] Despite the fact that some propaganda might have worthy or justifiable aims, Biddle argued that its "total effect is to increase the uncritical acceptance of the process of regimentation." Thus, he sought to place the increase of critical thinking, the development of skepticism, and the diminution of gullibility among the very highest of educational goals, so that students would have the facilities with which to question the propaganda in which they were increasingly being surrounded.[83] For Biddle, education represented the only defense against this onslaught of propaganda, because all propaganda, whether having admirable aims or not, leads to increased gullibility, and because legally set standards of truth would likely result in a censorship that would be even worse than the propaganda it sought to control. Yet, for Biddle, the very notion of democracy as a political ideology that "gives opportunity to the greatest number to live, in their own way, full, complete, and well adjusted lives," was at stake, and the future of democracy would depend on how well educators met this challenge. "A society that continues to exist by allowing skillful and wealthy minorities to regiment and manipulate the majority by a sort of 'invisible government,' " wrote Biddle, "is obviously not the ideal society from the point of view of such a democracy. A majority manipulated into increasing gullibility is not living to the full."[84]

Biddle relied on a psychological definition of propaganda that characterized it as essentially comprising direct and indirect emotional appeals to change behavior, and he identified four general principles that were in wide use by post-World War I propagandists. First, the propagandist had learned to rely on emotions rather than arguments to produce the desired effects. Second, the principle of constructing an "us" versus "them" scenario with respect to the issue in question had been found to be effective. Third, in pitching his or her propaganda to groups as well as to individuals, the propagandist could arouse more widespread support for the particular issue. And, fourth, the propagandist learned that in order to be effective, he or she must remain hidden from those individuals and groups who are the targets of his or her manipulation.[85]

From Biddle's perspective, the propagandists were becoming increasingly masterful of these techniques and, in addition, he recognized that structural changes in communications were aiding the development of propaganda. "The consolidation of newspapers into country-wide chains and the purchase of influential dailies by large corporations," he argued in 1932, "open the way for more completely anonymous control of opinion." He noted that radio and motion pictures have proven themselves to be "efficient means for unconscious emotional conditioning."[86] His prognosis for a social order pervaded by this type of propaganda was not hopeful. Indeed, he saw as a major consequence of this propaganda the development of a kind of "autistic" or "infantile" mode of thinking, in which the individual becomes less and less able to distinguish the real world from the imaginary world created by the propagandist. Although not optimistic, Biddle attempted to counter this trend by creating an educational program that sought to "make the student critical of his own and others' thinking, and critical of the point of view which he is supposed to accept."[87]

Although Dewey would have been supportive of Biddle's efforts at developing such an educational approach, he would have also encouraged an attempt to understand the reasons why so many people were susceptible to the techniques used to standardize their views and opinions. For Dewey, this susceptibility was a consequence of the inability to sustain meaningful and genuine community life. "The individual cannot remain intellectually a vacuum," he wrote. "If his ideas and beliefs are not the spontaneous function of a communal life in which he shares, a seeming censensus [*sic*] will be secured as a substitute by artificial and mechanical means."[88] But the problem with such artificially and mechanically created consensus is that it does not spring from actually lived experience; the unity that is achieved remains superficial, it is not tied to genuine circumstances in the community, and it is easily changed and distracted:

> In consequence, our uniformity of thought is much more superficial than it seems to be. The standardization is deplorable, but one might almost say that one of the reasons it is deplorable is because it does not go deep. It goes far enough to effect suppression of original quality of thought, but not far enough to achieve enduring unity. Its superficial character is evident in its instability. All agreement of thought obtained by external means, by repression and intimidation, however subtle, and by calculated propaganda and publicity, is of necessity superficial; and whatever is superficial is in continual flux. The methods employed produce mass credulity, and this jumps from one thing to another according to the dominant suggestions of the day. We think and feel alike—but only for a month or a season. Then comes some other sensational event or personage to exercise a hypnotizing uniformity of response.[89]

In emphasizing the importance of individual experience in the context of community, Dewey was reflecting a traditional and time-honored view of the role of communication. Christopher Simpson reminded us that the word *communication* appeared in "the English language around the fourteenth century, derived from the Latin *com* (literally 'together') and *munia* ('duties') meaning 'the sharing of burdens.' In this traditional vision, communication, to the extent it was articulated, was seen as a process of sharing with others (through cultural interchange, ceremony, commerce, etc.)

within any particular social context, as distinct from existing primarily as a medium for giving directions."[90] Dewey wanted to reclaim this traditional view of communication. Moreover, he wanted to discriminate between social unity, which he understood to be a requisite of individual thought and expression, and the uniformity and conformity that he saw increasing at great pace in the first half of the 20th century. Propaganda and mass communication technologies were able to standardize thought and behavior in a society where genuine communication and social unity were absent. "Conformity," Dewey wrote, "is a name for the absence of vital interplay; the arrest and benumbing of communication."[91]

Dewey and Biddle's work, as well as the work of other educators who were critical of propaganda in the late 1920s and early 1930s, added fuel to the antipropaganda flame that began to take on institutional dimensions by the late 1930s. In 1937, the National Council for Social Studies devoted its Seventh Yearbook to the critical study of propaganda. This yearbook, entitled *Education Against Propaganda*, contained articles by both university professors and practicing teachers covering a range of issues. "How to Read Domestic News," "Propaganda Influences within the School," "Teaching Students in Social-Studies Classes to Guard Against Propaganda," and "Propaganda and the News in Grade XI" were among the many areas of concern represented in this volume, as well as an article by Biddle entitled "Teaching Resistance to Propaganda."[92] The book sought to introduce social studies teachers to the basic concepts involved in teaching resistance to propaganda, as well as providing examples of successful classroom techniques to achieve this goal.

That year, 1937, was also the year that Edward Filene and Columbia University Teachers College professor Clyde Miller established the Institute for Propaganda Analysis for the explicit purpose of creating antipropaganda teaching methods and curricular materials. Consisting of an advisory board of such scholars as Robert S. Lynd, Hadley Cantril, Leonard Doob, and Charles Beard, a small editorial staff, and led by Executive Secretary Alfred McClung Lee, the institute published a newsletter and several longer works dealing with the issues pertaining to deciphering and understanding propaganda.[93] A nonprofit organization, the institute sought to "throw light on the devices propagandists use in their efforts to swing us to their ways of thinking and acting. This purpose, the Institute believes, can only be accomplished through the candid and impartial study of the devices and apparent objectives of specialists in the distortion of public opinions."[94]

The institute defined *propaganda* broadly, so as to entail all forms of manipulation regardless of whether the ends were considered to be justifiable or good: "Propaganda is expression of opinion or action by individuals or groups deliberately designed to influence opinions or actions of other individuals or groups with reference to predetermined ends." Thus, the institute's objective was to teach people to critically understand the phenomenon of propaganda itself without reference to specific positive values that the propagandist may endorse. Counterpoising the propagandist with the scientist, the founders of the institute wrote in their first bulletin:

> The propagandist is trying to "put something across," good or bad, whereas the scientist is trying to discover truth and fact. Often the propagandist does not want careful scrutiny and criticism; he wants to bring about a specific action. Because the action may be socially beneficial or socially harmful to millions of people, it is necessary to focus upon the propagandist and his activities the searchlight of scientific scrutiny. Socially desirable propaganda will not suffer from such examination, but the opposite type will be detected and revealed for what it is.[95]

Such a stance toward analyzing propaganda suggested that the institute was willing to examine propaganda covering a range of issues, and propaganda that was coming from a range of different organizations. During its short existence, the institute published a significant body of literature and curricular materials relating to propaganda analysis. In 1939, the institute published *The Fine Art of Propaganda,* detailing the propaganda techniques employed by the profascist Reverend Charles E. Coughlin of Detroit.[96] In 1940, it published Harold Lavine and James Wechsler's *War Propaganda and the United States,* which analyzed the war propaganda that was being directed at the United States.[97] In its bulletin *Propaganda Analysis,* the institute published a series of articles on such topics as "How to Detect Propaganda," "How to Analyze Newspapers," "The Public Relations Counsel and Propaganda," and others that were to be used in both schools and adult study group settings.[98] The institute also published experimental curricular materials, including the two longer works *Propaganda: How to Recognize It and Deal with It* and *Group Leader's Guide to Propaganda Analysis,* which were used in junior and senior high schools as well as in some colleges.[99] These published materials were, for the most part, based on a scheme of propaganda analysis that entailed the identification of seven commonly used propaganda devices: the name-calling device, the glittering generalities device, the transfer device, the testimonial device, the plain folks device, the card-stacking device, and the bandwagon device.[100] The institute promoted the idea that identifying and understanding these seven devices in mass communications would enable the audience to more critically attend to the issues behind the propaganda.

In retrospect, the hope that simply having people learn to identify seven commonly used propaganda devices as a way of getting them to become more critical about the messages they encountered seems rather naive, and such a program was destined to failure. Nevertheless, the fact that the Institute for Propaganda Analysis, the National Council for the Social Studies, as well as a host of individual scholars attempted to develop educational programs as a defense against propaganda suggests that the rise of propaganda and mass communications, and the social effects that resulted from this development, were significant concerns among many educators and other observers of the social scene. The institute's goal as an educational institution was "to analyze the propaganda of today and to formulate methods whereby American citizens can make their own analysis of attempts to persuade them to do something that they might not do if they were given all of the facts," and the members of the institute seemed to possess an acute awareness of the tension between widespread governmental and commercial propaganda and the ideals of a democratic state.[101]

Despite such seemingly reasonable educational objectives, however, the institute faced mounting pressure to discontinue its operations. J. Michael Sproule reported that the Rockefeller Foundation refused to offer financial support "on the basis that the Institute's work was not 'unassailably scientific.'"[102] Phyllis Meadows Hojems pointed out that "the antagonism of various business and political groups was heavy, because they did not want their propaganda analyzed. The Catholic Church . . . also took part in the growing opposition to the work of the analysts of the Institute and even the Teachers College of Columbia University wanted him [Clyde Miller] to abandon the whole idea of propaganda analysis."[103] On February 21, 1941, *The New York Times* ran a front-page article on the institute entitled "Propaganda Study Instills Skepticism in 1,000,000 Pupils."[104] Two days later, *The New York Times* reported that the House Committee on Un-American Activities, chaired by Representative Martin Dies, had been investigating the institute for nearly 2 years "to ascertain whether its aims were dangerous to about 1,000,000 school pupils."[105] The Executive Secretary of the Institute, Alfred McClung Lee, said that he welcomed the investigation, but went on to point out that "the Dies Committee was 'a disgrace to the United States,' and said that he was speaking 'as a conservative.'"[106] Although no formal indictment was ever made against the institute, the continued harassment took its toll.[107] By May 1941, two institute board members resigned "because they believed the institute was too critical of the defense policies of the Roosevelt Administration."[108]

Once the United States became involved in World War II, the advisory board dismantled the institute because it was feared that the approach of propaganda analysis provided by the institute "might serve to disturb the unity needed for the war effort."[109] In addition, several other institute members, including Hadley Cantril and Leonard Doob, left the institute at the onset of the war only to become central figures in the organization and dissemination of United States' propaganda during World War II. Some social scientists and educators associated with the institute went through a kind of personal transformation, from being initially opposed to propaganda during the pre-World War II period to supporting propaganda during and after the war. In any event, the antipropaganda position became increasingly tied to the isolationist position as the United States moved closer to entering the war and the antipropaganda position became an increasingly difficult position to hold in the face of the Nazi menace.[110] Although there was a limited attempt to revive the Institute for Propaganda Analysis after the war, the attempt found little support.[111] The antipropaganda movement had died by the early 1940s; however, the term *propaganda* continued to possess negative, undemocratic implications among large segments of the population.

THE PROPONENTS OF PROPAGANDA

The demise of the antipropaganda movement was aided by the rise of a more powerfully financed group of academic leaders, who envisioned propaganda serving an essential social function. Despite the pervasive sentiment critical of propaganda, there sat on the other side of the ideological fence a group of individuals who were convinced of the necessity of propaganda in the proper functioning of the modern, urbanized, and highly industrialized state. Placing great emphasis on the values of efficiency and conformity, these individuals argued (with varying degrees of certainty and conviction) that the modern means of communication could be harnessed to achieve these goals through the skillful use of propaganda. Harold Lasswell, who had written his dissertation under World War I propagandist Charles Merriam at the University of Chicago, was one of those individuals who envisioned propaganda fulfilling a necessary societal function in the modern state, and who thus envisioned the study of propaganda techniques to constitute a legitimate and important concern. "Propaganda is a concession to the wilfulness of the age," Lasswell wrote in his highly acclaimed 1927 text *Propaganda Techniques in the World War:*

> The bonds of personal loyalty and affection which bound a man to his chief have long since dissolved. Monarchy and class privilege have gone the way of all flesh, and the idolatry of the individual passes for the official religion of democracy. It is an atomized world, in which individual whims have wider play than ever before, and it requires more strenuous exertions to coordinate and unify than formerly. The new antidote to wilfulness is propaganda. If the mass will be free of chains of iron, it must accept its chains of silver. If it will not love, honour and obey, it must not expect to escape seduction.[112]

Lasswell's 1927 text was representative of those works in which it was difficult to determine whether the author was pursuing a study of propaganda techniques in order to decipher it or in order to learn how to use it effectively. This befuddled one reviewer of the book, who maintained that Lasswell regarded the activity of propaganda "as objectionable at least."[113] To the young Foster Dulles, however, Lasswell's study was "a Machiavellian textbook which should promptly be destroyed!"[114] As Lasswell's career progressed, it became clear that he was not simply a neutral observer of the phenomena of propaganda but instead was actively involved in developing techniques that would sharpen its effectiveness. By 1941, Lasswell argued persuasively for the need of the "specialists on intelligence" who would "provide us with a picture of human reality that is true, clear and vivid."[115] This "public relations function" would be served by the reporters who would convey this picture of reality as well as by the researchers who would define it. Increasingly, Lasswell played an important role in defining the researchers' activities in serving this "public relations" function.

If Lasswell at times portrayed an ambivalence to propaganda that made it difficult to determine precisely his position on the matter, Edward L. Bernays, Sigmund Freud's nephew and generally considered to be the founding father of modern public relations, was both clear and vociferous on his position.[116] In his 1928 book, appropriately entitled *Propaganda,* Bernays wrote unabashedly of the phenomena:

> The conscious and intelligent manipulation of the organized habits and opinions of the masses is an important element in democratic society. Those who manipulate this unseen mechanism of society constitute an invisible government which is the true ruling power of our country. We are governed, our minds are molded, our tastes our formed, our ideas suggested, largely by men we have never heard of. This is a logical result of the way in which our democratic society is organized. Vast numbers of human beings must cooperate in this manner if they are to live together as a smoothly functioning society.[117]

To Bernays, propaganda was nothing less than the modern instrument by which "to bring order out of chaos," and he frequently expressed his belief in the inability of the average person to adequately conduct his or her own affairs, often counterpoising the "intelligent few" with the average people, whom he referred to as the "herd."[118] For his outspokenness, Bernays received considerable criticism from those individuals who questioned the legitimacy of this instrument, as well as the underlying ideology it reflected. Bernays, for instance, related his wartime experience with propaganda quite openly when he wrote:

> It was, of course, the astounding success of propaganda during the war that opened the eyes of the intelligent few in all departments of life to the possibilities of regimenting the public mind. . . . The manipulators of patriotic opinion made use of the mental clichés and emotional habits of the public to produce mass reaction against alleged atrocities, the terror and tyranny of the enemy. It was only natural after the war ended that intelligent persons should ask themselves whether it was not possible to apply a similar technique to the problems of peace.[119]

Yet, Everett Dean Martin took Bernays to task for applying "a wartime psychology to the accomplishments of any ends whatever," and Martin could see in Bernays and other propagandists' systematic attempts to prey on prejudice and human weaknesses a major cause for the growth of intolerance in American society in the period after the war. "In this way," Martin wrote in 1929, "fundamentalism, prohibition, the Ku Klux Klan, censorship, and other forms of organized crowd insanity have now become a serious menace to American liberty."[120]

The fact that this critical, antipropaganda perspective existed as a significant social and cultural current required those individuals who envisioned the necessity of propaganda to be very careful in establishing the parameters of discussion on issues relating to the use of propaganda. It was not uncommon, particularly as World War II became imminent, for those who shared this pro-propaganda perspective to discriminate between "good" propaganda, which they associated with U.S. ideals and policy objectives, and "bad" propaganda, often associated with any kind of propaganda that departed from these U.S. ideals and policy objectives, rather than to raise the larger issue about the legitimacy of propaganda in a democratic society.[121] The widespread critical position on propaganda forced propagandists to equivocate about the meaning of their vocation: "Propaganda" became what the other, less scrupulous, side did; they, on the other hand, were the nonideological proponents of truth and objectivity. In addition, there was a general movement to simply wipe the term *propaganda* from the vocabulary and replace it with such terms as *education, information, public relations, public affairs,* and other such terms. In 1935, one observer thought it would be best to simply replace the term *propaganda* with the term *mass communication,* a suggestion that was consciously heeded during and after World War II. He wrote:

> The term "propaganda" has acquired a connotation that renders its use particularly difficult. In popular usage and in some technical material, invidious meanings are associated with the word. Its untoward aspects are emphasized. It is not the intention here to enter a discussion of definitions, but it is necessary to point out that not all propaganda is vicious or unjustified. It would perhaps be less confusing to drop the word, and to use instead the term "mass communication," since propaganda, regardless of definition, must be regarded as a special form of mass communication.[122]

The attempt to paint propaganda in the best possible light increased dramatically with the onset of World War II. Indeed, one way of interpreting James Mock and Cedric Larson's *Words That Won the War,* a historical treatment of the Committee on Public Information that was published at the start of World War II in 1939, is as an attempt to change the public's negative attitude toward propaganda and to prepare people for the establishment of a new propaganda organization. The book is essentially an apology for the Committee on Public Information, and it concludes with a chapter entitled "Blueprint for Tomorrow's CPI."[123]

Of course, the perspective that Bernays, Lasswell, and others were expressing of the need for social control through the control of public opinions was not new. Indeed, there are expressions of this perspective throughout the history of Western sociology, in the work of such dominant figures as Comte, Durkheim, Le Bon, Pareto, and others, and educational institutions have historically been the dominant organs of this control. Nor was the pursuit of the techniques of, or arguments for, social control uncommon during the early part of the 20th century, and this view gained greater legitimacy as the United States became poised for entry into World War II. Yet this perspective emphasizing social control had traditionally found itself in conflict with an inherited set of traditional democratic values that emphasized personal autonomy and responsibility, and that was premised on the belief that people had the capacity to rationally understand their world.

Because the need for free and open communication was the cornerstone to these democratic values, any discussions about the control of the press and the use of propaganda would necessarily strike at the core of those values and could not be lightly dismissed. Thus, social theorists who were proponents of propaganda could believe, with University of Kansas Professor Carrol D. Clark in 1935, "that the development of a rational technique of social control as are today being contemplated will require the most effective utilization of the newspaper and all other instruments of public opinion." Yet, the inherited democratic values of the culture also made these social theorists contend with the idea, also with Clark, that "until democracy has abdicated, the realization of a planned society depends less upon further advances in the social sciences—the point of view most frequently emphasized—than upon the co-operative participation of the public in whose hands the fate of any planning scheme must rest."[124] This put proponents of propaganda in the difficult position of needing to secure cooperation and consent from the public for a program of social control of which the public would presumably by left unaware.

To be sure, not all proponents of propaganda as a means of social control were troubled by this conflict with the ideals of democracy. Many of these individuals were able to reconcile this conflict by emphasizing the pressing social problems that seemed to require extraordinary means of social control, and the cooperation or consent of the public being controlled was really quiet beside the point. There were other individuals, however, who, although generally supporting the use of propaganda, were deeply troubled about the implications of widespread state-sponsored propaganda in a democratic society.

Perhaps no one articulated the issues behind this conflict better than George Catlin, a political scientist at Cornell from 1924 to 1935, and at Yale from 1935 to 1956.[125] Catlin, setting out to determine the role of propaganda in a democratic state, correctly recognized that democracy had been conceived to represent, since its very earliest conceptualizations, not only a theory by which political power is popularly elected and held accountable but also essentially a theory of toleration. Plato made note of this, Catlin argued, and thus Plato came to the understanding that "the democrat in spirit is a relativist."[126] Plato thought this toleration would lead to the inevitable demise of democracy because the democrat, by principle, must permit oppositional viewpoints to be heard, even though these oppositional viewpoints would not necessarily grant the same courtesy to the democrat. "The dilemma of democracy," wrote Catlin, "is that the democrat, as tolerant, must concede to these people the right to their own convictions."[127] On the other hand, the "true believer" is not constricted by the same ethical system, and in fact is compelled, by its very nature, to deny the validity of all perspectives but its own: "A State that considers itself the authoritative guardian of an absolute morality has, not only a right, but a duty negatively to exercise a censorship and positively to forward a propaganda designed to control opinion."[128]

For Catlin, this was the great danger facing democracy—that it would be brought to its knees by the very toleration by which it was defined. Still, Catlin maintained that "a democratic *government,* as the custodian of the instruments of force, is completely precluded, by its own principles, from all use of propaganda, understood in the sense of the authoritative instillation of one view to the exclusion of the others."[129] Democracy's hour seemed late to Catlin, as it did to many of his contemporaries in 1936. Unable to endorse a democratic state-sponsored propaganda, Catlin argued in support of voluntary party organizations that would spread the word of democracy through propaganda. This, Catlin suggested, was perfectly commensurate with the principles of democracy, because the democrat is entitled within the "limits of voluntary association, to a disciplined insistence upon the acceptance of certain values, and to propaganda upon their behalf."[130] Interestingly enough, in Catlin's view, these voluntary propaganda organizations would need to be aided by the development of a science that would arm the democrat with effective propaganda techniques. "It is not enough merely to agree to the proposition of political philosophy that democratic values are sound and need propagandizing," Catlin wrote.

> It is also requisite that we consult political science to discover how that propaganda may be successful against the urge to power of its opponents. Political science is a quantitative study, concerned to supply principles for the art of associating predominant masses of men to achieve a given end. Democracy must permit the propaganda of other movements a free role within the law. It must, therefore, the more certainly assure the successful role of its own propaganda.[131]

Catlin, of course, was not the first person to argue for the development of a political science that would concentrate on the construction of effective propaganda techniques in the interest of controlling public opinion. Fourteen years earlier Walter Lippmann, who did not share Catlin's compunction for precluding the democratic state from engaging in propaganda, had argued vigorously for a political science that would master the techniques by which the opinions of the mass society could be regulated and that would supply the necessary expert insight to those in position to formulate policy.

A man of enormous influence on American life as a journalist, public philosopher, and trusted advisor to several U.S. presidents, Lippmann was instrumental in redefining democracy for the 20th century.[132] In his 1922 book, *Public Opinion,* Lippmann maintained that democratic theory had placed misguided hope on the ability of the individual citizen to know his or her social environment accurately and thoroughly enough to make wise decisions about social policy. This inability was in the very nature of the human condition, although there were certain features of modern life that accentuated people's distortion of reality. "The environment with which our public opinions deal is refracted in many ways, by censorship and privacy at the source, by physical and social barriers at the other end, by scanty attention, by the poverty of language, by distraction, by unconscious constellations of feeling, by wear and tear, violence, monotony," Lippmann wrote. "These limitations upon our access to that environment combine with the obscurity and complexity of the facts themselves to thwart clearness and justice of perception, to substitute misleading fictions for workable ideas, and to deprive us of adequate checks upon those who consciously strive to mislead."[133]

Lippmann's proposed remedy consisted of constructing a "central agency," an "independent, expert organization for making the unseen facts intelligible to those who have to make the decisions," as well as organizing public opinion for the press.[134] Lippmann devoted a considerable part of his book to the logistics behind establishing this central agency, which he argued should be free from having to rely on the "annual doles from what may be a jealous or a parsimonious congress."[135] This central agency would be comprised largely of the educated elite and would "have in it the makings of national university."[136]

When Dewey reviewed Lippmann's *Public Opinion* in 1922, he called it "perhaps the most effective indictment of democracy as currently conceived ever penned."[137] When James W. Carey, contemporary communication researcher and former Dean of the College of Communications at the University of Illinois, reviewed the history of mass communications research 60 years later, he called it the founding book of the field.[138] Wilbur Schramm included a chapter from *Public Opinion* in his widely read 1949 anthology, *Mass Communications.*[139] Lippmann had indeed laid the foundations for a new field in which the control of public opinion through propaganda would be a major goal when he wrote in 1922:

Public opinion must be organized for the press if they are to be sound, not by the press as is the case today. This organization I conceive to be in the first instance the task of a political science that has won its proper place as formulator, in advance of real decision, instead of apologist, critic or reporter after the decision has been made . . . the perplexities of government and industry are conspiring to give political science this enormous opportunity to enrich itself and to serve the public.[140]

If the perplexities of government and industry were conspiring to give this science the "opportunity to enrich itself and to serve the public," it would be World War II that would solidify the efforts behind this conspiracy. Prior to World War II, government-sponsored mass communications research on university campuses was not widespread. During that time, mass communications research was conducted in departments like the Princeton Office of Radio Research, sponsored largely by foundations and broadcasting networks. The war, however, would greatly alter the relationship between the university social science departments and the government, and the government began to rely much more heavily on the social sciences in the conduct of its wartime policy objectives. The war effort required sophisticated information relating to morale, public opinion on a range of issues, and propaganda techniques by which opinions could be regulated or changed. Several governmental organizations were established, such as the Office of Emergency Management, the Coordinator of Information, the Office of Strategic Services, the Office of Facts and Figures, the Office of War Information, and others, and these organizations required the detailed and specialized knowledge of the social scientist, particularly as this knowledge related to mass communications. Walter Lippmann's hope for the organization of public opinion through the techniques of the social sciences began to become a reality.

NOTES

1. As quoted in Porter Sargent, *Between Two Wars: The Failure of Education, 1920–1940* (Boston: Porter Sargent, 1945), p. 30.

2. Melvin L. DeFleur and Sandra Ball-Rokeach, *Theories of Mass Communication* (New York: Longman, 1975), p. 93.

3. Harold D. Lasswell, Ralph D. Casey, and Bruce Lannes Smith, *Propaganda and Promotional Activities: An Annotated Bibliography* (Minneapolis: University of Minnesota Press, 1935).

4. Interestingly, during the same period a parallel and closely related debate occurred regarding the role of indoctrination in educational practice. See Paul C. Violas, "The Indoctrination Debate and the Great Depression," in *Roots of Crisis: American Education in the Twentieth Century*, edited by Clarence J. Karier, Paul C. Violas, and Joel Spring (Chicago: Rand McNally, 1973). See also Gail Paulus Sorenson, "Indoctrination and The Purposes of American Education: A 1930s Debate," in *Issues in Education, 3* (Fall 1985), pp. 79–98.

5. It is important to note that the first large-scale research project on the effects of motion pictures, the Payne Fund Studies of the early 1930s, came to the conclusion that this medium's

effects were significant in many dimensions. For a review of the Payne Fund Studies, see Shearon A. Lowery and Melvin L. DeFleur, *Milestones in Mass Communication Research* (New York: Longman, 1988), pp. 31–54. See also Garth S. Jowett, Ian C. Jarvie, and Kathryn H. Fuller, *Children and the Movies: Media Influence and the Payne Fund Controversy* (New York: Cambridge University Press, 1996).

6. In recent years there has been some interest among scholars within the communications field in studying the movement critical of propaganda between World War I and World War II. The goal here seems to be to locate an alternative "paradigm" at the origins of communication study in the United States and to call the received history about a widespread early belief in the "Magic Bullet" view of communications effects into question. The best of this work has been done by J. Michael Sproule. [See, for instance, J. Michael Sproule, "Propaganda Studies in American Social Science: The Rise and Fall of the Critical Paradigm," *Quarterly Journal of Speech, 73* (1987), pp. 60–78; J. Michael Sproule, "Progressive Critics and the Magic Bullet Myth," *Critical Studies in Mass Communication, 6* (1989), pp. 225–246; J. Michael Sproule, "Propaganda and American Ideological Critique," *Communication Yearbook, 4* (1991), pp. 211–238.] Such work is interesting, although too narrow for our purposes here, because what occured was not merely a "paradigm shift" in the history of communication study, but the creation of something new altogether that was then labeled "communication study."

7. Leonard W. Doob, *Propaganda: Its Psychology and Technique* (New York: Henry Holt, 1935), p. 3. See also George E. Gordon Catlin, "Propaganda as a Function of Democratic Government," in *Propaganda and Dictatorship: A Collection of Papers*, edited by Harwood Lawrence Childs (Princeton: Princeton University Press, 1936), p. 125.

8. Raymond Dodge, "The Psychology of Propaganda," *Religious Education, 15* (October 1920), p. 241.

9. Harold D. Lasswell, *Propaganda Technique in the World War* (New York: Knopf, 1927), p. 2.

10. And United States journalist Will Irwin reiterated this sentiment, although expressing a class-based dimension to the term's meaning, when he wrote in 1936:

> Before 1914, "propaganda" belonged only to literate vocabularies and possessed a reputable, dignified meaning. Over the door of an ancient structure in Rome there stood — and still stands — a legend, "College of Propaganda." For Propaganda, before the World War, meant simply the means which the adherent of a political or religious faith employed to convince the unconverted. Two Years later the word had come into the vocabulary of peasants and ditchdiggers and had begun to acquire its miasmic aura. . . . Some of those great government press bureaus so busily engaged in persuading neutrals or keeping their own people friendly to "national aims" had at first called themselves "Departments of Propaganda." By 1918 they had begun changing the title to "Department of Counter-Propaganda" — a hint that what the other side put forth was tainted or false and that their own output was the sanitary and corrective truth. When we entered the war, we introduced a variant by calling our bureau of propaganda The Committee on Public Information. Anything to avoid the sinister word!

Will Irwin, *Propaganda and the News: Or What Makes You Think So?* (New York: McGraw-Hill, 1936), pp. 3–4.

11. Agnes Repplier, "A Good Word Gone Wrong," *The Independent and the Weekly Review, 107* (7 October 1921), p. 5.

12. Sydney Stahl Weinberg, "Wartime Propaganda in a Democracy: America's Twentieth-Century Information Agencies" (Ph. D. diss., Columbia University, 1969).

13. Stephen Vaughn, *Holding Fast the Inner Lines: Democracy, Nationalism, and the Committee on Public Information* (Chapel Hill: The University of North Carolina Press, 1980), p. 3.

14. Howard Zinn, *A People's History of the United States* (New York: Harper & Row, 1980), p. 355.

15. Ibid., p. 355.

16. James R. Mock and Cedric Larson, *Words That Won The War: The Story of the Committee on Public Information, 1917–1919* (Princeton: Princeton University Press, 1939), pp. 67–74.

17. As quoted in ibid., pp. 45–46.

18. Zinn, *A People's History of the United States*, p. 359.

19. For a critical analysis of the suppression of dissent during this period, see William Preston, Jr., *Aliens and Dissenters: Federal Suppression of Radicals, 1903–1933* (New York: Harper & Row, 1963).

20. Mock and Larson, *Words That Won the War*, pp. 138–139.

21. As quoted in ibid., p. 81.

22. Ibid., p. 83.

23. Ibid., p. 72.

24. Ibid., p. 121.

25. Joel Spring, *Images of American Life: A History of Ideological Management in Schools, Movies, Radio, and Television*, (Albany: State University of New York Press, 1992), p. 27.

26. For a biographical sketch of Ford, see the introduction to Guy Stanton Ford, *On and Off Campus* (Minneapolis: University of Minnesota Press, 1938).

27. For a detailed discussion of some of these scholars who worked for Ford and within other divisions of the CPI, see Carol S. Gruber, *Mars and Minerva: World War I and the Uses of the Higher Learning in America* (Baton Rouge: Louisiana State University Press, 1975).

28. Mock and Larson, *Words That Won the War*, p. 7.

29. Ibid., p. 159.

30. Guy Stanton Ford, "A New Educational Agency," *Addresses and Proceedings of the National Educational Association, 56* (1918), p. 208.

31. J. Joseph Huthmacher, *Trial by War and Depression: 1917–1941* (Boston: Allyn & Bacon, 1973), pp. 27–28.

32. Edward A. Krug, *The Shaping of the American High School, 1880–1920* (Madison: University of Wisconsin Press, 1969), pp. 407–427.

33. Guy Stanton Ford, "The Schools As They Have Affected Government Activities," *Addresses and Proceedings of the National Educational Association, 57* (1919), p. 540.

34. See especially Clarence J. Karier, *The Individual, Society, and Education: A History of American Educational Ideas*, second edition (Urbana: University of Illinois Press, 1986).

35. Huthmacher, *Trial by War, and Depression: 1917–1941*, p. 35.

36. H. C. Englembrecht and F. C. Hanighen, *Merchants of Death: A Study of the International Armament Industry* (New York: Dodd, Mead, 1934).

37. E. T. Saintsbury, "Memoirs of a Four-Minute Man," *The American Mercury, 10* (March 1927), pp. 284–291.

38. C. H. Hamlin, *The War Myth in the United States History* (New York: Vanguard, 1927), p. 92.

39. Arthur Ponsonby, *Falsehoods in War-Time* (New York: Dutton, 1928), p. 14.

40. Ibid., p. 29.

41. Jacques Ellul, *Propaganda: The Formation of Men's Attitudes* (New York: Knopf, 1971), p. xi.

42. George Sylvester Viereck, *Spreading Germs of Hate* (New York: Horace Liveright, 1930), p. 11.

43. Edward K. Strong, Jr., "Control of Propaganda as a Psychological Problem," *The Scientific Monthly, 14* (March 1922), p. 236.

44. Lasswell, *Propaganda Techniques in the World War*, pp. 8–9.

45. Doob, *Propaganda: Its Psychology and Technique*, p. 89.

46. For an excellent overview of these definitions of propaganda during this period, see Barry Allen Marks, *The Idea of Propaganda in America* (unpublished dissertation, University of Minnesota, 1957).

47. John Dewey, "The New Paternalism," *The New Republic, 17* (21 December 1918), p. 216.

48. Ibid., p. 217.

49. Ibid., p. 216.

50. Ibid., p. 217.

51. Dodge, "The Psychology of Propaganda," p. 252.

52. Ibid.

53. U.S. Bureau of the Census, *Historical Statistics of the United States: Colonial Times to 1970,* Part I (Washington, D.C.: United States Government Printing Office, 1975), p. 400.

54. Roscoe C. E. Brown, "The Menace to Journalism," in *The North American Review, 214* (November 1921), pp. 610–618.

55. Ibid., p. 611.

56. Ibid.

57. Ibid., p. 618.

58. For an excellent contemporary discussion of this, see John Stauber and Sheldon Rampton, *Toxic Sludge Is Good For You! Lies, Damn Lies and the Public Relations Industry* (Monroe, Maine: Common Courage Press, 1995).

59. Carl Dreher, *Sarnoff: An American Success* (New York: Quadrangle/The New York Times Book Company, 1977), p. 217.

60. Adolf Hitler, *Mein Kampf,* trans. by Ralph Manheim (Cambridge, MA: The Riverside Press, 1943), pp. 176–186.

61. Irwin, *Propaganda and the News,* pp. 267–268.

62. As quoted in O. W. Riegel, *Mobilization For Chaos: The Story of the New Propaganda* (New Haven: Yale University Press, 1934), p. 1.

63. "The American Fascists," *The New Republic, 98* (8 March 1939), pp. 117–118. In 1934, O. W. Riegel characterized the sentiments of many of these individuals when he wrote of the dangers of fascist ideology and its reliance on the activity of propaganda:

> The menace of our time is the insidious encroachment of the intolerance of nationalism upon all the channels of approach to the human mind. The method of enslavement has proceeded from vassalage and physical force to the regimentation of thought. The nationalistic states of today have recognized the fact that the surest and safest form of control is that which regulates the kind of information and opinion which is available to national subjects, for a subject by conviction is a stronger defense than a subject by force. Foremost among the channels of information which determines man's thinking is the world-wide organization of electronical transmission devices which carry the burden of news. News is the vital factor in international life, and the control of it is at the core of the problem of nationalism.

Riegel, *Mobilization For Chaos,* p. 17. During World War II, Riegel became a propaganda analyst for the Office of War Information, and spent much of his career at Dartmouth College and then at Washington and Lee studying propaganda. See Wolfgang Saxon, "O. W. Riegel, 94, Early Expert on Propaganda," *The New York Times* (26 August 1997), p. D21.

64. National Education Association, *Report of the Committee on Propaganda in the Schools,* presented at the Atlanta Meeting of the National Education Association, July 1929.

65. "Announcement," *Propaganda Analysis: A Bulletin to Help the Intelligent Citizen Detect and Analyze Propaganda, 1* (October 1937), p. 3.

66. See, for instance, Wisconsin Teachers Association, *Report of the Committee on Propaganda in Schools,* 1929 and 1930.

67. As quoted in Alfred McClung Lee and Elizabeth Briant Lee, "An Influential Ghost: The Institute for Propaganda Analysis, 1936–1942," *Propaganda Review,* (Winter 1988), p. 12.

68. Lucy Maynard Salmon, *The Newspaper and Authority* (New York: Oxford University Press, 1923), p. 452.

69. Everett Dean Martin, *The Meaning of a Liberal Education* (New York: Norton, 1926), p. 48.

70. Frederick Lumley, *The Propaganda Menace* (New York: Century, 1933), pp. 301–329.

71. Everett Dean Martin, "Are We Victims of Propaganda: A Debate," *The Forum, 81* (March 1929), p. 145.

72. As quoted in Lumley, *The Propaganda Menace*, p. 34.

73. John Dewey, *Individualism Old and New* (New York: Capricorn, 1962).

74. Dewey, *Individualism Old and New*, pp. 42–43.

75. Ibid., p. 24.

76. Ibid., p. 32.

77. Ibid., p. 114.

78. Ibid., p. 163.

79. Ibid., pp. 127–128.

80. Ibid., p. 127.

81. For a biographical sketch of Biddle, see "Biddle, William Wishart," in *Contemporary Authors—Permanent Series,* vol. 2 (Detroit: Gale Research, 1978), p. 59.

82. William Biddle, *Propaganda and Education* (New York: Bureau of Publications, Teachers College, Columbia University, 1932), p. 2.

83. Ibid.

84. Ibid., p. 3.

85. William W. Biddle, "A Psychological Definition of Propaganda," *The Journal of Abnormal and Social Psychology, 26* (October–December, 1931), pp. 283–295.

86. Biddle, *Propaganda and Education*, p. 25.

87. Ibid., p. 36.

88. Dewey, *Individualism Old and New*, p. 83.

89. Ibid., p. 84.

90. Christopher Simpson, *Science of Coercion: Communication Research & Psychological Warfare, 1945–1960* (New York: Oxford University Press, 1994), p. 18.

91. Dewey, op. cit., pp. 85–86.

92. The editor of the volume, Elmer Ellis, understood well the importance of addressing the problem of teaching students to resist propaganda. This problem, Ellis wrote:

has been greatly complicated by the vast growth of the agencies of communication, the increased knowledge in the hands of experts in "sucker psychology," and the extreme complication of the issues themselves. Propaganda on public affairs is not confined to the newspaper editorial pages, to magazines of opinion, and to political speeches as many people, including some teachers, fondly imagine. It includes many other sources ranging from the unctuous speeches that fill the intermissions in broadcast programs of classical music to the emotionally toned radio news comment; from the movie censorship that keeps *It Can't Happen Here* off the screen to the news reel with a sharply pointed selection of pictures and comment; from the comic strips syndicated by extremely propagandistic newspapers to the fiction in the smooth paper magazine. This type of propaganda, disguised as information or entertainment, is one of the most serious problems which faces democratic government everywhere.

Elmer Ellis, editor, *Education Against Propaganda: Developing Skill in the Use of the Sources of Information about Public Affairs* (New York: National Council for the Social Studies, Seventh Yearbook, 1937), p. iii.

93. For a brief overview of the Institute's activities, see J. Michael Sproule, "The Institute for Propaganda Analysis: Public Education in Argumentation, 1937–1942," in *Argument in Transition: Proceedings of the Third Summer Conference on Argumentation,* edited by David Zarefsky, Malcolm O. Sillars, and Jack Rhodes (Annandale, VA: Speech Communication Association, 1983).

94. Alfred McClung Lee and Elizabeth Briant Lee, editors, *The Fine Art of Propaganda: A Study of Father Coughlin's Speeches* (New York: Harcourt, Brace, 1939), p. viii.

95. "Announcement," *Propaganda Analysis, 1.*

96. McClung and Lee, editors, *The Fine Art of Propaganda*.

97. Harold Lavine and James Wechsler, *War Propaganda and the United States* (New Haven: Yale University Press, 1940).

98. *Propaganda Analysis, 1* (October 1937 to October 1938).

99. *Propaganda: How to Recognize It and Deal With It* (New York: Institute For Propaganda Analysis, 1938); Violet Edwards, *Group Leader's Guide to Propaganda Analysis* (New York: Institute for Propaganda Analysis, 1938).

100. In the "name-calling device," the propagandist attempts to associate a negative word or term with what he or she is trying to get his target audience to reject. In the "glittering generalities device," the propagandist seeks to ascribe a positive or favorable word or term for whatever he or she is trying to win approval. In using the "transfer device," the propagandist is attempting to get the population to "transfer" larger favorable symbols, for instance church and state, to the position being advocated. The "testimonial device" refers to the practice of having some well-known figure either endorse or reject the position being sought. The propagandist tries to make it seem that he or she is just an ordinary person by using the "plain folks device," and the "bandwagon device" is used to show people that everyone else is adhering to the desired position. Finally, the "card-stacking device" refers to the deliberate campaign of disinformation and deception. See "How to Detect Propaganda," *Propaganda Analysis, 1* (November 1937), pp. 5–8.

101. Clyde R. Miller, "Preface," *Propaganda Analysis, 1* (October 1938), p. iv.

102. J. Michael Sproule, "Propaganda Studies in American Social Science: The Rise and Fall of the Critical Paradigm," p. 70.

103. Phyllis Meadows Hojem, *A Study of Propaganda and of the Analyses of the Institute for Propaganda Analysis, Incorporated* (unpublished masters thesis, University of Colorado, 1950), pp. 130–131.

104. Benjamin Fine, "Propaganda Study Instills Skepticism in 1,000,000 Pupils," *The New York Times,* (21 February 1991), p. 1A.

105. "Dies Scrutinizes Propaganda Study," *The New York Times* (23 February 1941), pp. 1, 21.

106. Ibid., p. 21. For an excellent study of Alfred McLung Lee and his wife Elizabeth Briant Lee that connects their critical antipropaganda work to the marginalization they experienced in American sociological circles, see John F. Galliher and James H. Galliher, *Marginality and Dissent in Twentieth Century American Sociology: The Case of Elizabeth Briant Lee and Alfred McClung Lee* (Albany: State University of New York Press, 1995).

107. August Raymond Ogden, *The Dies Committee: A Study of the Special House Committee For the Investigation of Un-American Activities, 1938–1944* (Washington, D.C.: Catholic University Press, 1945), pp. 236–237.

108. "Propaganda Study Loses 2 Educators," *The New York Times* (31 May 1941), p. 13.

109. William Garber, "Propaganda Analysis—To What Ends?" *American Journal of Sociology, 48* (September 1942), p. 240.

110. Weinberg, "Wartime Propaganda in a Democracy," pp. 107–137.

111. J. Michael Sproule argued that after Edward Filene's death in September 1937, the directors of his philanthropic foundation, the E. A. Filene Good Will Fund, eventually discontinued their funding of the institute. Sproule, "Propaganda Studies in American Social Science: The Rise and Fall of the Critical Paradigm," p. 70.

112. Lasswell, *Propaganda Technique in the World War,* p. 222.

113. Lumley, *The Propaganda Menace,* p. 27.

114. Wilbur Schramm, *The Beginnings of Communication Study in America: A Personal Memoir,* edited by Steven H. Chaffee and Everett Rogers (Thousand Oaks, CA: Sage, 1997), 35. Foster Dulles was the brother of Eisenhower's Secretary of State, John Foster Dulles, and Director of the CIA, Allen Dulles.

115. Harold D. Lasswell, *Democracy Through Public Opinion* (Menasha, WI: Banta, 1941), p. 66.

116. Communications theorist Stuart Ewen interviewed Bernays shortly before Bernays' death in March 1995 at the age of 102. Ewen reported that Bernays retained his fundamental commitment to the need for a hierarchical social order and the public relations expert's place in this order. See Stuart Ewen, *PR!: The Social History of Spin* (New York: Basic, 1996).

117. Edward L. Bernays, *Propaganda* (Port Washington, NY: Kennikat, 1928), p. 9.

118. Ibid., p. 159.

119. As quoted in Martin, "Are We Victims of Propaganda? A Debate," p. 143.

120. Ibid., pp. 143–144.

121. Peter Odegard was representative of this point of view when he reviewed the National Council for the Social Studies Seventh Yearbook, *Education Against Propaganda:* "There is a lack of historical perspective [in the yearbook] and the impression is given the propaganda is a sort of twentieth century witchcraft. There is an unexamined assumption that propaganda, like witchcraft, is necessarily evil and that the important task is to exorcise the demon rather than to understand the witch. . . . Propaganda as an instrument of social control is neither good nor bad. Its effectiveness depends ultimately upon the extent to which it gives symbolic representation to existing satisfactions or current discontents." See Peter Odegard, review of *Education Against Propaganda*, in *Public Opinion Quarterly, 1* (October 1937), p. 145.

122. Malcolm M. Willey, "Communication Agencies and the Volume of Propaganda," *The Annals of the American Academy of Political and Social Science, 179* (May 1935), p. 194.

123. Mock and Larson, *Words That Won the War.*

124. Carrol D. Clark, "News and Social Control," *American Sociological Society Papers, 29* (August 1935), p. 139.

125. For a biographical sketch of Catlin, see "Catlin, George Edward Gordon," *Contemporary Authors—First Revision*, vols. 13–16 (Detroit: Gale Research, 1975), pp. 147–148.

126. George E. Gordon Catlin, "Propaganda as a Function of Democratic Government," p. 132.

127. Ibid., p. 134.

128. Ibid., p. 127.

129. Ibid., p. 138.

130. Ibid., p. 137.

131. Ibid., p. 139.

132. See Ronald Steel, *Walter Lippmann and the American Century* (Boston: Little, Brown, 1980).

133. Walter Lippmann, *Public Opinion* (New York: Macmillan, 1927), p. 76.

134. Ibid., pp. 31–32.

135. Ibid., p. 387.

136. Ibid., p. 329.

137. John Dewey, "Public Opinion," *The New Republic, 30* (3 May 1922), p. 286.

138. James W. Carey, "The Mass Media and Critical Theory: An American View," in *Communication Yearbook 6,* edited by Michael Burgoon (Beverly Hills, CA: Sage, 1982), p. 23.

139. Wilbur Schramm, editor, *Mass Communications* (Urbana: University of Illinois Press, 1949), pp. 435–453.

140. Walter Lippmann, *Public Opinion*, pp. 31–30.

CHAPTER TWO

Communications Research
Comes of Age

*If managerial problems for industry and the military are to
continue to dominate the research of leading social psychologists
and sociologists, the value orientation of the managerial technician
rather than the value orientation of the social science educator will
dominate what evolves and is called social science. The emphasis
can thus shift from service to citizens in a democracy to service
for those who temporarily control and who wish to continue
to control segments of our society.*

—Alfred McLung Lee, 1949[1]

THE SOCIAL CRISIS precipitated by the economic depression, and
the severe dislocation wrought by technological developments still
naively regarded as "progress," compelled many people in the 1930s to ask
fundamental questions about their principal institutions and the values on
which these institutions were sustained. "What should be the central purpose of our educational institutions?" asked thinkers of every ideological
orientation, and "What knowledge, what view of human being, and what institutional practices are necessary and appropriate to guide such purposes?"
The social foundations of education, as an integral component of teacher
education programs looking to break with the technique-driven normal
school tradition, was born of this kind of questioning. Teachers were to have
a deepened understanding of the social and historical context in which they
worked and be able to raise critical questions about the larger social order
and their own teaching in relation to it. The emerging mass media in many
ways supplanted the "educational" influence of traditional schooling, even
as they dramatically altered the social environment in which schooling took
place. But through the 1930s, at least, significant effort was made to expand
teachers' awareness of the vital role they played in shaping students' consciousness, and to inquire into whose political and economic interests this
was being done.

By 1939, Columbia University sociologist Robert S. Lynd had brought these fundamental issues to bear on the way knowledge was constructed in the social sciences. In his brilliant but soon forgotten book *Knowledge For What? The Place of Social Science in American Culture,* Lynd recognized that "the controlling factor in any science is the way it views and states its problems."[2] As with any social phenomena, the activity of social inquiry is conditioned by the larger culture of which it is a part, which in turn is determined considerably by the way power is manifest in any particular culture. Lynd argued that, increasingly, social scientists in the United States were merely accepting the problems, and the definitions of those problems, provided by those whose economic and political interests were firmly entrenched in the status quo. Social scientists were losing their independence, and knowledge in the social sciences was losing its human bearing, as social scientists gravitated to the funding sources offered by those of wealth and privilege. Moreover, social scientists were surrendering their pursuit of objectivity as they were "drawn deeper within the net of assumptions by which the institutions [they are] studying profess to operate." Technical expertise and fragmentation of knowledge multiplied as social scientists refrained from asking the troublesome question: "Where are our institutions taking us, and where do we want them to take us?"[3] The basic purpose behind much of what passed as serious inquiry in the social sciences was suspect to Lynd. Social scientists needed to critically raise foundational questions about their work; they needed to examine carefully why they were engaged in such work and who would profit from it.

For Lynd, this situation was especially urgent in the area of propaganda and mass persuasion research, where the undemocratic implications seemed quite clear to him: "In doing such work, the social psychologist tends to sell merely his technical proficiency, with only casual knowledge of, and often with a disregard for, the task of analyzing the functioning serviceability of man's economic and other institutions."[4] Yet guided by a pragmatism that permitted the ends to justify the means, and a rather superficial understanding of the difference between private and public interests, Lynd actually encouraged research into the kind of manipulation he purported to deplore.

> In a world bristling with dictators wielding all the arts of propaganda, democracy will no longer be able to survive with a laissez-faire attitude toward public opinion. It must take the offensive in its own behalf and use these new and potent instruments for the ends of democracy. Already in the United States the "management of public opinion" for private ends is highly developed. We must either discover a way to democratize this process or give over the pretense of being a democracy.[5]

It is difficult to imagine that Lynd was unaware of the essential contradiction in his analysis here: that these "new and potent instruments" used by dictators could not be utilized for democratic purposes, and that a managed public opinion is not truly reflective of a democratic public's opinion. Lynd's declaration in 1939 evinced a willingness to foreclose analysis of the larger meaning of "these new and potent instruments" and to assume that they represented neutral techniques that could be harnessed to achieve whatever ends were desired. This position became even more clear as Lynd joined the discussions of the Rockefeller Foundation Group on Mass Communications Research, which in many ways set the direction for much of the subsequent work in this area.

Despite the fundamental questions raised in the 1930s about education, the social sciences, and propaganda, the larger trend was against such circumspection. Instead, there was a growing interest among certain academic, business, and governmental circles in bringing the methods of the social sciences to bear on the problems of managing the opinions of a mass society. A cadre of young scholars, with precisely these intentions and skills, was introduced into the world of U.S. politics and business during the 1930s. George Gallup took his Ph.D. at the University of Iowa in 1928 to emerge as a leader of the new field of public opinion polling. Frank Stanton, the future president of CBS, graduated from Ohio State University in 1935 after having developed a sophisticated device that could be attached to radio receivers to determine surreptitiously the listening patterns of his subjects. And Paul F. Lazarsfeld, who emigrated from Vienna to the United States in 1933 on a Rockefeller Fellowship, quickly became a leading figure in conducting applied communications research for advertisers and broadcasting networks. By 1937, the *Public Opinion Quarterly* was founded to serve as "a clearing house of information and a meeting ground of thought for all interested in public opinion."[6] This journal was needed, argued its editors, because "scholarship [on public opinion] is developing new possibilities of scientific approach as a means of verifying hypotheses and of introducing greater precision of thought and treatment."[7] Even before war broke out in September 1939, there was a significant and growing body of researchers concerned with problems of social control through the use of the mass media.[8]

World War II both accelerated this trend and provided an unusual set of circumstances that gave rise to the demand for mass communications research in the United States and led to its institutionalization as an important area of study on university campuses in the postwar period. The war legitimized the ideology of social control undergirding mass communications research: The construction of propaganda organizations during the war provided an important training ground for mass communications researchers; and through these organizations, mass communications researchers made important personal contacts that facilitated the establishment of the field in the postwar period. As the mass media became the dominant educational institution in the 20th century, these communications specialists became key figures in training the "new educators" and defining the meaning of their work. This chapter reviews some of the major historical circumstances that gave rise to mass communications research during the war and provided fertile soil for its growth on university campuses after the war.

THE ROCKEFELLER FOUNDATION GROUP ON MASS COMMUNICATIONS RESEARCH

Shortly after the beginning of World War II, the Rockefeller Foundation convened a group of social scientists and educators to consider the broad social and disciplinary issues of mass communications research. This group of scholars—including Paul Lazarsfeld, Harold Lasswell, Robert Lynd, Lyman Bryson, and others—"intended to formulate a disciplined approach to the study of mass communication in present day society" through informal discussions. These discussions apparently occurred at several meetings and spanned at least 11 months. Out of these discussions emerged two lengthy memoranda entitled "Public Opinion and the Emergency," dated December 1, 1939, and "Research in Mass Communication," dated July 1940. Although these memoranda were not intended for publication, they represent a significant record of the early thinking about the social uses of mass communications research.[9]

The first of the two memoranda, "Public Opinion and the Emergency," sought to understand the role that mass communications research would likely play during the war. In many ways, this memorandum was a diversion from the stated goal of articulating the more general role of mass communications research in a society presumably at peace; yet it is clear that the contributors thought that the war would in no small measure advance the cause of mass communications research, and that accurate mass communications research would greatly add to the actual conduct of the war effort. The contributors had little doubt, in December 1939, that the emergency situation would require the government to establish specific organizations whose task it would be to monitor and shape U.S. opinions about war-related policy. "Whether one likes it or not," the contributors stated, "a state of full emergency necessitates the deliberate formation and control of public opinion."[10] The contributors also realized that, although much progress had been made in understanding how to best control America's collective consciousness, there still existed variations of that collective consciousness that remained largely unexplored. The emergency situation would provide an excellent laboratory for systematically studying those many aspects about public opinion that had not been treated extensively. Looking forward to the postwar world, the contributors wrote:

Students of public opinion . . . agree that the present emergency offers an opportunity which is perhaps uniquely advantageous for making the observations on which any solid undertaking of the operation of public opinion in the United States will have to rest. In emphasizing considerations of national interest such an emergency inevitably is characterized by a sharper focussing of public opinion than occurs in ordinary times. This focussing in turn results in an acceleration and an intensification in the formation of opinion which makes its development peculiarly quick and easy to observe. In a sense then, the unusual factors now in play would not make findings less valid for ordinary times. Rather they serve only to throw into sharper relief the ordinary operations of public opinion. Thus the emergency seems to provide what is almost a laboratory situation for obtaining needed knowledge of the formation of public opinion in a democratic society such as now exists in the United States.[11]

The writers of this memorandum knew that mass communications research would be beneficial to the war effort, and that the war effort would greatly expand existing knowledge of how best to influence U.S. public opinion through the use of the mass media. With this in mind, Lazarsfeld, Lasswell, and their colleagues from the Rockefeller Foundation discussions began to plan for a mass communications research program that would serve these ends during the wartime emergency.

In constructing this mass communications research program, a primary concern among the contributors was the need to identify those particular symbols that possessed strong persuasive powers over various parts of the population. The contributors thought they had a reasonably sound understanding of what basic symbols would surface as important guideposts for public opinion. The notion of "aliens" would most assuredly be associated with those things considered "subversive," whereas "pulling together for the common good," "nonpartisanship," "national defense," "national unity," and other such symbols would be associated with those things considered to be in the national interest.

However, the contributors knew that their knowledge was "patently insufficient" to predict precisely how such symbols would operate on the U.S. public.[12] In addition, the contributors realized that there existed great variability in U.S. public opinion that would need to be understood. Different types of people attend to different kinds of media, the contributors noted, and people in various parts of the country would be responsive to different symbols, as would people who belonged to various groups. "The diffusion and acceptance of symbols," the contributors wrote, "will vary among different class, racial, and special interest groups which both initiate and undergo pressure, as, for example, the American Legion, the United States Chamber of Commerce, the C.I.O., or the German American Bund. . . . Any adequate observation of American public opinion, then, must be largely concerned with such variations. For only as they are discovered and characterized by observation will it be possible to understand how public opinion operates in this country."[13] Among the many groups and classes of people who would be slated for close observations so as to ascertain how to most effectively influence them, were groups based on differences in gender and age. "It is very generally agreed, that whoever wins the minds of youth has a trump for the future," the memorandum stated. "Recent studies of youth movements and youth organizations in many lands have painted vivid pictures of the world-wide struggle for the control of the political attitudes of the young."[14] Therefore, the writers recommended that extensive surveys be conducted on young people in schools, in colleges, and at work to detect changes in "youth attitudes, the rise of emerging leaders, and the course of political activism." Likewise, "the activities, communications, and aims of organized women's groups should be observed and correlated."[15]

This 1939 memorandum considered many of the various methodological approaches to mass communication that were gaining acceptance by the late 1930s, including polls and short interviews, content analysis, community studies, and others, although panel studies were seen as particularly important in the construction of this research program. As opposed to straw ballots or traditional polling techniques that can only indicate whether or not public opinion has changed on an issue, panel studies provide a way of determining *which* people have actually changed their opinions. The panel studies consist of a process by which the same sample group can be polled or interviewed several times over an extended period, and it is consequently a more sophisticated method of determining what kinds of communication messages are most effective in shaping the opinions of particular groups of people. In order to establish an accurate picture of public opinion on key issues among various groups and in various parts of the country, the contributors to the memorandum sketched out a list of 100 cities where such panel studies should be established. "It would be desirable to have panels established in key cities with population of 10,000 and up," the contributors wrote, "chosen for their representativeness as to size, locality, ethnic-composition and major industries."[16] In addition, the contributors thought it would be important to establish connections in the metropolitan areas of Washington, D.C., Hollywood, and New York, which dominate "symbol manipulations" in the United States. "It is indispensable to provide trained interviewers in these cities to establish and maintain proper connections with the governmental and economic and communication interests which predominate in these places."[17] Finally, in a proposal strikingly similar to Walter Lippmann's in 1922, the contributors conceived of establishing a "central coordinating agency . . . to stimulate concurrent researches, to perform continuously approximate coordinations, and to provide for intercommunication and interstimulation between the separate studies."[18]

The writers of this memorandum were aware that they would face some resistance to their attempts to gauge U.S. opinions through panel studies and other methods. Yet they thought that this resistance could be surmounted if their actions were presented to the U.S. people in the proper way. "Properly handled, poll and panel procedures can strengthen community interest in cooperating with field investigations. A panel can be called 'an informal citizens' committee'. It can be presented as part of a great national program for the consultation of the people's will."[19] The contributors were perceptive to note that there existed significant resistance in the United States to attempts to manipulate public opinion, and that it was necessary to try to neutralize this resistance by putting the best face on one's own activities. The contributors were even more perceptive to note, however, that this very symbol of resistance could be tapped so as to shape opinion:

> One somewhat novel type of symbol may be anticipated—paradoxically enough—symbols of symbol manipulation. Different groups and individuals (administrators both civilian and military, journalists, broadcasters, film makers, and speakers) will find it desirable to maximize their influence by symbolizing how others are manipulating the public mind. Current concerns have already given *propaganda* such standing and all the *pro* and *anti* symbols are likely to gain new acceptance.[20]

There is some irony in the idea that the antipropaganda position, which had gathered so much momentum between the wars, could itself be considered for its propaganda value by late 1939.

If the December 1939 memorandum "Public Opinion and the Emergency" aimed primarily to address the role of mass communications research during the war, the July 1940 memorandum "Research in Mass Communications" sought to articulate the role for mass communications in the larger context of modern society. Like the earlier memorandum, "Research in Mass Communication" highlighted many of the research methods that were gaining favor among social science researchers during this period and that were applicable to mass communications research. And like the earlier memorandum, this July 1940 memorandum attempted to consider the costs and logistics of establishing a large-scale mass communications research program. Yet this memorandum departed from the earlier memorandum in that the writers referred to it as "a statement of belief." "Research in Mass Communication," therefore, represented a clear and significant ideological statement about the need for mass communications research by some of the field's founders. Understanding why these early researchers regarded mass communications research to be an essential activity in modern society, helps to explain what kind of society they observed and what kind of society they hoped to create.

This "statement of belief" of the need for mass communications research was premised on what the writers regarded as three "facts." The first, and most important, of these facts concerned what the writers saw as the increasing complexity of the modern world, coupled with the belief that the "public mind" would be unable to contend with this complexity on its own. Thus, echoing Walter Lippmann in his 1922 book *Public Opinion,* mass communication research was conceived to be a necessary tool for helping the "public mind" adapt to the swirl of social changes, and for helping governmental leadership to "secure consent" for its policy objectives. "The public mind today is and for years to come will be, subject to peculiar strains," the contributors wrote. They continued:

> The rapidity and complexity of developing events bewilders the mind, threatens sober judgment, and tends to call in question values, assumptions, and customary actions confirmed by habit in times less violently subject to change. Modern instruments of communication—the press, the radio, the film— have introduced new complications and new potentialities in our society, the import of which is even now but dimly understood. Our purpose is to throw light upon the ways and means by which, given the necessity for change, the public mind can most effectively be helped to adapt itself in time to necessary change—helped to reappraise prevalent beliefs, discarding what has become irrelevant and outworn, retaining whatever remains fundamental.[21]

The writers did not specify what beliefs they regarded as "irrelevant" or "outworn," or what beliefs they regarded to be "fundamental." Presumably, these decisions would have to be made by governmental policymakers, who would be scientifically apprised of the nature of the public mind by mass communications researchers. Appealing to a vague notion of an American way of life, however, the writers stressed the need for creating and sustaining consensus around these values:

> We believe . . . that in the exacting times which lie ahead, public opinion will be a decisive factor. If America is to meet the necessity of adapting to a changing world, and at the same time preserve the ways of life that Americans hold dear, that adaptation must be achieved with public consent. In securing that consent, public opinion and the influences affecting will be crucial.[22]

Some may argue that to assume there exist "ways of life which Americans hold dear" implies that there exists a consensus with respect to these ways of life, and therefore attempts to create and sustain conformity around these values is unnecessary. Yet, for the writers of this memorandum, the notion of consensus and the scientific means to achieve it were of primary importance.

The second belief offered by the memorandum's writers that they thought justified the need for widespread mass communications research concerned "the relevance of research to public policy." Counterpoising public policy with private enterprise, the writers argued that in times of crises, which they conceived to be the status quo in the modern world, "government must either obtain cooperation from private enterprise in the field of communication or impose its own controls in order to secure the ends of government."[23] In either case, the writers thought it was necessary that governmental policymakers possess the expertise and know-how to effectively shape public opinion. Mass communications research would provide the necessary knowledge base. "Government which rests upon consent rests also upon knowledge of how best to secure consent," they argued. "Research in the field of mass communications research is a new and sure weapon to achieve that end."[24]

Finally, Lazarsfeld, Lasswell, and their associates argued their case for mass communications research on the basis that the techniques of measuring and shaping public opinion were already at hand, and that these techniques should be utilized by government policymakers. Moreover, they appeared to assume a distinct divergence of economic and political interests between public governmental policy and private corporate policy, which is, of course, not widely true of the United States today: "Techniques for the study of communication have long since been developed and applied in the fields of market research, advertising, propaganda, publicity, and public relations. Studies using these techniques produce facts of great importance for *private* policy. The techniques themselves are transferable and should be used to support *public* policy."[25] Although these techniques for shaping public opinion had been greatly enhanced, the contributors admitted that there were limits to the "present state of technical research." Therefore, they argued vigorously for funding this mass communications research, which they envisioned as essential to the very functioning of modern society.

"Research in Mass Communication" provided a hypothetical example of how government policymakers could utilize mass communications research effectively; it offered a description of Lasswell's "who says what to whom and with what effect" model,[26] which clearly demonstrated the applied character of the model; and it discussed some of the logistics behind the establishment of a large-scale research program in mass communication. Yet, equally noteworthy is not what is included in this and the earlier memorandum, but what has been left out. There are no discussions, for instance, of the social implications of such a widespread program of mass communications research that aimed to manufacture consensus; no articulation of the differences or similarities between state and privately sponsored propaganda; no apparent understanding of how reducing public policy issues to the level of advertising might effect the workings of an alleged democracy, or might affect the critical abilities of alleged free and autonomous individuals within this society; and no articulation of whose problems would be addressed by this research and whose problems would go unexplored.

In any event, it is important from our perspective to note that these views on the efficacy of utilizing mass communications research in the construction of consensus were alive in the culture even before the United States entered World War II. Indeed, the memoranda that grew out of the Rockefeller Foundation discussion groups make it clear that several of the founding figures in the field, including Paul F. Lazarsfeld and Harold D. Lasswell, regarded the development of conformity of opinion as the main goal of their research. Likewise, it is important to note that these views, although accentuated by the war, were not confined solely to problems of the society at war, but rather were seen as directly relevant to modern society in times of relative peace as well. These views were at work in the establishment of propaganda organizations during the war and in their continuation in the postwar period.

PROPAGANDA AGENCIES DURING WORLD WAR II

As the United States' entry into World War II became imminent, the need to develop organizations that could monitor and shape public opinion seemed urgent to many policymakers in the Roosevelt administration. A poll conducted as late as November 1941 revealed that only about one third of the population would vote for the immediate entrance of the United States into the war.[27] In response to the growing World War, President Roosevelt began to establish a series of intelligence agencies and propaganda organizations that attempted to monitor and shape public opinion both at home and abroad. These propaganda and intelligence agencies served as major influences on the development of the mass communications field.

At first, Roosevelt was slow in establishing these institutions of propaganda and intelligence, and his early attempts lacked any real centralized organizational structure. Although he had utilized publicity campaigns throughout his attempt to gain acceptance for his New Deal programs, and although he himself was a persuasive speaker who used radio to his advantage, Roosevelt had remained acutely aware of the pejorative connotation that the term *propaganda* had come to possess in the wake of the activities of the Committee on Public Information. He was therefore not anxious to repeat the mistakes of Woodrow Wilson and George Creel by establishing a centralized and highly powerful propaganda agency, or any agencies that could be obviously regarded as such.[28]

In 1939, Roosevelt established the Office of Emergency Management (OEM) to serve as an umbrella organization for the many war-related executive agencies that were developing. He appointed Nelson Rockefeller to head the Coordinator of Inter-American Affairs (CIAA) in 1940, which was to oversee the propaganda campaigns in Latin America. In May 1941, Roosevelt set up the Office of Civilian Defense (OCD), under the direction of New York City Mayor Fiorello La Guardia, which existed as a unit within the Office of Emergency Management. The OCD was the initial organization to deal with domestic matters relating to morale, public opinion, and civilian defense in the years preceding U.S. involvement in the war. In July 1941, Roosevelt created the Office of the Coordinator of Information (COI) to gather and analyze intelligence information relating to national security and to carry out limited espionage activities abroad, and appointed Colonel William Donovan as its head. In August of that same year, Roosevelt appointed playwright Robert Sherwood to direct the Foreign Information Service (FIS), a branch of Donovan's COI, which was to provide the rest of the world with carefully selected information concerning the United States' activities as well as collect intelligence data abroad. The Voice of America, the pro-American propaganda network, was at first situated within Sherwood's Foreign Information Service. In October 1941, Roosevelt created the Office of Facts and Figures (OFF) from a branch of the Office of Civilian Defense, and appointed poet and Librarian of Congress Archibald MacLeish to head that unit. The Office of Facts and Figures was to evaluate public opinion on a range of issues and, in Roosevelt's words, "to facilitate a widespread and accurate understanding of the status and progress of the national defense effort . . . and activities of Government."[29]

There was considerable overlap in the functions and activities of these various organizations, and consequently they were not as efficient or as effective as they might have been had they been situated within a centralized organization. In addition, these organizations generally were understaffed and lacked the authority to act independently of normal channels of government decision making. Then, with the Japanese attack on Pearl Harbor on December 7, 1941, the nature of these organizations were changed dramatically. The United States' entrance into the war required a much stronger and more pervasive propaganda effort, both against the enemy and against the domestic and allied populations. On June 13, 1942, Roosevelt created the Office of War Information (OWI), and appointed Elmer Davis of CBS to serve as its head. Davis was empowered to coordinate, "formulate and carry out, through the use of press, radio, motion picture, and other facilities, information programs designed to facilitate the development of an informed and intelligent understanding, at home and abroad, of the status and progress of the war effort and of the war policies, activities, and aims of the Government."[30] The OWI was constructed around both a domestic and foreign component, and it incorporated early propaganda organizations such as MacLeish's Office of Facts and Figures and Sherwood's Foreign Information Service into its structure, although Rockefeller's CIAA was to remain a separate organization.[31] Also on June 13, 1942, the Coordinator of Information became the new Office of Strategic Services (OSS). William Donovan was retained to direct the new OSS, which contained various operational branches such as Research and Analysis (R&A), Secret Intelligence (SI), Morale Operations (MO), and other divisions relating to espionage, intelligence gathering, and psychological warfare. Donovan was to exercise considerable power over the operations of the OSS, which was to employ almost 30,000 people by the time of the war's end.[32]

Because the OSS, the OWI, and other organizations within the various military branches and War Department were involved in the activity of persuasion, mass communication, and propaganda, it is not surprising that they would draw many of their employees from the ranks of those occupations that required the careful and skillful manipulation of language — publicists, journalists, radio broadcasters, advertisers, radio and newspaper executives, and so on. Among the many people who worked in this capacity during the war were William Paley, the President of CBS, who served as Deputy Chief of the Office of Psychological Warfare under General Eisenhower; Frank Stanton, who at the time was Director of Audience Research for CBS; David Sarnoff, the President of RCA, who coordinated press and radio communications for the Allies; *Newsweek* journalist Edward Barrett; newspaper magnate Gardner Cowles, Jr.; and scores of people from the entertainment industry, including actors, musicians, movie directors, athletes, and others. In addition, from the very beginning these organizations drew heavily from America's literary and intellectual elite — historians, novelists, social scientists from a range of disciplines, and so on — to staff these organizations and to direct research projects to be used by these organizations. People like psychologists Jerome Bruner, Carl Hovland, and Daniel Katz; public opinion poll experts George Gallup, Elmo Roper, and Rensis Likert; sociologists Leonard Doob, Paul Lazarsfeld, Morris Janowitz, and Robert Merton; political scientists Harold Lasswell and Daniel Lerner; historians William Langer and Arthur Schlesinger; literary humanist Wilbur Schramm; anthropologist Margaret Mead; librarian Bernard Berelson; and educators Lyman Bryson and George Stoddard were but a small number of the many university-based researchers who would lend their services to the war effort in the wartime propaganda and intelligence agencies.

Within the first 6 months following the United States' entrance into World War II, one observer noted that the number of social scientists who took jobs with the federal government "was as great as the number of social science positions in the entire federal service in 1938."[33] Although not all the social scientists who rushed to aid the war effort were to engage in mass communications research for the wartime propaganda agencies, those social scientists who did perform such research would form the nucleus around which the discipline of mass communications began to develop. It was here in the OSS, the OWI, and various military branches that these researchers began to establish close professional contacts, and these contacts became important when communication departments and units began to appear on university campuses in the postwar period. Not only did researchers become acquainted with colleagues with whom they would increasingly share academic departments, but these researchers also became acquainted with those governmental officials and with those governmental agencies who would find the results of their research so useful. It is difficult to overstate the significance of the kinds of professional contacts that developed among these researchers during the war years; and the feeling of duty and patriotism that must have accompanied their work should not be diminished. Nevertheless, it is equally important to recognize that these researchers coalesced around the study of mass communications in attempt to solve certain applied problems of the government at war. The ideological commitments of such applied work would thus be at the very foundations of the field.

On the foreign front, social scientists developed propaganda techniques that could be used to create disunity and rebellion among enemy nations in preparation for large-scale U.S. military invasions, and to sustain morale and conformity among the United States' allies. The research and analysis branch (R&A) of the OSS, headed by Harvard historian William Langer, was to be a main contributor to this kind of research. Langer would recall in 1947 that it was Donovan's "chief aim" in establishing the OSS "to bring into government service scholars who, in addition to their specialized knowledge of foreign countries, were trained in particular disciplines and thoroughly grounded in the methods of assembling, selecting, evaluating and presenting evidence."[34] Working primarily through the Library of Congress and such university departments as the Institute of Human Relations at Yale, and other institutes at Stanford, the University of California at Berkeley, the University of Denver, Columbia, and Yale, R&A sought to collect information concerning the social and cultural tendencies of the society to be propagandized, develop particular propaganda techniques that would be effective in that society, and evaluate the effectiveness of various propaganda operations.[35] From the very earliest days of the war, Donovan had sought to wage war on this psychological level, as official OSS historian Kermit Roosevelt wrote of Donovan's plans:

> The fruits of the intelligence processed by research and analysis would be available to strategic planning and to the propaganda service. Propaganda, as the "arrow of initial penetration," would become the first phase in operations. Special operations in the form of sabotage, fifth column work and other types of subversion would be the next phase. Then would come the commando raids and the harassing guerrilla tactics and uprisings behind the lines. With all of these reaching a peak at H-Hour, the softening-up process of a target territory would be complete. then would follow actual invasion by the armed forces.[36]

The OSS employed a full range of activities in achieving these ends, including radio broadcasts, leaflet drops, newspapers, planting rumors, and other forms of "black" propaganda (propaganda in which the true identity of the communicator is concealed), and the success of these endeavors doubtlessly ensured that these operations would be continued once the OSS was institutionalized as the CIA in the postwar period.

The Office of War Information also employed social scientists in its overseas branch, although the OWI did not possess the "operational" espionage arm that the OSS did, nor is the OWI generally regarded as having widely engaged in the kind of "black" propaganda that was characteristic of the OSS. By the end of 1943, the overseas branch of the OWI operated with a budget of $34 million, with which it published books and pamphlets, and created films, broadcast radio news programs, and other items.[37] Social scientists were employed in the overseas branch of the OWI primarily to measure the effectiveness of these various propaganda campaigns and to make recommendations concerning propaganda policy to be directed at both allies and enemies. After the war, Leonard Doob, a Yale sociologist who served as Chief of the Bureau of Overseas Intelligence for the OWI, would downplay the usefulness of social scientists in the overseas branch. Doob argued that the research provided to the policymakers of the OWI was generally completed too late to be of much use, and it was often presented in such an abstract and lengthy manner that it could not be easily utilized by the policymakers. Nevertheless, Doob argued that the social scientist could be of value to the policymakers if he or she was willing to step outside of the normal functioning of his or her discipline. Doob wrote in 1947:

> Social scientists who deliberately sought to be useful, therefore, were impelled to adapt themselves to the people and problems confronting them. This required a kind of plasticity which had no relationship whatsoever to social science and the organization chart, but which the individual had to possess or acquire as quickly as possible. He learned to function in a situation teeming with problems in social science, but lacking the data of social science.[38]

Doob was no doubt accurate in his assessment of the need for social scientists to alter their normal course of conducting research in order to be effective during the war. In most cases, the war effort required immediate information; the slow and methodical pace by which most social science research is conducted would not fulfill the needs of that effort. In the absence of optimal research conditions, social scientists had to rely on more commonsensical or intuitive assessments of particular techniques of propaganda and manipulation. Yet, this does not mean that social scientists were unsuccessful in making these kinds of adjustments and thus unable to provide policymakers with important and insightful analysis. Indeed, as the many published accounts of the successes of allied propaganda attest, social scientists were indispensable in the effective and efficient conduct of the war.[39]

It should be noted that not all social scientists who were engaged in research relating to the control of foreign populations were working under inferior or rushed conditions. Some social scientists were able to study literally captive audiences. Shortly after U.S. citizens of Japanese descent were imprisoned in early 1942, the War Relocation Authority dispatched a team of social scientists to the relocation center at Poston in the Colorado River Valley. Under the direction of psychiatrist Alexander Leighton, the social science team engaged in the threefold task of (a) aiding the internment camp administrators "by analyzing the attitudes (and responses) of the evacuees . . . to administrative acts and to draw practical conclusions as to what worked well, what did not work so well and why"; (b) preparing for the eventual U.S. occupation of Japan by gathering "data of a general character that might be of value in the administration of dislocated communities in occupied areas"; and (c) "training field workers of Japanese ancestry in social analysis so that they could be helpful in occupied areas of the Pacific, during or after the war."[40] Before the end of the war, with his practical experience in hand, Leighton was placed in the Foreign Morale Analysis Division of the Office of War Information, from which he directed psychological warfare operations on Japan.[41]

Social scientists were also utilized extensively in the domestic branch of the OWI. The domestic branch was broken down into several divisions, including the News Bureau, the Radio Bureau, the Bureau of Publications and Graphics, and the Bureau of Motion Pictures, from which the OWI created, dispersed, and censored news reports, radio programming, a wide variety of publications, and (in collusion with Hollywood's movie moguls) a series of films. Social scientists were housed primarily within the Bureau of Intelligence and the Bureau of Special Operations, from which they conducted large-scale surveys of U.S. opinion on a range of issues in efforts to ascertain areas that required modification, and to evaluate the success of various attempts to modify opinions. No area of U.S. opinion of importance to the war effort escaped their close and careful scrutiny. The domestic branch of the OWI, in cooperation with the National Opinion Research Center (which was then located at the University of Denver), conducted surveys of public opinion on such seemingly obscure topics as "Public Attitudes Toward the Ban on Pleasure Driving and the Equalization of the Gasoline Ration," "Worker Reaction to the Employment Stabilization Plan for the Louisville Area," "A Study of Boy Scout Distribution of Posters in Twelve Cities," ""Effectiveness of the Campaign to Collect Waste Fats," and "Home Canning Plans of American Women." On issues apparently more directly relevant to morale, the OWI conducted surveys on such topics as "The American Public Views our Russian Ally," "Public Appreciation of the Problem of Inflation," "How the Populace Regards the Government's Handling of War News," "Women Appraise the Food Situation," "Negro Attitude Toward Certain War-Connected Problems," "Urban–Rural Differences in People's Attitudes Toward the War and Related Matters," "Consumer Attitudes Toward Rationing and Related Problems," "Business Men Talk About Nazism and The German People," "War Information and the Changing Outlook Toward Russia and England," and "The Public Looks at Manpower Problems."[42]

The alliance between the Soviet Union and the United States during the war required the OWI to attempt to counter 2 decades of anti-Soviet propaganda. Several OWI-sponsored movies—such as *Mission to Moscow, Song of Russia, Three Russian Girls,* and *North Star*—were produced with the explicit intention of creating a positive image of the Soviet Union among U.S. audiences.[43] The need to ration food, gasoline, and other items, and the need to conserve and collect resources for the war effort, required the OWI to counter the strong currents of an incipient consumer culture. In the face of great inequities of wealth, strong appeals were made to an already restricted population to scrimp, save, and accept rationing regulations. Finally, the exigency of war required the OWI to face inherent U.S. racism and chauvinism. Although the war required full employment at home, an OWI survey in January 1943 indicated that two thirds of the population was against hiring recent immigrants for war industry work, at least one third of the public opposed the idea of giving African Americans equal access to war jobs, and that a majority of women had been conditioned to believe that their greatest contribution to the war effort would be made by remaining in the home.[44] In addition, a 1942 survey conducted by the Office of Facts and Figures revealed that 49% of African Americans thought that they would be no worse off, and 18% thought that they would be better off, if Japan were to win the war.[45] Obviously, these were not the kinds of attitudes from which those in power could hope to build a unified and enthusiastic war machine. In response, the OWI sought to diminish the image of the bomb-throwing radical immigrant, to promote an image of African Americans as possessing greater access to the fruits of the American dream, and to encourage the image of "Rosie the Riveter" in place of the image of women as homebound, domestic servants.[46]

The tasks faced by the domestic branch of the OWI, as well as those faced by the foreign branch of the OWI and the other intelligence and propaganda organizations established during the war, were formidable. The relative successes of these organizations in shaping opinions is a matter for debate. Yet, any failures that can be attributed to the OWI can hardly be seen as the result of a lack of a commitment on the part of the government to fund the massive propaganda organization. Indeed, from the time the OWI was established in June 1942 up until the time it was formally dismantled on

September 15, 1945, the OWI had spent almost $133 million on its propa-
ganda activities.[47] During this same time period, the OSS operated with a
budget of over $100 million.[48] The need for these organizations during a
time of war was not lost on those who controlled the governmental purse
strings, nor was the perceived need for these organizations diminished during the Cold War (as we see later in this text). The OWI and the OSS, as well
as several organizations dealing with propaganda and intelligence, would be
reconstituted, under different names, during the postwar period.

In his "Final Report to the President" at the war's end, Elmer Davis, the
Director of the OWI, attempted to draw lessons from the experience of the
organization for future wartime propaganda agencies. Davis argued that
future wartime propagandists would profit from an examination of the successes and failures of the OWI's organizational structure, but would not
profit from an examination of the successes and failures of particular propaganda techniques and methods. "Our technical experience has perhaps little pertinence for the future," Davis wrote. "The next Office of War Information might well have to operate with methods and instruments as much more
complex than ours (and probably as much more expensive) as ours were
more complex and expensive than Creel's."[49] Davis was perceptive to note
that the future would bring more complex communication instruments as
well as more accurate and complex methods by which to change and measure changes in opinions and attitudes. However, he was mistaken to assume
that the OWI's technical experience would be of little value to future propagandists. No greater experimental training ground existed for those interested in the study of propaganda and mass communications. Many scholars
and researchers who would lead the field in the study of mass communications during the postwar period had cut their teeth while working in the
wartime propaganda agencies. For at least the 2 decades following the war,
scholars would return again and again to the reservoir of propaganda techniques that were employed by both Allied and Axis forces during the war.

Social scientists who held primary interests in mass communications and
propaganda had come of age during World War II. As one observer noted,
the wartime activities of these social scientists enabled them to:

> increase their knowledge in depth and breadth. The studies they made of
> wartime manpower mobilization, intelligence and occupational testing, mili-
> tary and civilian morale, and psychological warfare activities provided them
> with a greater range of material for observation and analysis than they had
> ever had before. At the same time, the world-wide commitments of the United
> States brought them into contact with a wide variety of peoples on which to test
> their concepts. . . . After the war social scientists needed to consolidate and
> evaluate the gains that had been made; they also had to train a rising genera-
> tion of social scientists in the new methods of investigation that had under-
> gone rapid development during the war.[50]

Basked in the righteousness of combating a most heinous enemy, and carefully shielded from the negative repercussions which beset World War I's propagandists, these social scientists returned to their university positions to pursue their primary interests more systematically. Having experience in both foreign and domestic propaganda, these social scientists became favored consultants and researchers by the burgeoning national security state in the Cold War period.

COLD WAR DEVELOPMENTS

World War II created many deep and profound changes in the social, political, economic, and cultural fabric of the United States. Escaping the wholesale destruction experienced by other industrialized nations, the United States emerged as the clear dominant world power. Whereas other nations could only hope to rebuild their devastated cities and economies, the United States—its cities and economy considerably stronger than before the war—could look forward to an unparalleled period of growth and expansion at both home and abroad. Federal expenditures on the war effort had replenished the coffers of the large corporations that were awarded defense contracts, fueling the largest growth in industrial production in U.S. history and significantly diminishing the Depression-era unemployment rate. Fifteen million new jobs came into being during the war years, and the gross national product soared from $91 billion to $166 billion.[51] Wartime production contracts were greatly skewed in favor of the 30 largest industrial corporations, which received half of such contracts.[52] These corporations were thus equipped with the capital and organizational and technical skills to dominate foreign and domestic markets. The federal government, which had grown by leaps and bounds during the war and increasingly aligned itself with the interests of big business, instituted policies that sought to stimulate this growth, making distinctions between private and public policy on the national level rather moot. Large research universities reaped the financial benefits of massive research and development contracts during the war: "MIT alone was awarded $117 million in R&D [Research and Development] contracts, Caltech $83 million, and Harvard and Columbia about $30 million each."[53] Returning GIs profited under the GI Bill, which provided educational benefits, mortgage guarantees, and job placement services. The universities grew, the suburbs grew, and the power and influence of the U.S. government and U.S. corporations grew during this period of postwar development.

Of course, with the end of the war and the ensuing economic expansion came significant changes in U.S. foreign and domestic policy. The wartime alliance with the Soviet Union was severed, and an inherent anticommunist ideology was resurrected to shape both foreign and domestic concerns. It was the term *Iron Curtain,* apparently first used by Joseph Goebbels and then by Winston Churchill, that was used to characterize the Soviet menace.[54] In September 1945, soon after the surrender of Japan, President Truman began drafting his plans for postwar U.S. foreign policy.[55] In March 1947, Truman delivered his speech outlining this policy of containment by announcing to the American people that they faced an urgent and direct threat from the Soviet Union, and that it would be the United States' foreign policy to contain communism. This new Cold War would require the nation to remain in a permanent state of war mobilization, with national security as its highest value. And although the size of the standing army that was utilized during World War II could be diminished somewhat, the Cold War would require the federal government to continue its massive expenditures for the development and production of military weaponry, which was becoming increasingly sophisticated and lethal. Thus, the relationship among the military, industry, and the academy, which received a significant share of R&D defense-related contracts, continued to grow and strengthen.[56] In addition, this Cold War required the continued sustenance of those intelligence and propaganda organizations used during the war, which made use of social science research relating to mass communication.

Ironically, what should have been a period of great optimism and hope among U.S. citizens was a period more accurately characterized by pessimism, insecurity, and paranoia, as the public was continuously warned of the threat of war with the Soviet Union. Anticommunist messages inundated the postwar media, including films, radio programming, newspapers, books, and eventually television programming.[57] The Gallup Poll and National Opinion Research Center, which had worked so closely with the Office of War Information during the war, documented the effects of this barrage of anticommunist messages. At the end of 1945, just 32% of the U.S. public thought that another world war was inevitable within 25 years. By the end of 1946, this population grew to 41%; by 1947, it grew to 63%; and by March 1948, 73% of the U.S. population thought that another world war was inevitable.[58] That U.S. public opinion could be changed so quickly was no small feat, especially when it is noted that just a few short years earlier, as a result of OWI propaganda measures, U.S. public opinion of the Soviet Union was favorable. Indeed, in April 1943, Americans generally thought that the Soviet Union was trying harder to win the war than all other allies.[59]

The effects of the anticommunist messages went beyond simply preparing people to accept the threat of war as a permanent aspect of their existence; it also instructed them to be on constant vigilance for the threat of domestic subversion. People were told that the international communist conspiracy had infiltrated all U.S. institutions and that it was essential to national security to expose these communists. People were warned that these communists could be relatives, neighbors, or coworkers; nevertheless, these communists were bent on subverting U.S. values and clearing the way for an eventual takeover of the United States by the Soviet Union. Educators, governmental employees, and people employed by the communication industry came under particularly close scrutiny by the House Un-American Activities Committee (HUAC), and by the several state-supervised investigating committees. As early as October 1947, the public was treated to HUAC's public hearings on alleged communism in the film industry, leading to the blacklisting of several motion picture writers and directors. Also in 1947, three "former" FBI agents began publishing the newsletter *Counterattack: The Newsletter of Facts on Communism,* listing alleged communists in the broadcasting industry. In 1951, these same three ex-agents published *Red Channels: The Communist Influence in Radio and Television.* By the early 1950s, loyalty oaths, blacklistings, and extensive personal background checks of employees by the FBI were common fare in governmental, educational, and communication institutions.[60] By the time the more virulent form of this anticommunist crusade took shape in the rantings of Senator Joseph McCarthy, a number of careers and lives had been ruined. Yet, the effects of this "red scare" had implications beyond the personal level; the red scare also significantly shaped the ideology of governmental, educational, and communication institutions by defining who would, and who would not, be allowed to work in these institutions. This was especially true in the communication industry, which was to a large degree still in its formative years during the postwar period. McCarthy, for instance, was able to make key appointments to the Federal Communication Commission during the early 1950s, a time when the FCC was busy deciding who would and who would not be allowed to obtain television broadcast licenses.[61] No doubt these kinds of events continued to influence the character of the communication industry long after McCarthy was censured by the Senate in 1954.

With respect to higher educational institutions, the red scare not only went a long way in defining the character of the research and teaching that went on, but also substantially excluded certain voices and perspectives from the conduct of this research and teaching. This was a problem that had university-wide implications, because the acceptance of classified and secret research projects by a university often required its administrators to permit only those individuals who accepted the dominant ideology to be employed by that university. Individuals who were labeled "red" or "communist" (or who advocated any number of "dissident" views) were denied appointments to public institutions like the University of Illinois, as George Stoddard, President of the University from 1946 to 1953, wrote:

> The fact is that while (my critics) shout themselves hoarse about Communism in the University, those of us in charge have worked quietly, through our own security officers, the Federal Bureau of Investigation, the State Department

and the military establishment, to make sure that no Communists are on the staff. This is important for we have a number of classified and secret research projects at the University. All staff members of the University have signed a standard loyalty oath, and the Security Officer has announced publicly that there is not, to his knowledge, a single Communist in the University of Illinois.[62]

Contrary to popular belief, the 1950s had not been "academia's finest hour" with respect to sustaining freedom of speech and inquiry. In some instances, university faculty and administrators held more repressive views than did the general public on the issue of academic freedom: For instance, during this time 91% of the Rutgers University faculty endorsed a board of trustee statement that "There is no place on a university faculty for a member of the Communist Party."[63] This is all very understandable given the enormous financial interests involved and that the intellectual or educated class of any society is frequently the most deeply indoctrinated group in that society.[64] It is also important to keep in mind, however, the various activities that were utilized for the purpose of marginalizing dissident scholars and social activists.[65] The creation of FBI dossiers on writers and educators, for instance, began early in the 20th century, and it is probably safe to say that there are few (if any) significant U.S. intellectuals, regardless of ideological perspective, who were not kept under surveillance.[66] John Dewey had an FBI file that was started in 1930 and continued (at least) until 1957, 5 years after his death.[67] Such dossiers, of course, provide the grist for the blackmailer and the blackballer, and there is really no way of determining how many people were kept out of teaching, research, and administrative positions, at all levels of instruction, as a result of these activities. Educational historians will need to place this campaign of surveillance and harassment at the center of their attempts to understand education during the Cold War period.

It was this Cold War atmosphere, driven by a mass media system that had redirected its efforts from winning support for World War II to now continuously (and in near unison) warning of the threat of an international communist conspiracy, that shaped political, social, cultural, and economic life in the United States during the postwar years. Although some people would look at these developments and see striking similarities between this notion of an international communist conspiracy and the notion of an "international Jewish banking conspiracy" that Hitler had used so effectively in his rise to power, others would wonder how the Soviet Union, as the leader of this conspiracy, could come to pose such a threat.[68] Journalist I. F. Stone observed that "The U.S. emerged from World War II, as from World War I, virtually unscathed, enormously enriched and—with the atom bomb—immeasurably more powerful than any nation on earth had ever been. The notion that it was in danger of attack from a devastated Soviet Union with 25 million war dead, a generation behind it in industrial development, was a wicked fantasy."[69]

Regardless of whether the Soviet threat was real, imagined, or fabricated, there were several powerful forces at work within American society that profited from a continued confrontation with the Soviet Union. From the large corporations that continued to be awarded lucrative defense contracts and whose interest in dominating foreign markets and resources required a rationalizing principle as well as military assistance, to the Nazi war criminals who were recruited by the Central Intelligence Agency for their expertise in Soviet affairs, to the great public and private research universities who provided technical expertise and trained personnel to a nation permanently at war, to the ruling political and military elite who used the notion of "national security" to ward off opposition and to restrict other voices and perspectives, the forces that profited from the widespread fear of the Soviet Union and a continued Cold War were among the most powerful in the nation.[70] If one could trace the source of each of the anticommunist messages that appeared in the U.S. mass media and other educational sources during the postwar period, one would find that these powerful forces had underwritten many of them.

THE COLD WAR AND SOCIAL SCIENCE EXPERTISE

Many social scientists at U.S. universities, particularly those dealing with issues relating to mass communications, also profited greatly from a prolonged period of Cold War. The waging of a "Cold War" required even more sophisticated techniques of psychological warfare and propaganda than was required during World War II, as well as more general knowledge concerning the attributes of various regions of the world. Because so many of the battles waged in the Cold War would be fought on ideological grounds, learning to use the various media of mass communication to manipulate various foreign populations would be essential. In response to this situation, the Truman Administration, Congress, and the various military branches created a series of propaganda and intelligence agencies, largely out of the wartime OWI, OSS, and the intelligence divisions of the various military branches, that operated to carry out the ideological mission of the U.S. Cold War policies. These propaganda and intelligence agencies, possessing a complicated web of interconnections, looked to major public and private universities for research assistance in pursuing Cold War policies. Many of these universities responded by establishing communication units, regional studies programs, and various psychological and sociological research institutes where much of this research was conducted and for which they were rewarded profitable governmental contracts.

As World War II came to a close in 1945 and the United States began its extended period of occupation of Japan and Germany, the United States actually intensified its international propaganda activities, although appearing to dismantle the massive propaganda organizations it sustained throughout the war. This was necessary, argued one observer in *Public Opinion Quarterly* at the war's end, because the United States' wartime activities were open to alternative and unfavorable interpretations: "We shall have, for example, to keep straight, before the world, the story of our military bombing. We aimed to blast tyranny out of the world. But the fact of the destruction of Monte Cassino, Abbey, of Cologne and Aachen, of Hiroshima and Nagasaki, could be subject to misinterpretation by trouble makers who will ignore the reason for it, having no reason to love us."[71]

In both Germany and Japan, the United States established extensive "political reorientation" programs in these former enemy areas through controlling the information activities in these areas and flooding the communication channels with U.S.-created propaganda. Even before the Office of War Information was officially dismantled on September 15, 1945, President Truman began to transfer the functions and personnel of the OWI and Nelson Rockefeller's Latin America-based Coordinator of Inter-American Affairs (CIAA) to the Interim International Information Service (IIIS), which was created on August 31, 1945. The IIIS, which was placed within the jurisdiction of the Department of State, was directed by William Benton, former advertising executive of *Benton and Bowles* fame and later U.S. Senator from Connecticut, who was appointed Assistant Secretary of State for Public Affairs. Benton immediately set out to win congressional approval "for a new peacetime propaganda service including the necessary funds with which to operate . . . and to establish effective liaison, adapted to peacetime conditions, with responsible intelligence-collecting and policy making officers both inside and outside the Department of State."[72]

The IIIS was liquidated only to become the Office of International Information and Cultural Affairs (OIC) in early 1946. In 1948, the OIC's name was changed to the Office of International Information and Educational Exchange, and it was divided into an Office of Educational Exchange and an Office of International Information. Both of these organizations remained housed in the Department of State. The organizational structure of the growing international propaganda apparatus was thus well established by the time the U.S. Information and Educational Exchange Act of 1948 (also known as the Smith-Mundt Act) was enacted by Congress. The Smith-Mundt Act provided funds for a range of activities, including the preparation and dissemination of information concerning "the United States, its people, and its policies, through press, publications, radio, motion pictures and other information media, and through information centers and instructors abroad."[73]

The objectives of the Smith-Mundt Act sounded peaceful enough when it was drafted in 1947: "The objectives of this Act are to enable the Government of the United States to correct misunderstandings about the United States in other countries, which constituted obstacles to peace, and to promote mutual understanding between the people of the United States and other countries, which is one of the essential foundations of peace."[74] Nevertheless, it was clear from the outset that the Smith-Mundt Act was conceived to be an important weapon in the ongoing Cold War. As cosponsor of the Act, Senator Karl E. Mundt would recall: "Immediately following the close of World War II when we realized that we were leaving a hot war only to enter a cold war, many of us recognized the importance of fashioning programs to meet effectively the non-military challenge confronting us. It was out of this era that the Smith-Mundt Act emerged. . . ."[75] Such measures were necessary, argued Mundt, because the United States faced "an alien force which seeks our total destruction."[76] The perceived gravity of the situation faced by these postwar policymakers ensured that the organization, administration, and necessary research would not be left to amateurs. Instead, they turned to the social scientists who had conducted research for the wartime propaganda agencies for assistance in developing the research necessary for these programs. The Department of State, through its Office of International Information, thus contracted with university-based social scientists for research relating to its propaganda programs overseas. This practice of funding university-based social science research would continue once the Office of International Information became the United States Information Agency in 1953 and was transferred to the jurisdiction of the National Security Council.

Like the OWI, the OSS was liquidated in name only when World War II ended. On October 1, 1945, President Truman terminated the OSS but transferred the Research and Analysis Division of the OSS to the Department of State, where it continued in operation under the direction of Harvard historian William Langer.[77] On January 22, 1946, President Truman established the Central Intelligence Group from personnel of the OSS, and situated it within the temporary National Intelligence Authority. Then, with the passing of National Security Act on July 26, 1947, which created the National Security Council (NSC), an independent Air Force, the Joint Chiefs of Staff, and the Secretary of Defense, President Truman established the Central Intelligence Agency from the earlier Central Intelligence Group.[78]

With the passing of the National Security Act one could begin to see the contours of the national security state that would grow to an unwieldy size in the postwar period. At the heart of this national security state were the various planning and advisory boards, including the National Security Resources Board, the National Security Council, and the several agencies within the Department of Defense. These planning and advisory boards required the careful and systematic research of the social scientist. Like its organizational precursor the OSS, the new CIA placed primary emphasis on the recruit-

ment of social scientists into its ranks, and it increasingly became a centralized social science research storehouse for these national planning and advisory boards. Although the Research and Analysis Division of the OSS was
placed within the jurisdiction of the Department of State immediately following the war, it was reconstituted as the Office of National Estimates
within the CIA in 1950.[79] As early as November 20, 1947, William Langer,
Director of the Research and Analysis Division of the OSS and founder and
first director of the CIA's Office of National Estimates, explained to the
American Philosophical Society that:

> What we have. . . in the government is something like a huge social science re-
> search institute devoted to the exploration of certain types of problems bear-
> ing directly on the national security. . . . The principle has been established
> and the need recognized. I cannot conceive of the government ever being will-
> ing to dispense with it, and I am confident that, for the future, the work of
> the organization will serve as an incentive to closer coordination in the social
> sciences.[80]

Highly reminiscent of Walter Lippmann's 1922 plans for the establishment of a "central agency" for the coordination of information on public
opinion, Langer's vision for the CIA required close collaboration with leaders from across the social sciences in the United States. Langer recognized
that this "huge social science research institute" aimed at national security
problems was unprecedented in times of relative peace, and he was optimistic about its success in meeting the perceived national security needs of
the country. Nevertheless, Langer recognized that even this "huge social science research institute" was facing a severe manpower shortage and that
necessary intelligence research would go unfulfilled. He wrote:

> This new departure, like most others, has its shady side. The question of per-
> sonnel is and undoubtedly will remain for a long time the controlling factor in
> determining success or failure. During wartime the staff was built up by drain-
> ing the universities, but that could never be anything more than an emergency
> procedure. It stands to reason that, with the end of the conflict, many mem-
> bers of the staff and more particularly the senior, directing members, should
> have returned to their habitual callings—after all, the needs of the universi-
> ties after demobilization were just about as great and as urgent as those of the
> government during hostilities. The result has been that the intelligence re-
> search has been decapitated and generally depleted, with only faint prospect
> of improvement in the immediate future. The plain fact of the matter is that
> we have far from enough trained people in these fields to staff both the uni-
> versities and the government.[81]

To remedy this shortage of available social scientists for the intelligence
community, Langer hoped that there would be a "concerted" effort between
the universities and the government to both train necessary researchers and
conduct research relating to the national security problems. "My hope," he

wrote, "is that, as appreciation of the problem spreads, something larger and more systematic will be undertaken and that, ultimately it will be realized that the country has a real stake in the type of study that is clearly essential for any nation which, whether it likes it or not, is called upon to play a major part in world affairs."[82]

Langer's message was apparently well heeded. The CIA, like other agencies of the national security state, funded a significant number of communications and social science research programs (as well as research programs in other physical and biological sciences) at U.S. universities throughout the Cold War period. The full extent of this funding is unknown, and will likely remain unknown given the continued secrecy that surrounds it. The CIA deliberately tried to limit the maintenance of records on these research programs, and most of the remaining records of the CIA's extensive MKULTRA program on behavioral and biological research, which was alleged to have taken place between 1953 and 1966, were destroyed in 1973 by order of then-CIA Director Richard Helms.[83] Yet, even the incomplete records discovered in 1975 suggests a significant undertaking: The CIA surreptitiously funded at least 149 known MKULTRA subprojects, mostly at universities, but also involving research foundations and hospitals; at least 185 private researchers participated in studies ranging from drug experiments on unwitting subjects, to electroconvulsive treatments and sleep-deprivation experiments on psychiatric patients, to mass communication studies on cities and towns in the United States. In 1985, the U.S. Supreme Court refused to order the disclosure of the names of the researchers and institutions involved.[84] Nevertheless, the list of known participants includes some of the most prestigious educational institutions in the United States (including the Educational Testing Service, Cornell University, Harvard University, and many others), and some of the most prominent researchers in sociology and psychology (including B. F. Skinner, Carl Rogers, Charles Osgood, and many others).[85]

The best-known work on the topic of covert CIA funding of biological and behavioral research is John Marks's *The Search for the "Manchurian Candidate": The CIA and Mind Control,* which includes many stark revelations concerning the CIA's MKULTRA program, the CIA front organization "The Society for the Investigation of Human Ecology," and the research programs this organization supported at various U.S. and Canadian universities. Marks emphasized the LSD experimentation carried on by the CIA, and argued that the CIA was principally concerned with controlling the behavior of individuals who might be used as assassins or in other lurid operations. Still, one cannot help but to notice that many of the known MKULTRA subprojects had little to do with the control of individuals, and much to do with finding ways to manage and control the thinking and behaviors of large social groups. Testifying at a U.S. Senate joint committee hearing in 1977,

John Gittinger, a CIA psychologist and major figure in its MKULTRA program, argued that the Society for the Investigation of Human Ecology "was established to undertake research in the general area of the behavioral sciences. It definitely had almost no focus or interest in, say, drug-related type of activities except in a very minor way, because it was largely set up to attempt to gain a certain amount of information and to fund projects which were psychological, sociological, anthropological in character."[86] Likewise, many MKULTRA researchers were motivated by quite definite social ideologies that fit in well with the authoritarian character of the agency and its mission of social control during the Cold War. This is clearly in evidence when one examines the work of Dr. Ewen Cameron who, as a Professor of Psychiatry at McGill University in Montreal and the director of the Allan Memorial Institute of Psychiatry in the 1950s and 1960s, conducted the notorious "depatterning" experiments on unsuspecting psychiatric patients for the CIA's Society for the Investigation of Human Ecology. Harvey Weinstein argued that Cameron was strongly influenced by his experience as a member of a team of psychiatrists who evaluated Rudolph Hess during the Nuremberg Trials. Cameron took from this experience a strong, if perverse, desire "to make the world a better place." Weinstein pointed out that "Cameron's solution to the ills of society was simple: Experts should decide who can parent and who should govern. These experts must develop methods of forcefully changing attitudes and beliefs."[87]

The various military branches also supported mass communications research projects in university social science and communication departments. The Office of Naval Research (ONR) ran a substantial program for social science research through its Human Resource Division. Starting with a yearly budget of just $100,000 in 1946, it expanded to over $1,000,000 by 1948, and to over $1,500,000 by 1950, a full third of which was devoted to psychological warfare and group psychology research.[88] Like the CIA and the USIA, the Human Resource Division would contract with university-based researchers such as B. F. Skinner, Margaret Mead, Daniel Katz, Angus Campbell, and others, and would contract with departments in universities such as the University of Minnesota, the University of Chicago, the University of Southern California, the University of Michigan, and numerous others.[89]

The Army took a somewhat different approach to the funding of social science research. In 1948, it established the Operations Research Office (ORO) and housed it within Johns Hopkins University. In 1951, the Army contracted with George Washington University for the establishment of the Human Resources Research Office (HumRRO).[90] ORO and HumRRO, both of which were engaged in psychological warfare research, subcontracted some of this research to other university departments and researchers.[91] A number of mass communication experts assisted the ORO and

HumRRO in developing their training manuals in psychological warfare, including Harold Lasswell, Morris Janowitz, Daniel Lerner, Leo Lowenthal, Wilbur Schramm, Joseph Klapper, and others.[92] In addition, ORO and HumRRO were the two social science organizations that engaged in indoctrination experiments on U.S. military personnel who were ordered to participate in above-ground atomic bomb tests during the 1950s.[93]

Finally, the Air Force also supported psychological warfare research in several different university communication and social science departments, primarily through the RAND Corporation and the Human Resources Research Institute (HRRI). The roots of the RAND Corporation reach into the closing days of World War II, when Air Force and industry leaders perceived the need to retain the services of both physical scientists and social scientists within the military-industrial complex. Initially, the RAND Corporation was situated as a division within the Douglas Aircraft Corporation, but was established as an independent, nonprofit corporation in 1948 largely through the financial backing of the Ford Foundation.[94] The Air Force, however, remained RAND's primary contracting agency; the RAND Corporation, in turn, subcontracted some of their psychological warfare and other social science research to various university social science departments.[95]

The Air Force's Human Resource Research Institute also funded several psychological warfare and social science research programs at U.S. universities. Established by Air University at Maxwell Air Force Base in 1949, HRRI contracted research with, among others, the Bureau of Applied Social Research at Columbia University, the Educational Testing Service, the Laboratory of Social Relations at Harvard University, the Institute of Communications Research at the University of Illinois, and the Washington Public Opinion Laboratory at the University of Washington.[96] HRRI was disbanded during the 1953–54 academic year following an undisclosed congressional inquiry.[97] As we discuss later, however, at least some of the research programs initially contracted by HRRI were continued by the CIA, through front foundations, long after HRRI's operations were ended.

These several social science divisions within the military branches, as well as the research divisions of the CIA and USIA, represented the most significant source of funding for social science research during the postwar period. Even though corporate foundations would fund a considerable part of the social science research conducted during this period, it became increasingly difficult to discern between corporate foundation interests and the military and intelligence interests. In 1976, the U.S. Senate Select Committee to Study Governmental Operations with Respect to Intelligence Activities, also known as the Church Committee, wrote: "The CIA's intrusion into the foundation field in the 1960s can only be described as massive. Excluding grants from the "Big Three"—Ford, Rockefeller, and Carnegie—of the 700 grants over $10,000 given by 164 other foundations during the period

1963–1966, at least 108 involved partial or complete CIA funding. . . . In the same period more than one-third of the grants awarded by the non-"Big Three" in the physical, life and social sciences also involved CIA funds."[98]

Yet, even the Big Three foundations must be examined in light of this Cold War funding. Heads of some of the Big Three also retained positions on the advisory councils of the military and intelligence research divisions. For instance, Charles Dollard, the Carnegie Corporation president, served on the advisory council for HRRI and for RAND.[99] When Dollard set about to provide funds for social science and educational research to university departments through the Carnegie Corporation, one could legitimately wonder whether this research was being funded according to national security interests or the alleged philanthropic interests of the Carnegie Corporation.

The institutional mechanisms of the federal government for funding of social science research were firmly in place by the late 1940s, yet they were not going to remain at their current rate of funding for long. In his presidential address to the American Psychological Association in 1948, Donald G. Marquis was prophetic when he told his colleagues that he anticipated that governmental funding for the social sciences would increase twofold, perhaps threefold, in the years to come.[100] With the outbreak of the Korean War on June 25, 1950, these various propaganda, research, and intelligence organizations increased their activities dramatically. Congress tripled the funds for the United States' international propaganda agencies,[101] with the estimation that the federal government was spending as much as $1 billion annually on propaganda and psychological warfare activities.[102] And the budgets of these various military and intelligence research divisions for mass communications research also increased; the division spent between $7 million and $13 million each year in this area of social research alone.[103] The social science research budget of the Office of Naval Research, for instance, grew from just over $1,500,000 in 1950 to over $3,500,000 in 1951.[104] The CIA, with its unconstitutional secret budget, would step up its "black propaganda" programs through *Radio Free Europe* and *Radio Liberation,* financed with millions of dollars from the Crusade for Freedom of the American Heritage Foundation.[105] Reports were heard of the extraordinary brainwashing techniques of the "Reds," as the prestige and value of those social scientists engaged in mass communications research continued to soar.

The United States' propaganda and intelligence activities expanded throughout the 1950s and 1960s, as the CIA's efforts at clandestine radio broadcasting stations multiplied around the globe.[106] The CIA, in operations in Greece, the Philippines, Iran, Guatemala, Italy, Costa Rica, Albania, Germany, Syria, Vietnam, and many other countries, continued to require the knowledge of mass communications experts in shaping public opinion in order to achieve its Cold War policy objectives.[107] And the United States

Information Agency would also continue to solicit the assistance of mass communications experts in its ongoing ideological war throughout the 1950s. The social scientists who were skilled at creating mass communication "effects" became important functionaries in the national security state.

In 1949, Robert S. Lynd reviewed the first three volumes of what would be Samuel A. Stouffer's four-volume work, *The American Soldier.* This comprehensive, four-volume study was a classic work in the emerging communications field, utilizing a variety of novel survey and experimental techniques and operating with a huge budget and a ready pool of subjects, for the purpose of finding the means to control the attitudes and thinking of the people who would be soldiers. Lynd's review, appropriately titled "The Science of Inhuman Relations," allowed him to return to the interests that had informed his work from 10 years before, *Knowledge For What? The Place of Social Science in American Culture,* although now from a much surer vantage point. Lynd did not mince his words:

> These volumes depict science being used with great skill to sort out and to control men for purposes not of their own willing. It is a significant measure of the impotence of liberal democracy that it must increasingly use its social sciences not directly on democracy's own problems, but tangentially and indirectly; it must pick up the crumbs from private business research on such problems as how to gauge audience reaction so as to put together profitable synthetic radio programs and movies, or, as in the present case, from Army research on how to turn frightened draftees into tough soldiers who will fight a war whose purposes they do not understand. With such socially extraneous purposes controlling the use of social science, each advance in its use tends to make it an instrument of mass control, and thereby a further threat to democracy.[108]

Lynd also wondered what American society would be like if its social sciences were actually put to the service of addressing the real problems of real people in a real democracy: "not by discovering how to lessen men's fear in battle but how to lessen the massive insecurities of civilian life; not by developing the synthetic morale of an army but the living tissue of democratic social solidarity."[109] The overwhelming trend, however, was against such reasoning, and Lynd's lonely musings were not well heeded during this period of economic boom and Cold War hysteria.

NOTES

1. Alfred McLung Lee, "Book Department," *Annals of the American Academy of Political and Social Science, 265* (September 1949), p. 174.

2. Robert S. Lynd, *Knowledge for What? The Place of Social Science In American Culture* (Princeton, N.J.: Princeton University Press, 1939), p. 202.

3. Ibid., p. 120.

4. Ibid., p. 163.

5. Ibid., pp. 219–220.

6. "Forward," *The Public Opinion Quarterly, 1* (January 1937), p. 5.

7. Ibid., p. 3.

8. For a discussion of the prewar development of mass communication research, see Daniel J. Czitrom, *Media and the American Mind: From Morse to McLuhan* (Chapel Hill: University of North Carolina Press, 1982), pp. 121–146.

9. "Public Opinion and the Emergency," on microfilm at the State Historical Society Archives Wisconsin, Division of Manuscripts, Rockefeller Foundation: "Documents Re. A Study of Mass Communication." Other contributors included Lloyd A. Free, Geoffrey Gorer, John Marshall, Charles A. Siepmann, Donald Slesinger, Douglass Waples, R. J. Havighurst, Stacy May, I. A. Richards and David H. Stevens.

10. Ibid., p. 2.

11. Ibid., pp. 6–7.

12. Ibid., p. 4.

13. Ibid., p. 5.

14. Ibid., p. 52.

15. Ibid., p. 52.

16. Ibid., p. 38.

17. Ibid., p. 51.

18. Ibid., p. 53.

19. Ibid., p. 37

20. Ibid., p. 4.

21. "Research in Mass Communication," pp. 1–2. State Historical Society of Wisconsin, Division of Archives and Manuscripts, Rockefeller Foundation: "Documents Re. a Study of Mass Communication."

22. Ibid., p. 1.

23. Ibid., p. 3.

24. Ibid., p. 2.

25. Ibid., p. 5.

26. The "who" in Lasswell's model does not suggest an extensive analysis of the role and structure of power within a society, as some mass communications researchers continue to argue. Instead, the question regarding the "who" is concerned with the particular qualities of the speaker that make him or her, or that do not make him or her, credible.

27. Richard W. Steele, "Preparing the Public for War: Efforts to Establish a National Propaganda Agency, 1940–1941," *The American Historical Review, 75* (October 1970), p. 1640.

28. Ibid., p. 1642.

29. As quoted in Allan M. Winkler, *The Politics of Propaganda: The Office of War Information, 1942–1945* (New Haven, CT: Yale University Press, 1978), p. 23.

30. As quoted in ibid., p. 34.

31. Ibid., pp. 8–37.

32. For a discussion of the development of the OSS, see the U.S. Congress, Senate Select Committee to Study Governmental Operations with Respect to Intelligence Activities, *Supplementary Reports on Intelligence Activities, Book VI, 94th Cong.* (Washington, D.C.: U.S. Government Printing Office, 1976), pp. 138–155.

33. As quoted in Gene M. Lyons, *The Uneasy Partnership: Social Science and the Federal Government in the Twentieth Century* (New York: Russell Sage, 1969), p. 83.

34. William L. Langer, "Scholarship and the Intelligence Problem," *Proceedings of the American Philosophical Society, 92* (March 1948), pp. 43–44.

35. See Kermit Roosevelt, *War Report of the O.S.S.* (New York: Walker and Company, 1976), pp. 48–49; Robin W. Winks, *Cloak and Gown: Scholars in the Secret War, 1939–1961* (New York: Quill William Morrow, 1987), pp. 43–79.

36. Roosevelt, *War Report of the O.S.S.*, p. 16.

37. Winkler, *The Politics of Propaganda*, p. 105.

38. Leonard W. Doob, "The Utilization of Social Scientists in the Overseas Branch of the Office of War Information," *The American Political Science Review, 41* (August 1947), p. 667.

39. See, for instance, Daniel Lerner, *Psychological Warfare Against Nazi Germany: The Sykewar Campaign, D-Day to VE-Day* (Cambridge, MA: MIT Press, 1949).

40. Alexander H. Leighton, *The Governing of Men: General Principles and Recommendations Based on Experience at a Japanese Relocation Camp* (Princeton, NJ: Princeton University Press, 1945), p. 373.

41. Alexander H. Leighton, "Personnel Utilization in Strategic Psywar Evaluation," in *A Psychological Warfare Casebook*, edited by William E. Daugherty and Morris Janowitz (Baltimore: Johns Hopkins Press, 1958), pp. 214–224.

42. Bureau of Special Services, "Public Attitudes Toward The Ban on Pleasure Driving and the Equalization of the Gasoline Ration, Final Report" no. 63, August 13, 1943. Bureau of Intelligence, "Worker Reaction to the Employment Stabilization Plan for the Louisville Area" no. 51, February 25, 1943. Bureau of Special Services, "A Study of Boy Scout Distribution of OWI Posters in Twelve Cities" no. 74, March 15, 1944. Bureau of Special Services, "Effectiveness of the Campaign to Collect Waste Fats" no. 52, May 15, 1943. Bureau of Special Services, "Home Canning Plans of American Women," no. 57, June 14, 1943. These materials are located in the Main Library at the University of Illinois, Urbana-Champaign. Bureau of Special Services, "The American Public Views Our Russian Ally" no. 55, June 10, 1943. Bureau of Special Services, "Public Appreciation of the Problem of Inflation" no. 62, August 12, 1943. Office of Facts and Figures, "How the Populace Regards the Government's Handling of War News," January 22, 1942. Bureau of Special Services, "Women Appraise the Food Situation," no. 57, June 10, 1943. Bureau of Intelligence, "Negro Attitudes Toward Certain War-Connected Problems," March 9, 1942. Bureau of Intelligence, "Urban–Rural Differences in People's Attitudes Toward the War and Related Matters." Bureau of Special Services, "Consumer Attitudes Toward Rationing and Related Problems," no. 70, November 23, 1943. Bureau of Special Services, "Business Men Talk About Nazism and the German People," no. 56, June 9, 1943. Bureau of Intelligence, "War Information and the Changing Outlook Toward Russia and England" no. 40, December 23, 1942. Bureau of Intelligence, "The Public Looks at Manpower Problems" no. 43, January 5, 1943. Located in the Main Library at the University of Illinois.

43. Clayton R. Koppes and Gregory D. Black, *Hollywood Goes to War: How Politics, Profits, and Propaganda Shaped World War II Movies* (New York: Free Press, 1987), pp. 185–221.

44. Bureau of Intelligence, "The Public Looks at Manpower Problems," no. 43, January 5, 1943.

45. Koppes and Black, *Hollywood Goes to War*, p. 86.

46. For a discussion of the attempt to create a new image of women's role in American society see Maureen Honey, *Creating Rosie the Riveter: Class, Gender, and Propaganda During World War II* (Amherst: University of Massachusetts Press, 1984).

47. Elmer Davis, "Report to the President," *Journalism Monograph, 7* (August 1968), p. 75.

48. Roosevelt, *War Report of the OSS*, p. 247.

49. Davis, "Report to the President," p. 75.

50. Lyons, *The Uneasy Partnership*, p. 82.

51. Alan Brinkley, "World War II and American Liberalism," in *The War in American Culture: Society and Consciousness During World War II*, edited by Lewis A. Erenberg and Susan E. Hirsch (Chicago: University of Chicago Press, 1996), p. 317.

52. Stuart W. Leslie, *The Cold War and American Science: The Military-Industrial-Academic Complex at MIT and Stanford* (New York: Columbia University Press, 1993), p. 6.

53. Ibid.

54. James Aronson, *The Press and the Cold War* (New York: Bobbs-Merrill, 1970), p. 31.

55. Ibid., p. 32.

56. Between 1955 and 1994, federally funded R&D for national defense projects averaged 61.6% of expenditures, whereas R&D civilian functions averaged only 38.4%. From 1955 to 1959, defense-related R&D expenditures were at 84.1% of all federally funded projects, with only 15.9% for civilian functions. See A. D. Van Nostrand, *Fundable Knowledge: The Marketing of Defense Technology* (Mahwah, NJ: Lawrence Erlbaum Associates, 1997), p. 3.

57. For an insightful study of the anticommunist messages that were pervasive on television, see J. Fred McDonald, *Television and the Red Menace: The Video Road to Vietnam* (New York: Praeger, 1985).

58. Ibid., p. 37.

59. Bureau of Special Services, "The American Public Views Our Russian Ally," no. 55, June 10, 1943, p. 2.

60. For a discussion of the red scare on the communication industry, see Erik Barnouw, *The Golden Web: A History of Broadcasting in the United States, Vol. II — 1933 to 1953* (New York: Oxford University Press, 1968). See also John Cogley, *Report on Blacklisting I. — Movies*, and *Report on Blacklisting II. — Radio and Television* (New York: Fund For the Republic, 1956).

61. Erik Barnouw, *The Image Empire: A History of Broadcasting in the United States, Volume III — From 1953* (New York: Oxford University Press, 1970), pp. 10–11.

62. George D. Stoddard, *The Pursuit of Education: An Autobiography* (New York: Vantage, 1981), p. 130.

63. As Ellen Schrecker wrote: "In his 1954 survey of public opinion and civil liberties, the sociologist Samuel Stouffer found that 89 percent of a national cross section felt that Communists should not be allowed to teach in college." See Ellen Schrecker, "Academic Freedom and the Cold War," *The Antioch Review, 38* (Summer 1980), pp. 313–327.

64. For an elaboration of this point, see Noam Chomsky, "A Dialogue with Noam Chomsky," *Harvard Educational Review, 65* (Summer 1995), pp. 127–144.

65. For one scholar's experience pertaining to the Cold War and his academic career, see Sigmund Diamond, *Compromised Campus: The Collaboration of Universities with the Intelligence Community, 1945–1955* (New York: Oxford University Press, 1992).

66. See, for instance, Herbert Mitgang, *Dangerous Dossiers: Exposing the Secret War Against America's Greatest Writers* (New York: Donald I. Fine, 1988); Natalie Robbins, *Alien Ink: The FBI's War on Freedom of Expression* (New Brunswick, NJ: Rutgers University Press, 1992).

67. John A. Beineke, "The Investigation of John Dewey by the FBI," *Educational Theory, 37* (Winter 1987), pp. 43–52.

68. Aronson, *The Press and the Cold War,* pp. 112–113.

69. As quoted in Sidney Lens, *The Military Industrial Complex* (Philadelphia: Pilgrim Press & the National Catholic Reporter, 1970), p. 11.

70. For a discussion of the recruitment of Nazi war criminals, see Christopher Simpson, *Blowback: America's Recruitment of Nazis and Its Effects on the Cold War* (New York: Weidenfeld and Nicolson, 1988).

71. John A. Pollard, "Words Are Cheaper Than Blood," *Public Opinion Quarterly, 9* (Fall 1945), p. 303.

72. William E. Daugherty, "Post-World War II Developments," in *A Psychological Warfare Casebook,* edited by William E. Daugherty and Morris Janowitz (Baltimore: Johns Hopkins University Press, 1958), p. 136.

73. Ibid.

74. U.S. Congress, House, Committee on Foreign Affairs, *United States Information and Educational Exchange Act of 1947,* (Washington, DC: United States Government Printing Office, 1947), p. 3.

75. Karl E. Mundt, "Need for a National Freedom Academy," in *Propaganda and the Cold War,* edited by John Boardman Whitton (Washington, DC: Public Affairs Press, 1963), p. 75.

76. Ibid., p. 75.

77. Select Committee to Study Governmental Operations, *Supplementary Reports on Intelligence Activities, Book VI* (1976), p. 154.

78. U.S. Congress, *National Security Act of 1947—Public Law 253* (Washington, DC: U.S. Government Printing Office, 1966).

79. Winks, *Cloak & Gown,* p. 81.

80. William L. Langer, "Scholarship and the Intelligence Problem."

81. Ibid., p. 45.

82. Ibid.

83. U.S. Congress, Senate, Joint Hearing Before the Select Committee on Intelligence and the Subcommittee on Health and Scientific Research of the Committee on Human Resources, *Project MKULTRA, The CIA's Program of Research in Behavioral Modification* (Washington, DC: U.S. Government Printing Office, 1977).

84. C.I.A. v. Sims 108 S.Ct. 1881 (1985).

85. See John Marks, *The Search for the "Manchurian Candidate": The CIA and Mind Control* (New York: New York Times Books, 1979).

86. U.S. Congress, Senate, Joint Hearing Before the Select Committee on Intelligence and the Subcommittee on Health and Scientific Research of the Committee on Human Resources, op. cit., p. 59.

87. Harvey M. Weinstein, *Psychiatry and the CIA: Victims of Mind Control* (Washington, DC: American Psychiatric Press, 1990), p. 99.

88. John G. Darley, "Psychology and the Office of Naval Research: A Decade of Development," *The American Psychologist, 12* (June 1957), pp. 305–323.

89. Ibid., p. 313. See also Harold Guetzkow, editor, *Groups, Leadership and Men: Research in Human Relations* (Pittsburgh: Carnegie Press, 1951).

90. Lyons, *The Uneasy Partnership,* p. 141.

91. Letter from Wilbur Schramm to George Stoddard, November 13, 1951. University of Illinois Archives, Institute of Communications Research, Files of the Director, 13/5/1 Box 7, File: Operations Research Office.

92. William E. Daugherty and Morris Janowitz, editors, *A Psychological Warfare Casebook* (Baltimore: Johns Hopkins University Press, 1958), p. v.

93. See, for instance, Howard L. Rosenberg, *Atomic Soldiers: American Victims of Nuclear Experiments* (Boston: Beacon Press, 1980).

94. John McDonald, "The War of Wits," *Fortune, 43* (March 1951), pp. 99–158.

95. Erin Hubbert and Herbert H. Rosenberg, *Opportunities for Federally Sponsored Social Science Research* (Syracuse, NY: The Maxwell Graduate School of Citizenship and Public Affairs, Syracuse University, 1951), p. 13.

96. "The Human Resources Research Institute: A Brief Statement of Status at the End of the Second Year," prepared for the Fourth Meeting of the Advisory Research Council 6–8 December 1951, University of Illinois Archives, Institute of Communications Research, Files of the Director, 13/5/1, Box 5, File: Air Force Correspondence, 1950–51.

97. Lyons, *The Uneasy Partnership,* p. 144.

98. United States Senate, *Final Report of the Select Committee to Study Governmental Operations with Respect to Intelligence Activities: Foreign and Military Intelligence, Book I* (Washington, DC: U.S Government Printing Office, 1976), p. 182.

99. "Human Resources Research Institute," p. 32.

100. Donald W. Marquis, "Research Planning at the Frontier of Science," *The American Psychologist, 3* (October 1948), pp. 430–438.

101. Lois W. Roth and Richard T. Arndt, "Information, Culture, and Public Diplomacy: Searching for an American Style of Propaganda," in *The Press and the State: Sociohistorical and Contemporary Studies,* edited by Walter M. Brasch and Dana R. Ulloth (New York: University Press of America, 1986), p. 727.

102. Christopher Simpson, *Science of Coercion: Communication Research and Psychological Warfare, 1945–1960* (New York: Oxford University Press, 1988), p. 9.

103. Ibid.

104. Darley, "Psychology and the Office of Naval Research," p. 306.

105. John Scott, "Non-Governmental Agencies Engaged in Cold War Propaganda Operations," in *A Psychological Warfare Casebook,* edited by William Daugherty and Morris Janowitz (Baltimore: Johns Hopkins University Press, 1958), p. 154.

106. See Lawrence C. Soley, *Radio Warfare: OSS and CIA Subversive Propaganda* (New York: Praeger, 1989).

107. For a discussion of these operations, see William Blum, *The CIA: A Forgotten History—Global Interventions Since World War 2* (London: Zed, 1986).

108. Robert S. Lynd, "The Science of Inhuman Relations," *The New Republic* (29 August 1949), p. 22.

109. Ibid.

CHAPTER THREE

The Social Ideas of American Mass Communications Experts

*We have entered an era in which the mass media may be the
real public schools—the institutions in which the public is
not only formed and instructed but also brought into being
as a public with common standards and assumptions.*

—Philip H. Phenix, 1961[1]

IN 1935, HISTORIAN Merle Curti published the first edition of his land-
mark study *The Social Ideas of American Educators*.[2] Hailed by one reviewer
as "one of the most important contributions ever made to the literature of
American social and intellectual history," Curti's book sought to explore
how the social ideology of prominent 19th- and early 20th-century educators influenced the kinds of pedagogical approaches they advocated.[3] Curti
carefully examined the biographies of such key figures as Henry Barnard,
Booker T. Washington, William T. Harris, Francis Parker, G. Stanley Hall,
Edward L. Thorndike, John Dewey, and others, for insight into how their
views on what was deemed as socially "necessary, possible, and desirable"
translated into their various educational practices and programs. Acknowledging that, in some instances, these educators were not fully aware of the
social philosophy their educational work reflected, Curti maintained that
in each case this social philosophy was conditioned by a complex web of factors that included their personal temperament, the social and economic
class to which they belonged, the circumstances of their own education, the
prevailing intellectual currents of the time in which they lived and worked,
and so on. These factors, in turn, shaped how they explicitly and implicitly
came down on the big questions concerning the nature of human beings,
the conception ·of the ideal social order, the basis for making judgments
about knowledge and truth, and so on. Curti was especially interested in understanding how the social ideas held by prominent educational leaders
were reflected in their thinking about the education of women and other
subjugated and marginalized people, their views on the role of education in
issues of war and peace, and their attitudes concerning the function of edu-

cation in relation to the expansion of nationalism in the United States and around the world.

When the second edition of the book was published in 1959, however, the social and educational landscape had changed so dramatically as to require Curti to write a major retrospective essay concerning "the main developments in the social thinking of spokesman of American education in the past twenty-five years."[4] Curti maintained that the "quasi-biographical" approach he utilized when the book was first published was "not so suitable" for studying the years since the 1930s, because no clearly identifiable leaders had come to the fore to exert the kind of influence that Dewey, Thorndike, and others had done. This he attributed to the increasing specialization of educational theorists and administrators, the tendency for administrative research teams and committees to contend with the educational problems that formerly were the attention of individual scholars, and the rise in general "lay participation in the formulation of educational aims and of ways of realizing them."[5]

Moreover, Curti noted the conservative intellectual mood of the 1950s that tended to downplay conflict in historical interpretations and to "emphasize a more or less constant homogeneity," the movement toward much greater conformity in social and educational matters that sought to adjust individuals to prevailing institutional practices and group norms, and the general and widespread acquiescence to business values and interests by educational institutions.[6] Behind all this, Curti argued, stood the major and unprecedented social and economic changes that took place during the previous 25 years: the expansion of the federal government, the end of the economic depression, the challenges posed by fascism and communism, the pervasive fear precipitated by the Cold War. Curti mentioned, although did not explore, "the so-called communications revolution," which surely transformed the meaning and practice of education in untold ways. The scope and scale of those institutions responsible for education had been enlarged and transmuted greatly during this 25-year time span, and these changes could not be adequately seen as resulting simply from the social ideas of a few central educational theorists.

Curti was right: It would have been difficult to identify these influential educational leaders during this period in any event, and harder still to discern the implications of their social philosophies. On the one hand, historical circumstances had seemingly dwarfed the role of individual actors within educational institutions, even as these institutions took novel and varied forms. These changes seemed to occur regardless of what any one person or group of people thought was socially "necessary, possible, and desirable"; things were in the works, as it were, and they appeared to happen independent of human values and designs. On the other hand, it was becoming increasingly difficult to see the traditional school as the primary educational institution in contemporary society, and, thus, difficult to determine just who were the most influential educational leaders in this new society. "Two great new educational agencies—the armed services and industry—have entered the field," Margaret Mead pointed out favorably about these two agencies in 1958, "and there is little awareness of the ways in which operations in these institutions are altering traditional education."[7] In addition, there was little awareness of the ways in which the new predominant educator, television, had impacted on traditional educational activities—little awareness of how television was affecting learning and other social behavior, or how it was shaping public perceptions of education. The social ideas of American educators remained highly important, although now these educators were housed in a variety of new and transformed institutions, and now their social ideas seemed to be submerged beneath the larger structural realities of the period.

Within the context of this emerging "cacophony of teaching," to borrow a phrase from the late educational historian Lawrence Cremin, social ideas of mass communication experts hold special significance, because these experts proffered the most authoritative perspective on the social and educational implications of the new mass media, and because these experts became the leaders in training the workers for this new educational enterprise.[8] Christopher Simpson argued that communication research "underlies most college- and graduate-level training for print and broadcast journalists, public relations and advertising personnel and the related craftspeople who might be called the 'ideological workers' of contemporary U.S. society."[9] And, as Everett M. Rogers pointed out, "The field of communication study has been one of the fastest-growing academic units of U.S. university campuses for the past several decades."[10] Perhaps more important, the field of mass communications research has also served as the basis for most research into the impact of television on learning and other social behavior, and it has intersected significantly with the development of educational broadcasting in the United States. As the electronic mass media, especially television, began to compete with and then supplant the influence of other educational institutions in U.S. society, communication researchers at mid-century quickly became the experts who seemed to possess the authority to speak about the social, political, cultural, and educational effects of these mass media. Yet, the conditions that prompted and sustained their authority, or the social ideologies that informed their work, have not been adequately explored.

The constraints on this kind of exploration that Curti noted are still with us, although historical distance has permitted the opportunity to sketch the major contours of this development. The particular shape that mass communication research came to hold at mid-century was the work of many individuals who came from widely divergent backgrounds. Although interest in mass communication research was gaining before World War II, the field came into its own during that war and grew at a rapid rate in the Cold War years. Several thousand people contributed to the rise and development of the field through employment with the various propaganda and intelligence agencies that were an outgrowth of the war, and through appointments to the many communication research departments that were appearing at universities in the United States. Among these, several scholars came to the fore as important leaders of this new discipline either through the intellectual force or sheer output of their research, their organizational talents in running research units, or their important personal links with the various institutions who would fund this research. Coming from a wide range of disciplines and working primarily in large East Coast, Midwestern, and West Coast universities, these scholars converged to produce a formidable body of research on communication "effects" in the 1940s and 1950s, which remains the dominant focus of the field today.

Wilbur Schramm regarded Harold Lasswell, Paul Lazarsfeld, Carl Hovland, and Kurt Lewin as the "Founding Fathers" of the field,[11] despite the fact that Lasswell was never completely connected to a communication research institute, and despite the fact that Lewin's work was largely in the area of small group processes and not in mass communication research.[12] Lasswell's and Lewin's influence on the study of mass communications was significant, although Schramm was being unduly modest in not including himself among this list of "founding fathers." He, perhaps more than any other single person, defined the field of mass communications research. Schramm established communication research units at the University of Illinois, Stanford, and the University of Hawaii, remained in the field long after others had departed for other interests, and became the most often-cited mass communication researcher.[13] Several other individuals should also be considered to be among the list of contributors to the founding of the field: Bernard Berelson, Hadley Cantril, Stuart Dodd, Leonard Doob, George Gallup, Morris Janowitz, Daniel Katz, Daniel Lerner, Leo Lowenthal, Rensis Likert, John Marshall, Robert Merton, Elmo Roper, Ithiel de Sola Pool, Hans Speier, Frank Stanton, Samuel Stouffer, Douglas Waples, and several others must be considered for the contribution they made to the origins of mass communications research.

This chapter provides short professional biographies of five key contributors to the development of mass communications research, attempting to make clear the social ideas that informed their work. Of the many influential figures one could select, Bernard Berelson, Stuart Dodd, Hadley Cantril, Carl Hovland, and Frank Stanton have been chosen here for preliminary examination. Selecting these five individuals injects some regional and institutional diversity into the story behind the growth of mass communications research. In addition, an analysis of these five individuals demonstrates that mass communications research at mid-century was the handiwork of individuals who came from widely disparate personal and disciplinary backgrounds, even as they came to share common educational and social objectives for the mass media.

BERNARD BERELSON

The influence of Bernard Berelson on the development of the field of mass communications research has not yet been well documented. Nevertheless, his contributions were significant due to the extensive research he conducted at both the University of Chicago and the Bureau of Applied Social Research at Columbia University, and to his activities as Director of the Program in Behavioral Sciences for the Ford Foundation. Born on June 12, 1912, in Spokane, Washington, Berelson received an A.B. from Whitman College, and B.S. and M.A. degrees from the University of Washington. In 1941, he completed his Ph.D. at the University of Chicago in library sciences under the guidance of Douglas Waples, who would serve as Director of Psychological Warfare Studies at the University of Chicago after World War II.[14]

Berelson's dissertation, entitled "Content Emphasis, Recognition, and Agreement: An Analysis of the Role of Communications in Determining Public Opinion," was an attempt to analyze the effects of the content of political campaign messages in the 1940 presidential election, a decisive victory for President Roosevelt over opponent Wendell Willkie. The dissertation, an admixture of both quantitative and qualitative analysis, set the ideological tone that would characterize Berelson's future scholarship in the area of mass communications research:

> The development of media of mass communication facilitates the "production" of public opinion and thereby increases its importance. As the dominance of social control, the state progressively emerges as the agency in which are centralized the efforts to solve the insistent problems of a machine society. . . . Before governments can inaugurate far-reaching innovations in social organization which promise to deal basically with basic problems, they must be assured of popular confidence and support, or at least the temporary suspension of popular resistance. The effective limits of public action are ordinarily defined by public opinion. What the public will "take" in social policy depends upon what the public believes about social policy, that is upon what social myths the public accepts and rejects. Without popular approval or sufferance no governmental policies can be effective for long; either consent must be gained or the policies must be revised, in their symbolic connotations, if not in their actual operations.[15]

As this passage indicates, Berelson accepted a more or less functionalist understanding of government "progressively" emerging as the locus of social control, and he viewed mass communications as an important tool in the "production" of the public opinion necessary for government policy objectives. Moreover, he demonstrated in this passage that he believed public opinion about social policy resided primarily in the realm of "social myths" rather than on accurate appraisals by various publics of their own self-interests. These positions—concerning the role of government, the function of mass communications, and the characteristics of the public and of public opinion—represent the ideological foundation on which much of Berelson's later work was based.

In a paper read at a University of Chicago conference on "the administration of mass communications in the public interests" during the summer of 1941, Berelson presented a view of what he thought research in mass communications entailed. Like many of his colleagues, Berelson regarded the term *effect* to mean more precisely "effectiveness" or "efficacy." Thus, research into the "effects" of mass communications was not meant to imply research into how the mass media "affects" individuals or groups within the larger social order; rather, for Berelson, research into the "effects" of mass communication was research into how to effectively create mass communication messages to influence the individuals and groups within the social order. Speaking particularly about the role of print on public opinion, Berelson wrote:

> What is the effect of print upon public opinion? The question may be reformulated in any number of ways. How effective is print relative to the other factors which influence public opinion? How effective is it relative to other mediums of communication—both public (the radio) and private (conversation)? Under what social conditions is it more and less effective? What kinds of people respond to print in what ways, and why? What characteristic of print itself are more and less effective? Such questions could be multiplied at length; they serve simply to suggest the nature of the problem.[16]

For Berelson, as for nearly all his colleagues, the nature of the problem of mass communications research was the necessity of developing propaganda techniques that would effectively influence public opinion.

During World War II, Berelson was employed by the Foreign Broadcast Intelligence Service (FBIS), a Washington-based subdivision of the Office of War Information, which was responsible for analyzing German, and apparently Soviet, public opinion and morale during the war.[17] Before the war ended, Berelson moved to New York City and became a project director at the Columbia University Bureau of Applied Social Research.[18] While at the Bureau, Berelson collaborated with Paul Lazarsfeld and others on a series of studies concerning the voting habits of the American public. Their first such study, entitled *The People's Choice: How the Voter Makes Up His Mind in a Presidential Campaign,* was funded by the Rockefeller Foundation, Life Magazine, and Elmo Roper, and aimed at understanding:

modern American political behavior—specifically on the formation of votes during a presidential campaign. Every four years, the country stages a large-scale experiment in political propaganda and public opinion. The stimuli are comprised of everything the two parties do to elect their candidates.... We are interested here in all those conditions which determine the political behavior of people.[19]

Employing what were, at that time, rather sophisticated sampling, interviewing, and statistical techniques, the study provided a detailed picture of how variously stratified social groups responded to campaign messages. The researchers observed that a large portion of the population was politically apathetic, and that public opinion was in a significant way the result of smaller, more politically active groups influencing those less active segments. The researchers thus began to develop the theory of "the two-step flow of communications" to explain how the mass media messages shape public opinion through the personal influence of the "opinion leader" on the larger society. This theory of a two-step flow of communications research, which became the "dominant paradigm" in the field, is examined in the next chapter.

Berelson, Lazarsfeld, and William McPhee conducted another major study of American voting habits through the bureau, entitled *Voting: A Study of Opinion Formation in a Presidential Campaign,* which was financed by the Carnegie Corporation, the Rockefeller and Ford Foundations, the Readers' Digest Association, and the Standard Oil Company, among others.[20] This time studying the public's reaction to the presidential campaigns of Dewey and Truman in 1948, the researchers again located a large segment of the population who were politically apathetic.

Berelson took these results as an opportunity to expound on the nature of democracy in chapter 14, entitled "Democratic Practice and Democratic Theory." In this chapter, Berelson noted that the data from the study "reveal that certain requirements commonly assumed for the successful operations of democracy are not met by the behavior of the 'average' citizen."[21] Although classical democratic theory assumes as requirements that the average citizen will be politically motivated and interested, that he or she will have sufficient knowledge to make prudent decisions, that he or she will "cast his [her] vote on the basis of principle—not frivolously or impulsively," and that the average citizen will exercise rational judgments in the voting process, the study revealed that most citizens fell far short of these requirements. Instead, Berelson found that, for large portions of the population, the motivation to vote "is weak if not almost absent," and that "even when he [the average citizen] has the motivation, he finds it difficult to make decisions on the basis of full information when the subject is relatively simple and proximate; how can he do so when it is complex and remote?" Furthermore, the average citizen does not vote on the basis of principle but in accord with how his or her group votes. Berelson wrote: "The ordinary voter, bewildered by the complexity of modern political problems, unable to determine clearly what the consequences are of alternative lines of action, remote from the arena, and incapable of bringing information to bear on principle, votes the way trusted people around him are voting."[22]

Finally, the average citizen does not exercise rationality in making voting decisions. "For many voters," Berelson wrote, "political preferences may better be considered analogous to cultural tastes—in music, literature, recreational activities, dress, ethics, speech, social behavior."[23]

Yet, rather than conclude that the study's results reveal that the U.S. political system does not therefore represent a democracy, Berelson argued that classical democratic theory was mistaken in placing too much emphasis on the "requirements" of the average citizen in a democracy. Indeed, the U.S. political system *did* represent a democratic system for Berelson, because the larger society appeared to him to function smoothly. He wrote:

> *Individual voters* today seem unable to satisfy the requirements for a democratic system of government outlined by political theorists. But the *system of democracy* does meet certain requirements for a going political organization. The individual members may not meet all the standards, but the whole nevertheless survives and grows. This suggests that where the classic theory is defective is in its concentration on the individual citizen. What are undervalued are certain collective properties that reside in the electorate as a whole and in the political and social system in which it functions.[24]

It is clear, however, that Berelson not only felt that the "collective properties that reside in the electorate" have been undervalued by the classical political theorists who overemphasized the requirements for the average citizen in a democracy, but that these requirements are, in and of themselves, an anathema to the concept of a democratic society. Because the classical ideal democratic citizen does not succumb to persuasive techniques too easily, he or she presents a threat to Berelson's notion of a smoothly running "democratic" society. He wrote:

> How could a mass democracy work if all the people were deeply involved in politics? Lack of interest by some people is not without its benefits, too. True, the highly interested voters vote more, and know more about the campaign, and read and listen more, and participate more; however, they are also less open to persuasion and less likely to change. Extreme interest goes with extreme partisanship and might culminate in rigid fanaticism that could destroy democratic processes if generalized throughout the community. . . . Curiously, the voters least admirable when measured against individual requirements contribute most when measured against the aggregate requirement for flexibility. For those who change political preferences most readily are those who are least interested, who are subject to conflicting social pressures, who have inconsistent beliefs and erratic voting histories. Without them—if the deci-

sion were left only to the deeply concerned, well integrated, consistently-principled ideal citizens—the political system might easily prove too rigid to adapt to changing domestic and international conditions.[25]

Although Berelson's view on the "virtues of apathy" might appear to be antithetical to the very meaning of democracy, it is clear that such views, in Tom DeLuca's words, "resonate cleanly within the outlook on democracy held historically by many political elites, including political theorists and writers."[26] Yet, understood as such, education and communication for "democracy" take on a very specific meaning and a very definite approach, one in which the goal is to keep the public at large uninformed, uninterested, or otherwise distracted so as not to be able to contend with the policy issues that have bearing on their lives.

Berelson remained a central contributor to the growing body of mass communications research throughout the 1940s and 1950s. He published several articles on mass communications and public opinion, and he wrote three additional books. In 1949, Berelson conducted an extensive survey of the types of people who utilize public libraries, through University of Michigan's Survey Research Center, entitled *The Library's Public.*[27] In 1950, he published an anthology of readings, *Public Opinion and Communication,* with Morris Janowitz.[28] Additionally, he published a methodological treatise, *Content Analysis in Communication Research,* in 1952.[29] Berelson's most important contribution to the development of communication research followed his appointment as Director of the Program in Behavioral Sciences for the Ford Foundation in 1952. In this capacity, Berelson played a significant role in establishing the Center for Advanced Study in the Behavioral Sciences at Stanford. He was also in a position to define the nature of much of the mass communications and educational research that the Ford Foundation funded. For instance, it was under Berelson's tenure that the Ford Foundation granted $875,000 to the Center for International Studies at MIT in 1952, for a 4-year research project in the field of international communications.[30] Berelson remained in this position until 1957, at which time he returned to the University of Chicago to assume the position of Dean of the School of Library Sciences.[31]

Berelson brought many diverse talents to the development of the mass communications field. His ability to participate in both the world of the corporate foundations as well as the world of the university-based social sciences made him an important liaison between the national elite and the managerial class of which mass communications researchers were a part. Not unlike his friend and colleague Wilbur Schramm, who was also liberally trained, Berelson seemed to thoroughly understand the shortcomings of the very behavioral approach that he so vigorously endorsed. Also like Schramm, Berelson recognized that he and his colleagues were making bold ventures into an uncharted applied field. He, too, became an important figure in chronicling and defining the dimensions of the field's origins.[32]

FRANK STANTON

Perhaps more so than any other single event, Frank Stanton's appointment to the position of president of the Columbia Broadcasting System in 1946 demonstrated the increasing importance that mass communications research was coming to hold in the United States. Born in Muskegon, Michigan, on March 20, 1908, Stanton received a B.A. from Ohio Wesleyan University in 1930, and a Ph.D. from Ohio State University in 1935. After that he rose from a lowly position in what was, at that time, the small research department at CBS to hold the highest post in the nation's largest communication and advertising operation.[33] Yet, Stanton's success in the world of commercial broadcasting was more than just a symbolic achievement for the value of mass communications research; it also helped to establish firm personal and institutional ties between the commercial broadcasting industry and university-based mass communications research organizations.

It was Stanton's dissertation, entitled "A Critique of Present Methods and a New Plan for Studying Radio Listening Behavior," that first brought him to the attention of CBS. In this work, Stanton argued that current methods of determining radio listening habits (e.g., surveying people about their previous day's radio listening habits; telephoning people to ascertain if they were presently listening to the radio, and, if so, what program they were listening to; having people keep a record of their own radio listening habits; etc.) were inadequate. These methods were costly and inefficient, Stanton argued, and people could not be trusted to give accurate accounts of their radio listening behavior. In place of these methods, Stanton developed a small recording device that could be attached to the radio to determine what time of day, and for how long, the radio was used. He wrote:

> The proposed method involves the installation of recording devices in radio-homes with the listener's consent but without his knowledge of the real purpose of the device. These instruments give information concerning when the radio was in use during the period of observation. When the recorder is removed an interview is held with a member of the family. In this way information is secured regarding listening habits and certain aspects of the economic status of the family. At the same time small questionnaires are left with the person interviewed, one for each listener in the family. . . . The information from the questionnaires together with the interview data are studied in relation to the objective listening record.[34]

Stanton's innovation was an important advancement in broadcasters' and advertisers' attempts to correlate information about the social characteristics of the population with information about the population's radio listening habits. Yet, like so much of this type of research, there was deception at the heart of Stanton's dissertation. Stanton made it clear, in the previously cited passage and in several others in his dissertation, that the people who volunteered to have these measuring devices attached to their radios were not to know the actual motives behind the study, for fear that they would change their radio listening behavior if they realized that they were being observed. Stanton falsely told his subjects that the radio device was used to facilitate a study of the amount of electrical current radios were drawing. In asking people to participate in his study, Stanton identified himself as being connected with the university, but "departmental affiliation was not mentioned because it was feared the subjects might suspect the real nature of the investigation."[35]

In 1935, Stanton's dissertation came to the attention of Paul Kesten, then head of promotional department at CBS. Kesten recognized early on that Stanton possessed some unique talents with respect to understanding audience behavior, and Kesten offered him a research position within the promotion department, paying him $55 a week.[36] CBS historian Robert Metz's description of Stanton during this period could not have been more inaccurate when he wrote that Stanton was "a thoroughgoing pedagogue, with what amounted to a reverence for the sanctity of pure research, he could hardly been prepared for the . . . cynical molders of public opinion who welcomed him to his new job."[37] On the contrary, Stanton fit right in at CBS, and his dissertation had prepared him well for the kinds of work he would conduct while he was there. During this period, Stanton's same talents were also recognized by people within the Rockefeller Foundation and Princeton University and, in 1937, Stanton was offered the position of Director of the Office of Radio Research at Princeton, an offer he considered but declined. Paul Lazarsfeld was then offered and accepted the position, and Stanton agreed to serve as an Assistant Director.[38]

The relationship between Stanton, the CBS mass communications researcher, and Lazarsfeld, the university-based mass communications researcher, was a long and important one, and it facilitated many personal as well as institutional collaborations. In the late 1930s, Stanton and Lazarsfeld developed the first "program analyzer," an electronic device that permitted researchers to measure audience reactions to various media stimulation, and thus provided a means by which the success or failure of planned programming could be predicted. As Robert Metz wrote:

> Stanton's "analyzer" calls for a small screening room with about a dozen seats spaced evenly before a long table. Each location has a pair of push buttons, which are wired to a central recording device. CBS pulls in people from tourist centers in Los Angeles and New York and flatters them by asking if they would like to help pick the shows the nations' viewers will watch on CBS. The partic-

ipants sit at the table, their left hands on the red buttons, their right hands on the green. They watch pilot shows on the screen and are asked to give their push-button reactions. Anything the viewer deplores gets the red button, anything he particularly likes gets the green button. The responses are graphed on the control-room board where a network observer watches.[39]

In the 1940s, Stanton and Lazarsfeld co-edited and published a series of general readers, *Radio Research 1941*, *Radio Research 1942–1943*, and *Communication Research 1948–49*.[40] Lazarsfeld looked to Stanton for CBS funding of many of the research projects he devised, and CBS came through with financial support for many of Lazarsfeld's projects. Stanton looked to Lazarsfeld for the preparation of mass communications research personnel for CBS. Stanton hired Lazarsfeld's student, Joseph Klapper, to serve as Director of Research for CBS in the early 1960s,[41] and CBS funded such important Bureau studies as Gary A. Steiner's 1963 text *The People Look at Television*.[42] In many ways, Stanton and Lazarsfeld enjoyed a symbiotic relationship. CBS gained by remaining closely associated with the university, and the university gained by remaining closely associated with CBS.

Stanton increasingly drifted away from personally conducting mass communications research after he became CBS president in 1946, yet he remained committed to supporting this research in managing the affairs of CBS for the next 25 years. In addition, Stanton came to hold key positions in the national security apparatus, including the chairmanship of the United States Advisory Commission on Information, which oversaw the operations of the United States Information Agency; the chairmanship of the Board of the RAND Corporation; and the chairmanship of the Executive Committee of Radio Free Europe, which was revealed in 1967 to be a CIA conduit.[43] Stanton's influence on the development of mass communications research thus deserves to be given a closer and more thorough scrutiny.

HADLEY CANTRIL

By the time of his death in 1969, Hadley Cantril had earned a reputation among his social scientist peers of being rather difficult to get along with and being somewhat removed from mainstream mass communications research. This might explain why his significant influence on the origins of the field has been overlooked by historians. In a 1942 letter to R. Keith Kane of the Bureau of Intelligence for the Office of War Information, Paul Lazarsfeld characterized Cantril as a man of mere "general intelligence," who had "hardly done any original research" and who had difficulty handling research funds. As a popularizer of other people's research, "his social graces are tinged with just enough liberalism to make him acceptable and useful to a lot of people," Lazarsfeld wrote of Cantril. "I just want to be sure that in the field of research, moral and intellectual standards are not set by him."[44]

Yet Lazarsfeld's interpretation notwithstanding, Cantril was to become a central figure in establishing the moral and intellectual standards of mass communications research. It was his 1935 book *The Psychology of Radio,* co-authored with Gordon Allport, that first led John Marshall of the Rockefeller Foundation to consider funding an institute dedicated to mass communications research.[45] Marshall approached Cantril about heading this institute, although Cantril declined the directorship and recommended Lazarsfeld in his stead. Cantril did, however, serve as an Assistant Director of this new Office of Radio Research at Princeton, and he was responsible for founding several public opinion research institutes in the years to come. He published widely in the area of mass communications research, helped found the journal *Public Opinion Quarterly* in 1937, and cultivated personal contacts with government and philanthropic interests that would greatly facilitate the development of mass communications research.

Born in 1906, Cantril took his B.S. from Dartmouth College in 1928, where he roomed with Nelson Rockefeller. He studied for 2 years in Munich and Berlin before completing his Ph.D. at Harvard in social psychology under Gordon Allport in 1931. After a short stint on the faculty of Columbia University's Teachers College, in 1935 Cantril moved to Princeton University, where he remained for the next 34 years, eventually serving as chairperson of the psychology department.[46]

Cantril was representative of those social scientists who underwent a shift in ideological perspective with the onset of World War II. Prior to the war, Cantril often voiced a critical stance toward propaganda and the mass media. However, during and after the war, Cantril's research interests turned to the development of techniques relating to shaping public opinion. He was an active member and President of the Institute of Propaganda Analysis in 1937. Before the war, it was not uncommon to find Cantril arguing for the development of a critical pedagogy to thwart the pervasive and persuasive influence of the mass media. His 1940 study of the public's reaction to Orson Welles' *War of the Worlds* broadcast, which created widespread panic among at least 1 million of the estimated 6 million listeners, suggested this critical stance. Among Cantril's conclusions as to why people reacted as they did to the broadcast were that people had developed an uncritical faith in radio as a purveyor of accurate and legitimate announcements, the historical timing of the broadcast coincided with a general feeling of crisis in world affairs, the broadcast itself was constructed in such a way that it sounded like a legitimate newscast, and many people who were frightened by the broadcast had simply tuned in late and had not heard the disclaimer that preceded the broadcast. To remedy the situation that seemed to make people so easily manipulated by radio, Cantril called for "extensive educational opportunities" so that a person "can be taught to adopt an attitude of readiness to question the interpretations he hears."[47]

Yet, if Cantril often adhered to a critical perspective on propaganda and the mass media during the years before the war, the seeds of a more accepting position on the use of propaganda and the mass media were also evident in Cantril's prewar writings. In his 1935 text *The Psychology of Radio*, co-authored with Gordon Allport, one can locate this pro-propaganda position that came to dominate Cantril's thinking during World War II and during the Cold War. *The Psychology of Radio* was in many ways a groundbreaking work, and it accurately recognized many of the social changes radio was creating. "The radio is a recent innovation that has introduced profound alterations in the outlook and social behavior of men, thereby creating a significant social problem for the psychologist," Cantril and Allport wrote in the preface. "Radio is an altogether novel medium of communication, preeminent as a means of social control and epochal in its influence upon the mental horizons of men."[48]

Cantril and Allport noted that radio had diminished the importance of the "physical presence" of the speaker and audience, freeing "the listener from the necessity of conventional politeness toward public performers" and interposing "a serious psychological barrier between the broadcaster and his audience through the destruction of the normal circular relationship."[49] In addition, Cantril and Allport were insightful to recognize the profound differences between radio and the screen, and between radio and the printed word. Finally, Cantril and Allport realized that this new communication technology had the potential for greatly altering the relationship between the ruler and the ruled. "We realize that the day cannot be far off when men in every country of the globe will be able to listen at one time to the persuasions or commands of some wizard seated in a central palace of broadcasting, possessed of a power more fantastic than that of Aladdin," they wrote. Yet, despite what some people may regard to be a gloomy prognosis, Cantril and Allport did not, for the most part, conceive the social changes that radio was creating to be negative. Rather, they saw radio as essentially an instrument that would serve as an aid to the development of democracy.

Cantril and Allport viewed radio as a positive development for democracy for several reasons. Radio provided an inexpensive and quick means of communication, and it penetrated the sociological barriers that traditionally kept groups of people separated. "Any device that carries messages instantaneously and inexpensively to the farthest and most inaccessible regions of the earth, that penetrates all social, political, and economic barriers, is by nature a powerful agent of democracy," they wrote. "Distinctions between rural and urban communities, men and women, age and youth, social classes, creeds, states, and nations are abolished." In addition, Cantril and

Allport believed that radio would be a boon to the development of democracy, because it helped to create the "crowd mind" that they saw as a necessary characteristic of a democracy. They wrote:

> One of the characteristics of a democracy is the ease with which individuals acquire a "crowd mind." The radio, more than any other medium of communication, is capable of forming a crowd mind among individuals who are physically separated from one another. (To a lesser degree, of course, the newspaper does the same thing. But newspaper readers do not have as marked an "impression of universality.") The daily experience of hearing the announcer say "This program is coming to you over a coast-to-coast network" inevitably increases our sense of membership in the national family. It lays the foundation for homogeneity. In times of potential social disruption the radio voice of someone in authority, speaking to millions of citizens as "my friends," tends to decrease their sense of insecurity. It diminishes the mischievous effects of rumor and allays dread and apprehension of what is unknown.[50]

Cantril and Allport harbored a particular view of democracy that placed great importance on the values of consensus, conformity, and security, and it was this particular view of democracy that radio would serve to facilitate. Although some would take exception with this particular notion of democracy, it is clear that this notion of democracy would permit, and even require, the development of those communication techniques that would foster consensus, conformity, and security. Therefore, one can understand why Cantril turned increasingly to the study of how to create these communication techniques as the World War II began to threaten these values.

Although many social scientists rushed off to service in the Office of War Information, the Office of Strategic Services, and the other military intelligence and propaganda agencies established during the war, Cantril lent his social science expertise from a rather unique position. In 1940, the Rockefeller Foundation provided funds for Cantril to establish an Office of Public Opinion Research. Housed in attic space at Princeton University, the purposes of the Office of Public Opinion Research, as Cantril recalled, were "(1) to learn and study public opinion techniques systematically; (2) to gain insight into the psychological aspects of public opinion, how and why it changes, what motivates large segments of the public; (3) to build up an archive of public opinion data for the use of qualified scholars; and (4) to begin to follow the course of American public opinion during the war that had already started in Europe, in which I felt the United states would soon be involved."[51] The office experimented widely with survey techniques, and Cantril began to develop sampling methods that would permit him to "obtain quite precise representations of opinions of a whole nation's population with surprisingly few cases."[52] In addition to what Cantril called the "intrinsic theoretical interest" of these sampling methods, he pursued these methods for two practical reasons:

I felt that if the United States became involved in the war and we had established the reliability of small samples, there would be the possibility of obtaining information on the reactions of the American people with maximum
speed and minimum cost. Second, I foresaw the potentiality of utilizing the
survey technique clandestinely in enemy or neutral territory to get information that might in one way or another help the war effort.[53]

After successfully predicting voting behavior in gubernatorial and other
elections from the small samples, Cantril and his colleagues sent a team of
researchers to Canada to surreptitiously interview Canadians about an up-
coming plebiscite on conscription. Simulating conditions under which a researcher would make a survey in enemy territory, or in an area where the
population remained resistant to such methods to control them, Cantril
armed his researchers with skills and techniques that would keep their true
motives hidden from the people being interviewed. "The interviewers had
to memorize the questions, ask them in casual conversations, make no written notes during the interview, but record the answers as soon as possible
after they had left the respondent."[54] Cantril's methods proved successful,
as the difference between the vote on the plebiscite predicted from the
small sample and the vote on the actual plebiscite was 4.5%.[55]

Cantril's success in these endeavors brought him increasingly to the attention of people within the Roosevelt administration. In September 1940,
Cantril was asked by Nelson Rockefeller, who was at that time Coordinator
of Inter-American Affairs, to establish operations to gauge public opinion
in Latin America. Together with George Gallup, Cantril established American Social Surveys, a nonprofit research corporation. Utilizing funds from
the U.S. Office of Emergency Management, Cantril and Gallup placed
researchers throughout Latin America to gauge public opinion on issues
of importance to the United States, and to carry out various research assignments.[56]

Requests from the Roosevelt administration for research into public
opinion increased after Pearl Harbor. In early 1942, Cantril established The
Research Council, Inc., with funds from wealthy advertising executive Ger-
ard Lambert. Cantril and Lambert began to set up a "nationwide survey
mechanism," enabling them "to launch studies at any time they were required."[57] Housed in the same headquarters as Cantril's Office of Public
Opinion Research at Princeton, The Research Council, Inc., worked with almost limitless funds. "At the end of each month, I sent Lambert's New York
office a report of the amount of money spent during the month, and a check
was returned to the Research Council immediately," Cantril wrote. "There
was no special limit placed on our expenses: we undertook any research
Jerry and I thought would be helpful or any that was requested by the White
House."[58] Reports on the status of U.S. public opinion on a range of topics
—including labor and economic problems, issues relating to U.S. percep-

tions of the war's progress and likely outcome, and U.S. concerns about the postwar world—were fed to Roosevelt's six "anonymous assistants," who in turn relayed the reports to Roosevelt. Cantril and Lambert attempted to keep public knowledge of their own involvement with this research to a minimum: "We deliberately made a point of being seen as little as possible in Government offices or agencies in order to minimize curiosity and preserve the informality of our relationships."[59]

Although retaining a low profile, Cantril and Lambert's work within The Research Council, Inc., would have significant influence on White House policy both before and after the war. Roosevelt was apprised of the ebb and flow of U.S. opinion through a series of charts that Cantril routinely updated. In several instances, Roosevelt heeded Cantril's recommendations about the content and tone of his speeches, and followed Cantril's policy recommendations in still others. Cantril argued that such research as provided by The Research Council, Inc., was needed because "no President can successfully implement a policy he believes in unless the people are concerned about that policy and are educated to its implications. And the President can become a more successful educator if he knows something about the extent to which people have any information about the problems he faces and how much they are concerned with them."[60] Engaging in research for the Psychological Warfare Branch of Military Intelligence on North Africa, the Department of State on American attitudes toward international affairs, and the Office of Strategic Services on German public opinion, The Research Council, Inc., proved itself to be a valuable organization both during and after the war. The Research Council, Inc., continued its operations into the postwar years under the direction of Cantril and his colleague Lloyd Free. In this capacity, Cantril continued to provide policy recommendations concerning the United States' relationships to Cuba, the Dominican Republic, Poland, India, and other countries, as well as to provide recommendations to President Eisenhower about what should be said to the U.S. people in his public addresses.

In the spring of 1952, Cantril studied public opinion in Holland and Italy to gauge attitudes toward the United States and its intentions, in order to determine what might serve as "plausible appeals" to each population and "to measure the impact of these appeals in changing the mind of a nation."[61] "The Cantril Report on Plausible Appeals in Psychological Warfare," as the report was called, sought to provide U.S. propagandists with a method by which they "can measure IN ADVANCE the effectiveness of any communication in psychological warfare. That is, they can predict how well any approach or appeal will get across to the people for whom it is intended."[62]

In December 1977, *The New York Times* revealed that The Research Council, Inc., had been covertly funded by the CIA. "The council, founded by Hadley Cantril, the late chairman of the psychology department, and his associate Lloyd Free, derived nearly all its income from the CIA in the decade in which it was active," the *Times* reported.[63] That Cantril and Free were aware of the funding source there can be little doubt. Free told *The New York Times* that Cantril and he had "sort of run" the council for the CIA. During this time period, Cantril and Free were heavily involved in analyzing and making recommendations about U.S. domestic public opinion while under CIA contract. In their study, *The Political Beliefs of Americans: A Study of Public Opinion,* Cantril and Free examined U.S. public opinion on a range of domestic and foreign policy issues, including attitudes toward federal antipoverty programs, federal expenditures for Head Start and other educational programs, the role of labor unions, and the classification of public opinion across the ideological spectrum. In this work, Christopher Simpson pointed out, "Cantril introduced an important methodological innovation by breaking out political opinions by respondents' demographic characteristics and their place on a U.S. ideological spectrum he had devised—a forerunner of the political opinion analysis techniques that would revolutionize U.S. election campaigns during the 1980s."[64]

Although the full story behind The Research Council, Inc., has not been reported, and Cantril's influence on the development of mass communications research in the United States has not been thoroughly documented, both considerations remain central to any adequate understanding of the field's origins.[65] What Cantril regarded as the "basic idea" of mass communications research needs to be explored in order to see how it became the major aspect of the dominant paradigm of mass communications research at mid-century. The "basic idea," argued Cantril, "is that it is possible by means of research to design more effective ways of talking to people about the point of view one is trying to get across and lessen the time, energy, and money wasted in scattered efforts to influence people with arguments that do not get their attention or do not ring true to them."[66]

CARL I. HOVLAND

Carl Hovland's chief contribution to the field of mass communications research was his application of experimental design procedures in laboratory settings to test various methods of changing opinions and attitudes. Born in Chicago, Illinois, on June 12, 1912, Hovland received both his A.B. and M.A. degrees from Northwestern University. He obtained his Ph.D. in 1936 from Yale University, where he became enamored of Clark Hull's behaviorist approach, one he would employ throughout his productive yet short life. After graduation, he stayed on at Yale to assume a position within Yale's Institute of Human Relations, and in 1941 he was appointed director of graduate studies in psychology at Yale.[67]

During Word War II, while the Institute of Human Relations was placed in the service of the OSS, Hovland temporarily left the institute to become Chief Psychologist for the Information and Education Division's Research Bureau of the War Department. It was here, within the Research Bureau, that Hovland had access to almost limitless resources and subjects with which to test his hypotheses concerning the conditions for attitude and opinion change. Hollywood director Frank Capra created the series of films *Why We Fight,* which aimed at strengthening the morale among U.S. servicemen. Hovland, together with six graduate students he had culled from Yale, was asked to evaluate the effectiveness of these films in persuading servicemen to adopt a more vigorous prowar attitude. With full access to the Army's files on the social and personal characteristics of soldiers, Hovland selected soldiers for placement in both control and treatment groups, devised "before and after" questionnaires to measure changes or status in opinion, and ran several tests by showing films to the treatment group. The results of these experiments, published after the war in *Experiments on Mass Communication,* suggested that the films did not have a significant impact on strengthening morale, although these conclusions doubtlessly were conditioned by the fact that morale was already high, with 38% in the control group and 41% in the treatment group who wished to be sent to battle.[68]

Hovland ran several other experiments on issues relating to opinion formation during the war, including measuring the short- and long-term effects of the morale films, measuring the factual war knowledge of both the control and treatment groups, and comparing the effectiveness of presenting one side or two sides of a controversial issue on changing opinions. This last experiment, that of comparing the effectiveness of presenting one or two sides of a controversial issue, suggested that certain individual characteristics, including educational attainment, makes one more amenable to opinion change if two sides of an issue are presented.[69] In these experiments, Hovland went to great lengths in keeping the servicemen unaware of the fact that they were being tested, by hiding the pertinent questionnaire items within larger surveys. When soldiers asked why they were given this survey a second time, during the posttest, they were told that they were now responding to a revised version of the survey.[70] As Chief Psychologist and Director of Experimental Studies for the Research Branch of the Information and Education Division of the U.S. War Department (Hovland's official title), he was certainly in a unique position from which to conduct opinion management research unfettered by concerns for costs or ethics. As Wilbur Schramm recalled: "Hovland was in charge of a research program that could get as much research money (within reason) as it needed. Furthermore, he could move out of the laboratory into the field when necessary and still retain a high degree of control over experimental conditions. He could use very large samples of human subjects on whom large amounts of data were already available, and he didn't have to pay them or persuade them to participate. They could be commanded to be there and they would."[71]

After the war, Hovland returned to Yale to establish and direct the Yale Program of Research on Communication and Attitude Change, from which he continued to conduct the same type of experimental research on the effects of communication messages that he had conducted during the war. From 1946 to 1961, the Yale Program conducted over 50 such experiments, largely through the funding of the Rockefeller Foundation.[72] Hovland, however, broadened his approach to developing the means by which opinions and attitudes could be changed. Although still working primarily within a laboratory created experimental design model and still utilizing the behavioral schema of stimulus and response, Hovland began to consider other dimensions of the communication process as well. He became interested not only in the characteristics of the audience, but also of other variables, such as the characteristics of the communicator and the nature of the message. Hovland conducted an experiment on how opinion change is affected by the credibility of the communicator. His conclusions, like those of much of the social science research created in this vein, were somewhat obvious:

> Communications attributed to low credibility sources tended to be considered more biased and unfair in presentation than identical one attributed to high credibility sources. . . . High credibility sources had a substantially greater immediate effect on the audience's opinions than low credibility sources. . . . The effects on opinion were not the result of differences in the amount of attention or comprehension, since information tests reveal equally good learning of what was said regardless of the credibility of the communicator; variations in source credibility seem to influence primarily the audience's motivation to accept the conclusions advocated.[73]

In another experiment, he sought to examine how messages of fear change people's opinions. Here, Hovland and his researchers suggested that threatful messages were indeed effective in changing opinions, although moderate threats were generally more effective than strong threats because strong threats tended to create unwanted emotional tension that distracted the receiver from attending to the content of the message.[74] In still another experiment, Hovland and his researchers hypothesized that "persons with psychoneurotic symptoms" tended to resist "persuasive communications." This hypothesis was supported, wrote Hovland, "by the personality inventory results: students who remained relatively uninfluenced had higher scores than others on items indicative of neurotic anxiety and obsessional symptoms."[75] It was not clear, however, if Hovland was suggesting that neurotics tended to resist persuasive communications or that persons who tended to resist persuasive communications were neurotics.

Hovland was aware of the importance and practical utility of the research he was conducting in the Yale Program. "The growing interdependence of ever larger numbers of people," wrote Hovland in 1953, "along with advances in the techniques of transmitting communication have led to a high degree of reliance upon mass media to convey information to various types of public and thereby mold their convictions."[76] Others, too, saw the practical utility of Hovland's work. Wilbur Schramm, for instance, reported Hovland's research results in his training text for employees of the United States Information Agency.[77] Yet Hovland understood the limits of the laboratory-based experimental design model that he employed; he could not reproduce the mass communication process in his laboratory, and therefore was aware that his assertions concerning the techniques to change opinions remained tentative and not necessarily generalizable to other situations. He wrote:

> Even when a controlled analytical experiment shows a given factor to be significantly related to communication effectiveness, the question still remains as to the generality of the relationship. For example, experimental results may show that a communication designed to induce people to volunteer for civilian defense activities is more effective when fear-arousing appeals precede rather than follow the action recommendation. Would the outcome be the same in the case of a different topic? Or a different type of communicator? Or another medium? Or a different type of audience? Or a different type of recommended action?[78]

Hovland thought that these questions could be answered by further experimentation under "carefully selected conditions." He wrote that "only in this way can one ultimately determine whether or not the hypothesis is a valid generalization."[79]

Hovland was neither a very imaginative nor forceful writer. Most of his articles were concerned very narrowly with details relating to the design of his experiments. He was careful to not let slip any overtly ideological written remarks. With respect to politics, Hovland listed himself as an independent.[80] He wrote no Cold War treatise, nor did he apparently take a public stand on any issue of national importance. Schramm described Hovland as a quiet and calm man, a man who took his own life in the spring of 1961 while afflicted with cancer.[81] Yet we know that while Hovland lived he did not conduct "pure science"; rather, he adopted a behaviorist approach to understanding human beings, with implicit ideological and normative commitments. In addition, Hovland held key positions on several major national boards, including the Air Force's Human Resources Research Institute, the Ford Foundation, the Rockefeller Foundation, the Office of Chief of Staff of the U.S. Air Force, and others, and he doubtlessly had input in determining the research agendas that these organizations pursued.[82] A shared ideological commitment with these organizations was at least suggested by his participation on their advisory boards.

Hovland, then, had significant influence on the development of mass communications research during the 1940s and 1950s. He established a major communications research program at Yale, and in that program trained several graduate students who later became prominent figures in communications research, including Irving Janis, Arthur Lumsdaine, Nathan Macoby, Gerald Lesser (the principal research advisor to the television program "Sesame Street"), and Lloyd Morrisett (who became the president of the John and Mary R. Markle Foundation, a major source of mass communications research funding).[83] Finally, Howland advocated the use of an experimental design model for understanding communication effects that gained some popularity during the 1940s and 1950s.

STUART C. DODD

Stuart Dodd's contribution to the emerging field of communications stands somewhat unique with respect to the other four contributors selected. Like Hovland and Cantril, Dodd also established and directed a research institute during this period, one that was engaged in government-sponsored mass communications research. Yet, Dodd stood somewhat outside the mainstream; he was both geographically and intellectually removed from the kinds of activities that were occupying the minds of East Coast and Midwestern mass communications researchers. Also, his work never received the recognition nor the favorable reviews that work of the other contributors did. There has been, as a consequence, less general acknowledgment of Dodd's influence on mass communications. Nevertheless, Dodd's influence on mass communications was significant. He, too, trained a generation of mass communications researchers, and his writings suggest a clear and profound ideological purpose that shaped his work.

Dodd was born in 1900 in Talas, Turkey, where his father was a medical missionary. He received B.S. and M.A. degrees and, in 1926, a Ph.D. in psychology, all from Princeton.[84] Although he would consider himself a sociologist and was widely recognized as such, he took no courses in this field.[85] As a student, Dodd came into contact with Robert Yerkes and Clark Hull, both of whom advised him on his dissertation. Heavily influenced by positivism and the testing movement, Dodd's dissertation, entitled "International Group Mental Tests," sought "to measure intelligence internationally . . . to measure intelligence with the use of test material which was free from the effects of limited or local culture."[86] Devising a list of "universal elements" or objects that he thought would be recognizable by all cultural groups, Dodd created an examination based on drawings of these universal objects, and asked his subjects to identify facial expressions, identify associations and similarities between these objects, work mazes, and engage in other such activities. Dodd used his tests to compare the intelligence of such groups as Princeton University juniors, people at the State Institution for the Feeble-

Minded, students at the New Jersey School for the Deaf, and children at the Hebrew Orphan Asylum in New York City. He also sent his test to psychologists for administration in other countries, including Austria, South Africa, Turkey, China, and India, although only the results from the administration of the examination in India were reported in his dissertation. Dodd reported that the Hindu students tested in India scored lower than did their U.S. counterparts. Summarizing the data, Dodd remained circumspect with respect to his conclusions:

> To account of the fact of lower means, several hypotheses, none of which are mutually exclusive, are possible. It is possible that Hindu children are not geared up to work as fast, so that the same time limits in a more leisurely civilization result in a smaller amount of mental work. It is possible that the tests present a task much more strange in a Hindu child's environment and demand a more difficult adaptation. It is possible that the attitude toward such work was much more that of getting every item right than of getting as many items done as possible, an accuracy rather than a speed set.[87]

Yet, true to the ideology of intelligence testing, Dodd did not rule out the possibility "that Hindu children are inferior in ability."[88] Dodd moved away from his interests in intelligence testing in later years. However, his interests in trying to locate common denominators, or universal elements, of human existence through the application of mathematical and statistical techniques would be a major current throughout his career.

Dodd developed and directed the Social Science Research Section at the University of Beirut from 1927 to 1947. During World War II, he served as Director of Surveys with the U.S. Army in Sicily. Then, in 1947, Dodd accepted an offer to direct the Washington Public Opinion Laboratory at the University of Washington, a position he held for the next 14 years.[89] Although the complete story about the research programs conducted by the Washington Public Opinion Laboratory has not yet been told, one of the larger contracts awarded to the laboratory came from the Air Force's Human Resources Research Institute (HRRI). In 1951, HRRI awarded the laboratory an initial $100,000 contract, ostensibly to research the effects of leaflet drops on U.S. communities. "Project Revere," the name given to the project, was funded with a third of a million dollars before the project ended in 1958.[90] Dodd served as the principal researcher for Project Revere, which turned out to be funded secretly by the CIA through HRRI and later through the Society for the Investigation for Human Ecology after HRRI was liquidated in the 1953–54 year.[91]

Project Revere was an extensive research study that targeted several U.S. communities for airborne leaflet drops, ostensibly to gather data concerning the speed by which information could pass through a community, the effects of the messages on members of the community, and the degree of compliance in following the message's direction among people in the community. A total of 13 communities were selected to receive the airborne leaflets, chosen mostly on the basis of their relative seclusion, small size (between 850 and 1,650 people per community), and relative close proximity to the University of Washington. Yet, Salt Lake City was also chosen, and 55,000 leaflets were dropped there in the early morning hours of July 26, 1951. The messages dropped on each community varied. For instance, the leaflets dropped on Salt Lake City read: "Urgent. If this were an enemy leaflet dropped to warn you of an atomic attack coming today, what would you do?"[92]

Following this statement, the leaflet provided four possible multiple choice responses and asked the person finding the leaflet to complete the question and mail the leaflet to the Utah Office of Civil Defense. Messages dropped elsewhere included "Operation Blood Bank," which sought to change people's attitudes toward donating blood; "Operation Krishna," which informed people about a "man calling himself Jesus Christ reincarnated" with the interest of measuring people's reaction to his claim; and "Pretest 1," which employed "a hypothetical news item about the President's death."[93] In each of the 13 communities, Project Revere researchers had the complete cooperation of all the media outlets in keeping people uninformed about both who had dropped the leaflets and for what purposes.[94] In the case of the Salt Lake City experiment, for instance, it was not until 24 hours after the last leaflet was dropped that the public was informed that the leaflets had been dropped; and this was done not by the Utah Office of Civil Defense, but instead by a research team from the University of Washington.[95] Dodd realized that gaining such widespread cooperation from mass communications agencies, including the national press and wire services, was no small accomplishment. Yet, under the pretension of aiding national defense, Dodd was able to effectively obtain this cooperation and thus created a research situation that he noted was rare for social scientists. "Such control of factors by the social scientist is difficult to obtain outside of a totalitarian society," he wrote, "except when one is operating on a defense contract and can invoke the public motivation of helping national defense."[96]

Apparently, Dodd was given considerable latitude in establishing the designs of these leaflet experiments. As Melvin DeFleur and Otto Larsen, two of the younger scholars who assisted in Project Revere and who later published the results, said of the project:

> To social scientists characteristically working on meager budgets it seems somewhat incredible that a group of researchers would have placed at its disposal almost unlimited funds for the purpose of deliberately conducting research into basic problems of communication without the insistence that practical problems were of importance. Yet, this is the context within which the present research was carried out. The United States Air Force felt that a truly practical research program into communication problems would be one that

had long range aims. They recognized the development of a full understanding of communication procedure requires first of all a good understanding.[97]

Thus, Dodd would be in the position to define the procedures and objectives of this large mass communication experiment, and the advances that accrued from this experiment must, in large measure, be seen as a result of Dodd's work. Yet, it is also important to recognize objectives and consequences of the Project Revere studies that may have transcended the pursuit of knowledge about mass persuasion and that Dodd may or may not have been fully aware. Christopher Simpson wrote that "Dodd's project was both a study of propaganda and a propaganda project in its own right. The sample messages clearly served to stimulate popular fear of atomic attacks by Soviet bombers at the height of the famous (and contrived) 'bomber gap' war scare of the 1950s. In reality, many of the communities targeted in Dodd's study were at that time inaccessible to American commercial airlines, much less Soviet Bombers."[98] Simpson went on to point out that the U.S. Air Force created the "purported bomber gap to shore up its position in internal Eisenhower administration debates over strategic nuclear policy."[99]

Dodd and the Project Revere researchers were concerned with the twofold problem of (a) determining the pathways by which messages pass through a community—the characteristics of people who first respond to messages and the social relationships that determine the diffusion of the message; and of (b) determining the optimal number of messages that must be entered into the community to ensure widespread and accurate awareness of the message—too few messages were thought to result in people not being sufficiently aware of the message, whereas too many messages were thought to reach a point of diminished returns, in which the number of people aware of the message does not substantially increase with an increase in messages. The fact that leaflets were chosen as the primary medium of communication in these experiments had more to do with technical considerations rather than with the attempt to understand the effects of leaflets per se. It was easy to quantify the ratio between the number of leaflets and the number of people in the community, and the leaflets (which included questionnaires regarding the characteristics of the person responding to the message), provided a means by which people could mail their responses back to researchers. Dodd and the Project Revere researchers assumed from the outset that their experiment would be applicable to message diffusion through other media of communications as well.[100]

After dropping leaflets on both Birmingham, Alabama, and Salt Lake City, Utah, to get a general understanding of the type of people who responded to the messages, Dodd and the Project Revere researchers moved to a smaller community in Washington State to understand the particulars by which a message would pass through a community. The researchers located a wholesale coffee distributor who was willing to serve as a front for their research activities and who would be willing to exchange coffee for the free advertising it would receive by participating in the study. The researchers then carefully selected 17% of the households in this rural Washington community to serve as rumor starters. These households were contacted and told that if they could remember the message "Gold Shield Coffee: Good as Gold!" when an interviewer returned in a few days, they would receive a free pound of coffee. They were also told to pass this message on to others who would also receive coffee for remembering the message. To motivate others to learn of the rumor, the researchers dropped 30,000 leaflets that read "one out of every five housewives in town already knew of the message" and informed people that if they learned what the message was and remembered it when an "advertiser" came to their door 3 days later, they too would receive free coffee. When the researchers, disguised as advertisers, returned in 3 days, they discovered that 84% of the population could recite the slogan accurately. The researchers distributed the coffee and interviewed the people in the community to ascertain social characteristics of the respondents and to learn from where they had heard of the message. With this information, as well as aerial photographs, maps of dwelling places, and the addresses of the respondents, the researchers were able to trace the flow of the message through the community and to determine the existence of several "interpersonal networks" through which the message was passed.[101]

Variations of this experiment were reproduced in eight different Washington communities, all with the local media cooperating in keeping people in the dark about who was conducting the experiments. Dodd and his researchers varied the number of leaflets dropped in the communities and experimented with different messages as well, in an effort to determine the optimal number of repetitions of a particular message that would lead to community awareness of the message, and to determine the accuracy of the respondents' recall of the message as it passed through different phases of diffusion. The researchers concluded, in DeFleur's words, "that the frequency or redundancy with which a message is presented to a target audience is a vital factor in determining the eventual level of communicative and compliance outcome."[102] Noting that many people who had received the message through third- and fourth-hand sources often garbled it, the researchers concluded that it was important for every member of the target audience to have direct contact with the medium. Finally, the researchers noted that children played an integral role in the flow of the message. Children retrieved the leaflets, and people who had small children were more likely to know about the message than were people who did not. This suggested to the researchers that "an important aspect of the dynamics of social diffusion . . . was that a flow of information took place *from children to adults*" (emphasis in original).[103]

It is not clear whether Dodd was aware that the CIA was covertly funding Project Revere. Yet, regardless of whether or not he knew the true source of the funding, his influence on the development and administration of this large research program had implications for the developing field of mass communications. At least eight dissertations were written from the data gleaned from this research, as well as more than 45 articles that appeared in various professional journals.[104] Some of the students who worked for Dodd on Project Revere would adopt his methodology and ideological perspective. As Everett M. Rogers, a Project Revere researcher in the 1950s and contemporary communication researcher, wrote:

> I did not know that the CIA may have been sponsoring Project Revere and using the Air Force as a front. . . . But I did absorb the diffusion research approach from the Revere studies, a scholarly specialty that I have pursued for the past 30 years or so. Certain of the mathematical formulae for the diffusion of air-dropped leaflets, worked out in Project Revere, are still useful in diffusion studies today. Like the Decatur study, Revere showed the importance of interpersonal networks in understanding the mass communication process.[105]

No doubt there were other mass communications research projects conducted by the Washington Public Opinion Laboratory during the period of Dodd's directorship. A review of the full record of this research would be necessary in order to understand Dodd's influence on the emerging field.

Dodd's published writings between 1939 and 1960 were extensive and varied, and they demonstrate the degree to which he sought to make social phenomena reducible to, and controllable by, mathematical formulae. "It is possible with our present knowledge to begin constructing a quantitative systematic science of sociology," he declared in his 1942 text *Dimensions of Society,* a companion volume to George A. Lundberg's *Foundations of Sociology.*[106] In 1951, he attempted to provide operational definitions, through the use of mathematical equations, for such concepts as "freedom," "equality," and "democracy."[107] In a 1951 article appearing in *Educational Theory,* Dodd sought "to translate the traditional concepts of the Christian religion into the terms of modern social science." Taking what he considered to be "seven of the most enduring of theological questions," Dodd explained how social scientists view good and evil, the soul, sin, prayer, and other such notions.[108]

Perhaps his most ambitious undertaking, one possessing direct bearing on how he viewed communication, was his 1959 article appearing in *Educational Theory,* entitled "An Alphabet of Meanings for the Oncoming Revolution in Man's Thinking."[109] Recognizing the rapid development that had taken place in communication technology since the turn of the century, and seeing a resultant inefficiency and imprecision in most communicative acts, Dodd proposed the development of a single, international language based on mathematics. "It seems likely to us" Dodd wrote, "that mankind could express all the meanings now expressed in language with perhaps one percent of the world's present number of written and spoken symbols. This estimate implies that ninety-nine percent of the world's symbols are now unnecessary and are increasingly becoming wasteful of human energy."[110] Dodd noted that his new ten-letter alphabet, referred to as "Tilp," would be a perfect symbolic system, capable of expressing every human meaning, without indefiniteness or waste of energy. After going through some mathematical steps, Dodd assured his readers "that an alphabet of meanings with as few as ten elements is theoretically ample to express all the meanings mankind can possibly express in a thousand years."[111] Dodd asserted that adoption of this new alphabet of meaning would revolutionize and streamline all thought, reduce conflicts and misunderstanding, and even shorten the extended period of time that students spend in school. Finally, according to Dodd, adoption of this new alphabet of meaning would "revolutionize human speech and thinking and thereby significantly accelerate man's cultural evolving."[112]

This article, written in all seriousness, demonstrates Dodd's intellectual distance from the other mass communications researchers examined in this chapter. This article also suggests an ideological perspective (e.g., a belief that replacing one symbolic system with another symbolic system would overcome the gulf between a symbol and its referent; an anxiety with multiple and diverse meanings; an excessive faith in the value of efficiency, etc.) that would need to be analyzed closely. Still, Dodd remains an important contributor to the development of mass communications research, and analyzing his contribution, as well as the ideological perspective undergirding it, is essential to an understanding of the field.

The institutionalization of mass communications research on university campuses at mid-century was a complicated affair, resulting from various external forces. The researchers who led in this development came from widely divergent disciplinary, methodological, and ideological backgrounds. Nevertheless, circumstances and institutional arrangements that were an outgrowth of World War II provided a powerful impetus to the development of the field, and this is reflected in the significant amount of research conducted for the military and the intelligence agencies both during and after the war. Also, despite the great differences existing among these leading researchers, certain commonalities remained with respect to how they understood the role of the mass media in modern society. The values of security, conformity, secrecy, and so on can be seen undergirding much of the mass communications research conducted by these important contributors, and without exception these researchers were interested in the mass media in terms of how they could be utilized most effectively in shaping the opinions of the larger society. Thus, a fairly consistent instrumentalist view of the mass media of communications had emerged by mid-century among mass communications researchers on university campuses—a view that understood the absolute importance in shaping and controlling the opinions of the emerging mass society. This was not, then, the "end of ideology" that some observers were proclaiming and celebrating in the 1950s, even if many social scientists refrained from examining (or even openly expressing) the ideological assumptions that guided their work. Indeed, one might well argue that these assumptions were so contrary to traditional values pertaining to democracy, rationality, and freedom as to require these researchers to conscientiously hide behind the veil of objectivity, methodology, and administrative research.

The next two chapters discuss how this scenario was played out in the early work of the two people widely regarded as the "founding fathers" of communications study in the United States: Paul F. Lazarsfeld and Wilbur L. Schramm.

NOTES

1. Philip H. Phenix, *Phi Delta Kappan, 43* (October 1961), p. 15.

2. Merle Curti, *The Social Ideas of American Educators* (Paterson, NJ: Littlefield, Adams, 1963). Originally published in 1935.

3. H. J. Carmen, "Review of Merle Curti's *The Social Ideas of American Educators*" *Survey, 71* (October 1935), p. 315.

4. Curti, p. xxv.

5. Ibid., p. xxvi.

6. Ibid., p. xxviii.

7. Margaret Mead, "Thinking Ahead," *Harvard Business Review, 36* (November/December 1958), p. 24.

8. Lawrence A. Cremin, *Popular Education and its Discontents* (New York: Harper & Row, 1989).

9. Chistopher Simpson, *Science of Coercion: Communication Research and Psychological Warfare, 1945–1960* (New York: Oxford University Press, 1994), p. 3.

10. Everett M. Rogers, *A History of Communication Study: A Biographical Approach* (New York: Free Press, 1994), p. 479.

11. Wilbur Schramm, "The Unique Perspective of Communication: A Retrospective View," *Journal of Communications, 33* (Summer 1983), pp. 6–17. See also his posthumously published book, *The Beginnings of Communication Study in America: A Personal Memoir,* edited by Steven H. Chaffee and Everett Rogers (Thousand Oaks, CA: Sage, 1997).

12. Jesse G. Delia, "Communication Research: A History," in *Handbook of Communication Sciences,* edited by Charles R. Berger and Steven H. Chaffee (Newbury Park, CA: Sage, 1987), p. 55.

13. William Paisley, "Communication in the Communication Sciences," in *Progress in Communication Sciences, 5,* edited by Brenda Dervin and Melvin J. Voight (Norwood NJ: Ablex, 1984), pp. 1–43.

14. David L. Sills, "Bernard Berelson: Behavioral Scientist," *Journal of the History of the Behavioral Sciences, 17* (July, 1981), pp. 305–311.

15. Bernard Berelson, *Content Emphasis, Recognition, and Agreement: An Analysis of the Role of Communications in Determining Public Opinion* (Ph.D. dissertation, University of Chicago, 1941), pp. 1–2.

16. Bernard Berelson, "The Effects of Print Upon Public Opinion," in *Print, Radio, and Film in a Democracy*, edited by Douglas Waples (Chicago: University of Chicago Press, 1942), p. 41.

17. Eric H. Boehm, "The 'Free Germans' in Soviet Psychological Warfare," in *A Psychological Warfare Casebook*, edited by William E. Daugherty and Morris Janowitz (Baltimore: Johns Hopkins University Press, 1960), p. 814.

18. Sills, "Bernard Berelson," p. 306. During the late 1950s, Berelson became the bureau's director.

19. Paul F. Lazarsfeld, Bernard Berelson, and Hazel Gaudet, *The People's Choice: How the Voter Makes Up His Mind in a Presidential Campaign* (New York: Duell, Sloan and Pearce, 1944), p. 1.

20. Bernard R. Berelson, Paul F. Lazarsfeld, and William N. McPhee, *Voting: A Study of Opinion Formation in a Presidential Campaign* (Chicago: University of Chicago Press, 1954).

21. Ibid., p. 307.

22. Ibid., pp. 308–309.

23. Ibid., p. 311.

24. Ibid., p. 312.

25. Ibid., pp. 314–316.

26. Tom DeLuca, *The Two Faces of Political Apathy* (Philadelphia: Temple University Press, 1995), p. 2.

27. Bernard Berelson, *The Library's Public* (New York: Columbia University Press, 1949).

28. Bernard Berelson and Morris Janowitz, editors, *Public Opinion and Communication* (Glencoe, IL: Free Press, 1950).

29. Bernard Berelson, *Content Analysis in Communication Research* (Glencoe, IL: Free Press, 1952).

30. Letter from Hans Speier to Wilbur Schramm, October 3, 1952. University of Illinois Archives, Institute of Communications Research, Files of the Director, 13/5/1, Box 8, File S-1952.

31. Sills, "Bernard Berelson," p. 307.

32. See, for instance, Bernard Berelson, "The State of Communication Research," *Public Opinion Quarterly, 28* (Spring 1959), pp. 1–17.

33. "Frank Stanton," in *Political Profiles — The Kennedy Years*, edited by Nelson Lichtenstein (New York: Facts on File, 1976), p. 483.

34. Frank Nicholas Stanton, *A Critique of Present Methods and a New Plan for Studying Radio Listening Behavior* (Ph.D. dissertation, Ohio State University, 1935), p. 90.

35. Ibid., p. 113.

36. Robert Metz, *CBS: Reflections in a Bloodshot Eye* (Chicago: Playboy Press, 1975), p. 59.

37. Ibid., p. 59.

38. David Morrison, "The Beginning of Modern Mass Communication Research," *European Journal of Sociology, 19* (1978), p. 348.

39. Metz, *CBS: Reflections in a Bloodshot Eye*, p. 62.

40. Paul Lazarsfeld and Frank Stanton, editors, *Radio Research 1941* (New York: Duell, Sloan and Pearce, 1941); Paul Lazarsfeld and Frank Stanton, editors, *Radio Research 1942–1943* (New York: Duell, Sloan and Pearce, 1944); Paul Lazarsfeld and Frank Stanton, *Communication Research 1948–1949* (New York: Duell, Sloan and Pearce, 1949).

41. Willard J. Rowland, *The Politics of TV Violence: The Policy Uses of Communication Research* (Beverly Hills, CA: Sage, 1983), p. 72.

42. Gary A. Steiner, *The People Look at Television: A Study of Attitudes* (New York: Knopf, 1963).

43. Herbert I. Schiller, *Mass Communications and the American Empire* (Boston: Beacon, 1971), p. 55.

44. Letter to R. Keith Kane from Paul Lazarsfeld, December 17, 1942. Paul F. Lazarsfeld Papers, Columbia University Archives, Box 1B: Correspondence D–G, Folder D.

45. Letter of Paul Lazarsfeld from John Marshall, July 12, 1969. Paul F. Lazarsfeld Papers, Columbia Univeristy Archives, Box 6: Ar–Bureau of Applied Social Research, File #18 – BASR.

46. William H. Ittelson, "Cantril, Hadley," in *International Encyclopedia of the Social Sciences, 18* (New York: Free Press, 1979), pp. 99–100.

47. Hadley Cantril, *The Invasion From Mars* (Princeton, NJ: Princeton University Press, 1947), p. 205.

48. Hadley Cantril and Gordon W. Allport, *The Psychology of Radio* (New York: Harper & Brothers, 1935), p. VII.

49. Ibid., p. 14

50. Ibid., p. 21.

51. Hadley Cantril, *The Human Dimension: Experiences in Policy Research* (New Brunswick, NJ: Rutgers University Press, 1967), p. 24.

52. Ibid., p. 26.

53. Ibid., p. 26.

54. Ibid., p. 27.

55. Ibid., p. 27.

56. Ibid., p. 28.

57. Ibid., p. 39.

58. Ibid., p. 40.

59. Ibid., p. 40.

60. Ibid., p. 69.

61. Hadley Cantril, *The Cantril Report on Plausible Appeals in Psychological Warfare,* (Princeton, NJ: The Office of Public Opinion Research, Princeton University, 1952), p. 5.

62. Ibid., p. 2

63. "Worldwide Propaganda Network Built by the CIA," *The New York Times* (26 December 1977), p. 37.

64. Simpson, op. cit., p. 81.

65. When Lloyd Free died in 1996, *The New York Times* made no mention of his CIA ties or its earlier exposé on the matter. See "Lloyd A. Free, 88, Is Dead; Revealed Political Paradox," *The New York Times* (14 November 1996), p. B15. Similarly, when Albert H. Cantril, Hadley's son and a public opinion expert in his own right, edited a collection of his father's writings, he made no mention of the important CIA connection. See Hadley Cantril, *Psychology, Humanism, and Scientific Inquiry: The Selected Essays of Hadley Cantril,* edited by Albert H. Cantril (New Brunswick, NJ: Transaction, 1988).

66. Cantril, *The Human Dimension,* p. 99.

67. Biographical information drawn from "Carl Iver Hovland," *The National Cyclopedia of American Biography* (New York: James T. White, 1970), pp. 263–264.

68. Carl I. Hovland, Arthur A. Lumsdaine, and Fred D. Sheffield, *Experiments on Mass Communication* (Princeton, NJ: Princeton University Press, 1949).

69. Ibid., p. 210.

70. Shearon A. Lowery and Melvin L. DeFleur, *Milestones in Mass Communication Research* (New York: Longman, 1988), pp. 113–114.

71. Schramm, *The Beginnings of Communication Study in America: A Personal Memoir,* p. 92. Emphasis in the original.

72. Ibid., p. 138.

73. Carl I. Hovland, Irving L. Janis, and Harold H. Kelly, *Communication and Persuasion: Psychological Studies of Opinion Change* (New Haven, CT: Yale University Press, 1953), pp. 269–270.

74. Ibid., p. 271.

75. Ibid., p. 277.

76. Ibid., p. 1.

77. Wilbur Schramm, editor, *The Process and Effects of Mass Communication* (Urbana: University of Illinois Press, 1954), pp. 261–288.

78. Hovland, Janis, and Kelley, *Communication and Persuasion,* p. 5.

79. Ibid., p. 5.

80. "Carl Iver Hovland," *The National Cyclopedia of American Biography*, p. 264.

81. Wilbur Schramm, "The Beginnings of Communication Study in the United States," in *The Media Revolution in America and in Western Europe*, edited by Everett M. Rogers and Francis Balle (Norwood, NJ: Ablex, 1985).

82. "Carl Iver Hovland," *The National Cyclopedia of American Biography*, p. 263.

83. Schramm, *The Beginnings of Communication Study in America: A Personal Memoir*, p. 95.

84. William A. Catton, Jr., "Stuart C. Dodd," in *International Encyclopedia of the Social Sciences* (New York: MacMillan–Free Press, 1980), pp. 147–150.

85. Otto N. Larsen, "In Memoriam: Stuart Carter Dodd, 1900–1975," *Public Opinion Quarterly, 40* (Fall 1976), pp. 411–412

86. Stuart Carter Dodd, "International Group Mental Tests" (Ph.D. dissertation, Princeton University, 1926).

87. Ibid., pp. 86–87.

88. Ibid., p. 87.

89. Catton, "Stuart C. Dodd," p. 148.

90. Shearon A. Lowery and Melvin L. DeFleur, *Milestones in Mass Communication Research* (New York: Longman, 1988), p. 190.

91. Ibid., pp. 435–437

92. "Postcards From Heaven," *Newsweek, 38* (13 August 1951), pp. 20–21.

93. Melvin L. DeFleur and Otto N. Larsen, *The Flow of Information* (New York: Harper & Brothers, 1948), p. 42.

94. Ibid., p. 59.

95. "Postcards from Heaven," pp. 20–21.

96. Stuart C. Dodd, "Can the Social Scientist Serve Two Masters?—An Answer Through Experimental Sociology," *Research Studies of the State College of Washington, 21* (September 1953), p. 197.

97. DeFleur and Larsen, *The Flow of Information*, p. xiv.

98. Simpson, *Science of Coercion*, p. 79.

99. Ibid., p. 79.

100. For a discussion of the Project Revere experiments, see Lowery and DeFleur, *Milestones in Mass Communication Research*, pp. 187–212.

101. Ibid., pp. 192–194.

102. Ibid., p. 207.

103. Ibid., p. 208

104. Simpson, *Science of Coercion*, "Appendix—Dr. Stuart Dodd's List of 'Revere-Connected Papers,'" pp. 118–122.

105. Everett M. Rogers, "Foreword" in Lowery and DeFleur, *Milestones in Mass Communication Research*, p. xiii.

106. Stuart Carter Dodd, *Dimensions of Society: A Quantitative Systematics for the Social Sciences* (New York: MacMillan, 1942), p. 1.

107. Stuart C. Dodd, "Historic Ideals Operationally Defined," *Public Opinion Quarterly, 15* (Fall 1951), pp. 547–556.

108. Stuart C. Dodd, "The Religion of the Social Scientist," *Educational Theory, 1* (August 1951), pp. 87–96.

109. Stuart C. Dodd, "An Alphabet of Meanings for the Oncoming Revolution in Man's Thinking," *Educational Theory, 9* (July 1959), pp. 174–192.

110. Ibid., p. 176.

111. Ibid., p. 180.

112. Ibid., p. 191.

CHAPTER FOUR

Paul F. Lazarsfeld and the
Bureau of Applied Social Research

*The dominant paradigm in the field since World War II has been,
clearly, the cluster of ideas, methods, and findings associated
with Paul F. Lazarsfeld and his school: the search for specific,
measurable, short-term, individual attitudinal and behavioral
"effects" of media content, and the conclusion that media are
not very important in the formation of public opinion.*
—Todd Gitlin, 1978[1]

PAUL FELIX LAZARSFELD'S enormous contribution to the field of
mass communications research has been widely recognized, thanks especially to his many former students and colleagues who have written in
honor and praise of him.[2] Such evaluations by former students and colleagues are rarely critical, and they are often conducted with an eye toward
aggrandizing one's own position by demonstrating one's own association
with the "great" individual being so honored. Yet, these motivations notwithstanding, Lazarsfeld's former students and colleagues were correct to ac-
knowledge his wide impact on the development of the field. One of these
former students, James S. Coleman, credited Lazarsfeld with nine significant contributions to the field of sociology generally, including such contributions to mass communication research as initiating the use of survey
panel methods in public opinion polling; creating the prototype for conducting large-scale, university-based social research; and becoming the chief
proponent of the "two-step flow of mass communications," which was to become the dominant paradigm in mass communication research.[3] Coleman
could have gone further still by noting that Lazarsfeld's Office of Radio Research at Princeton University was the very first academic unit in the United
States to be devoted solely to the study of mass communications research;
Lazarsfeld's published work dominated the mass communications research
field during its early years so much that he had to often use the pseudonym,
Elias Smith, in order to avoid the embarrassment of having his own name
appear on published communication research too frequently; and Lazars-

feld greatly influenced the thinking of many graduate students who assisted him and took their degrees under him.

If there has been wide recognition of Lazarsfeld's contributions to the origins of mass communication research, much of the work that elaborates on these contributions is based on some fundamental misconceptions about Lazarsfeld's aims in conducting this research. These misconceptions are made by those who are sympathetic as well as those who are critical of Lazarsfeld's research, and they have resulted in a great deal of confusion regarding the field's origins. David Morrison, one of the first individuals to examine Lazarsfeld's contributions, argued that Lazarsfeld "had no interest in mass communication as such," and instead gravitated to the discipline to pursue methodological interests.[4] Relying largely on Lazarsfeld's own interpretation of his early work, Morrison quoted Lazarsfeld as having told him: "Look you have to understand that I had no interest whatsoever in mass communications. I mean everything in a way is interesting to a methodologist."[5] Herbert Schiller, one of the most widely recognized critics of mass communications in the United States, maintained that the "Lazarsfeld contingent" at Columbia's Bureau of Applied Social Research had paid "little or no attention to the work of those who were concerned with the global arena and to the role of mass communication in securing the political attachment of people outside the United States."[6]

There is, of course, some truth to both Morrison's and Schiller's claims; Lazarsfeld *was* interested in methodology, and the "Lazarsfeld contingent" *did* perhaps pay *less* attention to the development of international propaganda techniques than did some other mass communication research groups. But it is equally true that Lazarsfeld possessed very early interests in propaganda and mass communications, and it is also equally true that Lazarsfeld and the bureau he directed engaged in extensive analysis of the role of mass communications in shaping political allegiances in foreign countries during the Cold War.[7] Such misconceptions concerning Lazarsfeld's research aims are undoubtedly based on an inadequate understanding of the particulars of his research as well as the historical context in which his research was conducted. But such misconceptions have far-reaching implications; attempts to paint him as a neutral methodologist, or those that do not account for the historical context in which Lazarsfeld was an important actor, necessarily lead to faulty appraisals of Lazarsfeld's research aims into mass communications.

At the heart of this confusion rests the very definition of *mass communications effects,* which Lazarsfeld used to describe his work, and which others have interpreted to entail an analysis of the degree of social, cultural, political, and educational impact caused by the introduction of various mass media into a social system. Yet, an examination of Lazarsfeld's work reveals no such wide-ranging analysis of the social, cultural, political, and educational impact of the mass media. Rather, Lazarsfeld, like his colleagues in the mass communications research field, used the term *mass communication effects* in a much more narrow sense; Lazarsfeld used it to describe the degree to which mass communication content, designed to change the opinions and behaviors of the audience, was successful in achieving its intended outcome. To state this in a different way, Lazarsfeld was interested in mass communication effects the way a propagandist is interested in effects—the concern is over effectiveness or efficacy, rather than with the social, political, cultural, and educational consequences of the mass media as such.

Lazarsfeld was forthright about how he used the term *mass communications effects* in, among other works, his 1955 text *Personal Influence: The Part Played by People in the Flow of Mass Communications Research,* which he co-authored with Elihu Katz.[8] In this work, Lazarsfeld noted that "the overriding interest in mass media research is in the study of the effectiveness of mass media attempts to influence—usually to change—opinions and attitudes in the very short run. Perhaps that is best described as an interest in the effects of mass media 'campaigns'—campaigns to influence votes, sell soap, to reduce prejudice."[9] Acknowledging that the sponsors of mass communications research played the most significant role in emphasizing this narrow definition of *mass communication effects,* Lazarsfeld maintained that the many subdivisions of this research, including audience research and content analysis, were "not autonomous at all, but in fact merely subordinate aspects of this dominant concern."[10] It was to these ends that Lazarsfeld's work was directed, as a preliminary analysis of his early career bears out. Like his contemporaries, Lazarsfeld's research in mass communications sought to develop "an understanding of how, and under what conditions, mass media 'campaigns' (rather specific short run efforts) succeed in influencing opinions and attitudes."[11]

It is interesting to note that *Personal Influence,* a work in which Lazarsfeld was particularly clear about the objectives of mass communication research, has become a source of endless confusion among scholars who write about the origins of the field. *Personal Influence* is widely considered to be a work central to the field's history, and a book in which the dominant paradigm of "the two-step flow of mass communications" is given its most extensive articulation. Basically, the conceptualization of "the two-step flow of communications" or the paradigm of "personal influence" argues that mass communications messages do not influence the entire population directly, but rather are filtered through "opinion leaders" who diffuse the messages to others within their domain. These "opinion leaders"—by reason of their social status, educational status, or personality traits—are able to exert influence in the areas of news and information, fashion, taste, or any other area in which opinions and attitudes are formed. These opinion leaders are supposed to serve as a conduit through which the mass media's message is interpreted to their domain of influence within the larger society.

The idea is certainly not a very complicated one, and is almost common-sensical; yet, such a conceptualization has had enormous practical utility to propagandists and advertisers, because identifying these opinion leaders and finding particular ways in which to persuade them has led to an increased capacity to persuade the larger population. This was precisely what was motivating Lazarsfeld and his colleagues in sharpening the conceptualization of "the two-step flow," and this conceptualization was widely used by propaganda organizations, including the Voice of America and the United States Information Agency. Nevertheless, historians of mass communication research have not interpreted *Personal Influence,* or the two-step flow conceptualization, to represent a more sophisticated and refined propaganda technique. Instead, these historians have interpreted *Personal Influence* entirely as an analysis that seeks to describe the larger social effects of the mass media. These historians have used Lazarsfeld's endorsement of the two-step flow conceptualization to support the view that Lazarsfeld believed the mass media to have an indirect, and therefore limited, effect (meaning larger social, political, cultural, or educational effect) on society. By treating *Personal Influence* as simply a descriptive account of mass communications effects, and by failing to recognize the narrow meaning that Lazarsfeld ascribed to "mass communication effects," these historians have greatly distorted the nature of this important work and also, therefore, the origins of the field as well.[12]

The purpose of this chapter is to clarify the objectives of Lazarsfeld's mass communication research by providing an overview of the many personal and social forces that shaped his work. It is argued that Lazarsfeld possessed a long-standing interest in propaganda, and that this interest was significantly enhanced by the many commercial and governmental agencies that contracted Lazarsfeld and the several social science research institutes he directed. Finally, the practical utility of the conceptualization of the two-step flow of communications also discussed.

EARLY VIENNA INFLUENCES

Paul Felix Lazarsfeld was born in Vienna on February 13, 1901, to a middle-class, educated, Jewish family with strong commitments to the socialist movement of the day. His father, Robert, was a lawyer who conducted a private practice; his mother, Sofie, was a psychotherapist trained in the Alfred Adler vein. The family nurtured close ties with many of the leading intellectual and socialist figures in Vienna during this period, and thus helped to create an environment for their children that was both intellectually stimulating and at the center of political controversy. Alfred Adler served as the family pediatrician, and the unrelated Friedrich Adler—mathematician, physicist, and socialist leader—advised the young Paul Lazarsfeld to pursue an academic career in mathematics. When Friedrich Adler assassinated the prime minister, Count Karl Sturghk, in August 1916, Lazarsfeld became an active protester against Adler's conviction and imprisonment.[13]

During the early part of the 20th century, Vienna was the site of great intellectual ferment, which significantly influenced Lazarsfeld and his contemporaries (many of whom who would later emigrate to the United States). Hans Zeisel, Lazarsfeld's childhood friend and adulthood colleague, pointed particularly to Freudian psychology, the Vienna Circle of philosophers (including Ludwig Wittgenstein and Rudolf Carnap), and the introduction of U.S. and British empirical social science research as important constitutive elements of the intellectual climate in which they were educated. Freudian psychology, said Zeisel, provided "an awareness of the limits of rational action and of the new, until then unknown, motives of human behavior." According to Zeisel, the logical analysis of language associated with the Vienna Circle "did not claim to know what is true, good, or beautiful but limited itself to the modest analysis of what was meant by statements in science, aesthetics, and ethics."[14] In addition, Zeisel maintained that the empirical social science research that was generating interest in the United States and England at the time began to make deep inroads into both his and Lazarsfeld's thinking about social phenomena.

However, Zeisel and Lazarsfeld would both recall that it was the socialist movement in Vienna that had the most significant influence on their early thinking and activities. "For a brief moment in history," Zeisel explained, "the humanist ideals of democratic socialism attained reality in the city of Vienna and gave new dignity and pride to the working class and the intellectuals who had won it."[15] Lazarsfeld internalized the ideals of this democratic socialism, in many respects, and it was within this socialist movement that Lazarsfeld demonstrated his earliest interests in the role of mass communications and propaganda. In his memoir, Lazarsfeld wrote: "I was active in the Socialist Student Movement, which was increasingly on the defensive before the growing nationalistic wave. We were concerned with why our propaganda was unsuccessful, and wanted to conduct psychological studies to explain it."[16]

Such attempts at explanation were not conducted simply for their own value, but rather as a means to create more effective and persuasive propaganda for the socialist cause. Presumably, Lazarsfeld utilized the results of such analyses in his activities associated with the socialist movement, including publishing a socialist newspaper, acting as a leader of socialist organizations, and contributing to the political theater of Vienna.[17]

From very early in his career, Lazarsfeld was interested in and committed to this notion of propaganda, and his career decisions were based, in no small measure, on these concerns. As the first examples of market research began to appear in Vienna in the 1920s, Lazarsfeld saw parallels between this market research and what he was trying to do with his socialist propaganda. After becoming acquainted with one Austrian study of "why people bought various kinds of soap," Lazarsfeld said he became deeply drawn into what he saw was the methodological importance of such market studies, and how these market studies related to his own thinking about public opinion. "Such is the origin of my Vienna market studies," Lazarsfeld wrote in his memoir, "the result of the methodological equivalence of socialist voting and the buying of soap."[18] Lazarsfeld's interest in developing techniques and methods that would make propaganda more viable and effective continued to grow throughout his years in Vienna, and he brought this with him as a major research interest when he emigrated to the United States.

If Lazarsfeld's concern for propaganda, communications, and advertising continued to develop in later years, his belief in the ideals of democratic socialism, which had originally brought him into this research area, waned as he came into adulthood. According to David Sills, Lazarsfeld once explained that "he was a socialist the way he was a Viennese: by birth, and without much reflection."[19] As Lazarsfeld passed through his doctoral program in applied mathematics at the University of Vienna, one could detect a gradual decline in his commitment to the ideals of democratic socialism that he had previously espoused so vigorously. By the time he emigrated to the United States in 1933, these same ideals were, apparently, no longer a significant part of Lazarsfeld's worldview. Although the issues surrounding Lazarsfeld's rejection of democratic socialism are many and complex, it is clear that he underwent such a transformation. Indeed, one would be hard pressed to find aspects of later Lazarsfeld's work that were particularly democratic or in any significant way reflective of socialism.

Lazarsfeld completed his Ph.D. in 1925 at the University of Vienna, where he came under the tutelage of child psychologists Karl and Charlotte Bühler. The Bühlers had established a psychological institute at the university, and hired Lazarsfeld to assist in the statistical analysis of some of the studies of child development they were conducting at the time. Lazarsfeld characterized Karl Bühler as a "prominent introspectionist" who had become well acquainted with both European cultural philosophy and American behaviorism. "The key to Bühler's thought," according to Lazarsfeld, "was the need to transcend any one approach or any one immediate body of information, to reach a broad conceptual integration."[20] Lazarsfeld was unsure as to the degree to which he was influenced by Karl Bühler's "ecumenical spirit;" but he admitted that he "never missed the chance to show that even 'trivial' studies, if properly interpreted and integrated, could lead to *important* findings, 'important' implying a higher level of generalization."[21] In later years, Lazarsfeld justified his continued interest in market research on the grounds that such "trivial" studies would lead to much greater generalizations about social relations. In addition, Lazarsfeld's penchant for utilizing both quantitative and qualitative methods in his analysis of social phenomena was, in part, a result of his association with Bühler and Bühler's emphasis on various methodological approaches. From Charlotte Bühler, who both served as the administrator of the institute and directed studies relating to child and adolescent psychology, Lazarsfeld adopted the style of organizing research units for which he was to be noted. Reflecting the characterization that would later be used to describe him, Lazarsfeld wrote that Charlotte Bühler "had a Prussian ability to organize the work activities of many people at many places." Like Lazarsfeld, "some felt exploited by her," but Lazarsfeld added that he "always appreciated her good training and help."[22]

By 1927, Lazarsfeld had constructed his own social science research division within the Bühlers' psychological institute. This division, known as the Wirtschaftspsychologische Forchungsstelle, would be the model on which his later research institutes in the United States would be based. The pattern for securing external funding for research (a hallmark of Lazarsfeld's later institutes), was established within the Forchungsstelle, and Lazarsfeld made his first mark as a director of social research there. Having become interested in market research and the construction of propaganda, it was not surprising that Lazarsfeld pursued this kind of research at the Forchungsstelle. As director of the Forchungsstelle, Lazarsfeld solicited contracts from a number of different commercial organizations to conduct market research in the interest of determining the most efficient and effective way to advertise their products. Among the list of such products studied within the Forchungsstelle to enhance their marketability were beer, butter, coffee, milk, vinegar, soup, shoes, rayon, and wool. In addition, Lazarsfeld conducted one of the first studies into radio listening while at the Forchungsstelle. Convincing manufacturers, distributors, and broadcasting stations about the value of this market research was not an easy task at first. "To sell market research in those days was about as easy as selling a bicycle to somebody who had never before heard of such an allegedly practical contraption," Hans Zeisel wrote. Yet, after a few of the studies were completed, the value of the research began to be demonstrated. "The ice broke," wrote Zeisel, "when one prominent Vienna industrialist wrote to us stating that, as a result of our study, sales of the investigated product had increased by 27 percent."[23]

Lazarsfeld's work within the Forchungsstelle helped to make market research "academically respectable."[24] Yet, the kind of research Lazarsfeld was championing, which entailed the close observation and scrutiny of the behavior of possible consumers and audiences, was not universally popular among the people who were the subjects of his studies. Indeed, the record suggests that these people did not always take kindly to Lazarsfeld's variety

of social analysis, and Lazarsfeld had to develop techniques by which to sur-
mount this resistance. Zeisel recalled one incident in which Lazarsfeld's applied social research, aiming to "help in the education of difficult children,"
ended with Zeisel and Lazarsfeld being pelted with stones by these "difficult
youngsters . . . until we got the message and decided to go home."[25] By the
time Lazarsfeld, Zeisel, and Lazarsfeld's first wife, Marie Jahoda, conducted
their study of Marienthal (an Austrian community suffering extreme unemployment), Lazarsfeld and his colleagues had developed several sophisticated techniques by which their activity of gathering personal information
from people would appear less obtrusive.

Attempting to develop a portrait of the psychological characteristics of an
unemployed community, Lazarsfeld and his colleagues sent a research team
into Marienthal to gauge the inhabitants' reactions to conditions relating to
their unemployment. Doubtlessly anticipating resistance to their attempts
to gather such information, Lazarsfeld and his colleagues created an approach that they thought would make their presence and activities more acceptable to the people who lived there. "We made it a consistent point of
policy," Lazarsfeld, Zeisel, and Jahoda wrote, "that none of our researchers
should be in Marienthal as a mere reporter or outside observer. Everyone
was to fit naturally into the communal life by participating in some activity
generally useful to the community."[26] In addition, Lazarsfeld and his colleagues engaged in several "special projects" that helped them gain access
to the personal and social lives of their subjects, including establishing a
clothing project, gaining access to the various political organizations in the
community, offering courses in pattern design and girls gymnastics, and
providing medical and parental guidance consultation to the people in the
community. The clothing project consisted of distributing used clothing,
which had been collected in Vienna, to the people in Marienthal. The distribution was preceded by a visit from one of the researchers, who inquired
about what items of clothing were needed by the family. "These visits," Lazarsfeld and his colleagues wrote, "gave us unobtrusive access to the home,
and enabled us to ascertain the particular needs of the family and discover
which members received special attention."[27] The distribution of clothing,
thus, provided an effective way of gaining insight into the behavior of the
people under study—insight that, under normal circumstances, the people
did not apparently want to share with social science researchers. Lazarsfeld,
Zeisel, and Jahoda wrote:

> While issuing the clothes we made detailed records of the behavior of the re-
> cipients, their reactions to this kind of assistance in particular and to their own
> predicament in general. Finally, contact with the population was facilitated by
> Dr. Lotte Danziger's preparatory work in connection with the clothing proj-
> ect; she inspired the confidence to which we owe the copious biographical ma-
> terial the workers confided to us.[28]

The free medical consultations were also utilized as a means to gain access to information about the personal lives of the impoverished people of Marienthal. Once a week, two doctors offered free medial consultation and, in urgent cases, free medicine. Yet, these consultations were not absolutely free, because the people of the community paid for this service with the personal information they revealed to the doctors. "Notes were kept of the conversations in the examination room," Lazarsfeld and his colleague wrote, and because these were based on consultations with doctors over health concerns the researchers could be assured that they were gathering accurate information: "These medical consultations provided our best opportunity to learn about the medical and economic circumstances of a family, since the very success of the examinations depended on the patient's truthful reporting. Here we also had an opportunity to check on some of the statements made to the welfare worker, which were at times not quite truthful."[29]

The unemployed people of Marienthal were no doubt very appreciative of the free clothing, medical consultations, and other services offered by the researchers, and Lazarsfeld, Zeisel, and Jahoda recorded no widespread resistance to their attempt to collect data from the people who lived there. Lazarsfeld's skill in developing unobtrusive means to gather personal information in his market and communication research also proved useful later, when his subjects were U.S. citizens, many of whom were also wary of attempts to measure their behaviors and opinions.

It was this Marienthal study that first brought Lazarsfeld to the attention of the Rockefeller Foundation, which offered him a fellowship to pursue his research interests in the United States. Lazarsfeld accepted this offer, left his wife and small child, and moved to the United States in September 1933, beginning a relationship with the Rockefeller Foundation that remained strong for at least the next 2 decades. During his first year in the United States, Lazarsfeld made extended visits to many of the major research universities in this country—including Harvard, Columbia, Chicago, Ohio State, and others—and engaged for a time in some research for the newly formed Psychological Corporation. His visits brought him into wide contact with a number of influential people in academia (including Robert Lynd, Gordon Allport, and Robert Hutchins), and he began to establish important contacts with many leaders in social research in the United States, a number of whom were just beginning to explore the terrain of mass communication research. Lazarsfeld had originally planned to return to Vienna after the fellowship ended to continue his work at the Forchungsstelle; yet, when in February 1934 the social democrats were overthrown by the fascist Conservative Party in Austria and most of Lazarsfeld's family was imprisoned, Lazarsfeld asked for an extension in his fellowship, which was granted by the Rockefeller Foundation. By 1935, Lazarsfeld was recommended by Columbia University's Robert Lynd to direct the University of Newark Research Center. Lazarsfeld accepted this offer, and remained in the United States for the rest of his life, during which time he established himself as a dominant figure in American mass communication research.[30]

MACHINE BUILDING IN THE UNITED STATES

Lazarsfeld was one of many German and Austrian émigrés to the United States in the 1930s and 1940s who had an enormous impact on American culture through either their criticism of the mass media or in the particular manner in which they proposed to use this mass media.[31] Whereas Bertolt Brecht, Theodor Adorno, and other émigrés would take the lead in criticizing the culture that was created and sustained by the mass media in the United States, Lazarsfeld's own contribution was found in his construction of several research institutes that provided the mass communicator with the "administrative research" necessary for the perpetuation of that culture. His close ties with many of the critics of that culture (including the Frankfurt theorists), his European academic training, and his early adherence to democratic socialism somewhat clouded the nature of his research and, to some people, lent a certain legitimacy to his activities; nevertheless, he was not critical of the mass media of communications and, in fact, labored arduously to perfect its use as a means of economic gain and social control.

Like other émigrés to the United States in the 1930s, Lazarsfeld faced the prospect of making a living and trying to fit into a society that was both economically depressed and often strange and alienating. Being Jewish, Lazarsfeld faced both the overt and subtle forms of anti-Semitism that run throughout American culture, and his earlier ties with socialism were considered by some people to be a mark on his record that would need to be overcome.[32] However, Lazarsfeld also carried with him some talents that made him particularly well suited for a leadership role in this new field of mass communication research in the United States, and some skills that made him particularly attractive to those powerful interests who would profit from his style of research. He had previous experience in winning contracts from commercial concerns for market research, which was increasing in demand among advertisers in the United States, and he also had experience in directing a social science research "machine" affiliated with a university, something that was uncommon during the 1930s in the United States.[33] Finally, Lazarsfeld realized that he represented a "connecting cog" between some of the various "speculative" and "empirical" approaches in the social sciences occurring at that time in the United States. As Lazarsfeld wrote 36 years after arriving in the United States: "A European 'positivist' was a curiosity welcomed by men aware of the subtler trends in the American social sciences."[34] And he would be welcomed as he introduced his own brand of positivism, along with highly developed administrative skills, into this germinating mass communication research field.

Lazarsfeld's earliest work in the United States reflected the same concerns that motivated his research at the Forchungsstelle at the University of Vienna. While at the University of Newark's Research Center in 1935 and 1936, Lazarsfeld again made it an explicit point to seek out commercial and other governmental organizations to fund the center's research activities. The Research Center had several objectives: to train and employ students, to develop new research methods, to assist Newark in understanding its economic and social problems, and so on. But Lazarsfeld also listed "to act as a consulting service to social and business agencies in the city" as a main objective of the center.[35] In addition to initiating a study of issues relating to unemployment for the New Jersey Relief Administration, Lazarsfeld also conducted a series of studies seeking to provide commercial agencies with insight into how they might more effectively market their products. For the Eastman Kodak Company, Lazarsfeld directed a study of how owners of home movie cameras used the product so that "consumers [could be] better organized," for the DuPont Company Lazarsfeld directed a study of "relative pleasantness" of various fabrics, and for the Milk Research Council Lazarsfeld directed a study into "why young people dislike milk."[36] For an unknown sponsor, Lazarsfeld conducted a study of "Magazine Reading in American Cities with a Population Over 100,000," which included an analysis of "educational expenditures, income tax returns, age of population, number of industrial workers, number of movies, number of negroes, number of foreigners, and the circulation of twenty-five leading magazines" for all cities with populations of more than 100,000.[37]

The Research Center at the University of Newark remained in a very tenuous position during its short existence, and the studies that Lazarsfeld conducted there were minor in comparison to those which he would later direct. Nevertheless, these studies demonstrated how closely Lazarsfeld's research interests were tied to the interests of industry and government from his very earliest days in the United States. These interests grew closer still when, in 1937, Hadley Cantril of Princeton University recommended Lazarsfeld to head the newly founded Office of Radio Research at Princeton. The stated objectives of the Office of Radio Research, which was initially funded by the Rockefeller Foundation for a 2-year period at $67,000, were "to determine . . . the role of radio in the lives of different types of listeners, the value of radio to people psychologically, and the various reasons why they like it."[38] Yet, the objectives of the office were, from its inception, closely aligned with the marketing interests of the mass communication industry and other commercially oriented agencies. In the stated plans for the office, the researchers noted that existing commercially sponsored research into radio "effects" had already established the foundation from which to examine the social role of radio, and that these commercial studies could be extended to create more general results:

> During the past decade commercial broadcasting has done a considerable amount of systematic research and has accumulated much practical experience which needs only slight modification to be useful for more general purposes. Unless we know who listens to an individual program, how it is received, and what accounts for its acceptance, no insight into the social effects and potentialities of radio is possible. . . . For this reason one of the groups of activities planned by the Princeton Radio Research Project is the adaptation and extension of the commercial sort of radio research toward more general use.[39]

However, the aims of the Office of Radio Research went beyond simply extending the insight of existing commercial radio research, and actively sought commercial contracts as an important source of revenue. Although the full extent of this commercial funding within the office during its early years remains undocumented, the studies supported by commercial contracts were many and considerably varied, with such titles as "Should Bloomingdale's Maintain Its Restaurant?" "Explanatory Study of the Psychology of Refrigerator Purchasers," "The Outlook for Testing Effectiveness in Advertising," "Psychological Techniques in Market Research," and many others.[40] From 1944 to 1949, after the office had been renamed the Bureau of Applied Social Research and moved to Columbia University, the commercially sponsored grants accounted for 48.5% of the total amount of income ($625,000) for this 5-year span.[41]

There were other important connections between the Office of Radio Research and commercial organizations that deserve to be noted. Frank Stanton, who was in the late 1930s Director of Research for CBS, served as Assistant Director of the Office of Radio Research, and Stanton and Lazarsfeld developed a close collaborative relationship throughout the years to follow. When Lazarsfeld began in 1956 to plan for the celebration of the 20th anniversary of the Bureau of Applied Social Research, he stated his indebtedness to Stanton in a letter to Columbia University President Grayson Kirk:

> During the first ten years it [the bureau] was helped in every conceivable way by Dr. Frank Stanton. He was first my collaborator and then a member of the Board until the time that it was decided that the governing board should consist of members only. But even now Dr. Stanton in his capacity as President of the Columbia Broadcasting System is still in many ways supporting the Bureau's activities.[42]

In addition, the Office of Radio Research provided the research ammunition needed by the communication industry to ward off attempts by the federal government to restrict monopoly control of the media. As Lazarsfeld recalled:

Just before the war, the FCC opened hearings on the question of whether newspapers should be permitted to own radio stations. We received funds to set up punched cards providing, for every station, data on ownership and on the way news programs were handled. These funds were provided by a committee including all radio stations owned by newspapers. This was, at the time, an important source of income for us, but I made it a condition of our work that the FCC would have complete access to our data.[43]

The institutional framework of the Office of Radio Research, and its relationship to important commercial sources of income, were thus well established by the time the office was transferred to Columbia University in 1939 and eventually renamed the Bureau of Applied Social Research in 1944. In 1941, Lazarsfeld explained to the National Association of Broadcasters and the Association of American Newspaper Editors what this relationship meant to the social scientists who were engaged in mass communication research:

Those of us social scientists who are especially interested in communications research depend upon the industry for much of our data. Actually most publishers and broadcasters have been very generous and cooperative in this recent period during which communications research has developed as a kind of joint enterprise between industries and universities. But we academic people always have a certain sense of tightrope walking; at what point will they shut us off from the indispensable sources of funds and data.[44]

Lazarsfeld proved himself to be a proficient tightrope walker, if that metaphor accurately captures the activities in which Lazarsfeld had to engage in order to ensure continued economic support from the industries. Research conducted by the Bureau of Applied Social Research was supported by commercial contracts at least through the middle 1960s.[45]

There can be little doubt that the commercial organizations that provided substantial research money to Lazarsfeld's Office of Radio Research, and later to his Bureau of Applied Social Research, played a significant role in defining its research perspective and agenda. From its earliest days, the notion of radio "effects" utilized by the office referred most precisely to the notion of radio "effectiveness." This was true whether the office was conducting program research and posed such questions as "How do you measure listener reaction to a program? . . . How can one measure the 'effectiveness' of a given information program?, How (to) determine the cumulative effect of a series of programs?," or whether the office was conducting more specific "effects studies" that Lazarsfeld maintained "pertains to the effectiveness of one section or element of a program."[46] In any event, it is, as Todd Gitlin suggested, "no secret" that the mass communication research for which Lazarsfeld would be noted descended "directly from the development of sophisticated marketing techniques." Furthermore, as Gitlin argued, "the theory of 'effects' was first developed for the direct, explicit use of broadcasters and advertisers."[47] Lazarsfeld, however, saw no problem with his close association with commercial agencies; nor was he apparently concerned about the way in which these commercial sponsors were shaping the research agenda for the Office of Radio Research, despite widespread opposition in academia during that time to attempts by industry to dictate the focus of social and educational research. Instead, Lazarsfeld thought that this kind of radio research seemed "to fulfill very well the definition of 'applied psychology' as the sum total of techniques used by psychologists when they are called upon to collaborate with agencies empowered to perform specific social functions." Even more to the point, Lazarsfeld was aware of what he and others like him could gain from the pursuit of this new mass communications research. "This field of radio research presents three important opportunities to psychologists," he wrote in 1939, "challenging problems, unusual data, and more jobs."[48]

There was another important source of research funds to the Bureau of Applied Social Research, and consequently a major influence in shaping the research agenda of the bureau, that has been largely ignored by bureau historians: The federal government, and particularly those aspects of it relating to national security, played an enormous role in the bureau's early development. As the war in Europe began to increase in intensity during the latter part of 1939 and the early part of 1940, Lazarsfeld was aware that the discussion concerning the role of propaganda in a democracy had to give way to a discussion about how to use propaganda effectively. In the introduction to his 1940 text *Radio and the Printed Page* (a careful analysis of the relative merits of radio and print in attracting and persuading audiences), Lazarsfeld recognized the importance of this shift. Noting that "until quite recently social psychologists were interested primarily in problems of propaganda," Lazarsfeld argued that the world situation had changed so dramatically that "the role of radio as a tool of propaganda has receded to the background because not what to do but how to do it has become the problem of the day."[49] Such a shift, of course, boded very well for Lazarsfeld and the bureau. The outbreak of World War II initiated a relationship between Lazarsfeld's bureau and various agencies of the U.S. government, and this relationship continued into the postwar period. During the war, the Office of War Information as well as the United States Army utilized the bureau and its personnel for a variety of services, including, in Lazarsfeld's words, "the testing of films and radio programs devised to maintain the morale of various sectors of the civilian and military populations. . . . The fees provided by these assignments were turned over to the Bureau and were an important financial help."[50] Leo Lowenthal, Robert Merton, Lowenthal's second wife, Majorie Fiske, and Lazarsfeld's second wife, Herta Herzog, were among the many bureau employees who worked in the United States' wartime propaganda agencies.

Because he was not a U.S. citizen during the early years of World War II, Lazarsfeld was denied a formal appointment to the Office of War Information.[51] Lazarsfeld was, however, hired as a consultant to the OWI as well as to the War Production Board and the War Department.[52] Lazarsfeld's actual work while serving as a consultant to the OWI and other propaganda-related agencies has not been well documented. He is acknowledged as having assisted in Carl Hovland's extensive experimentation on attitude change for the U.S. Army, and he apparently played an instrumental role in Samuel Stouffer's study of *The American Soldier.* His personal papers contain very little material relating to his wartime service, and a preliminary search of the National Archives for materials relating to Lazarsfeld's association with the OWI has not been fruitful. Still, one can get a general picture from his own published accounts, as well as from items that remain in his papers, that Lazarsfeld's involvement in propaganda research for the U.S. national security apparatus was significant both during and after the war. Lazarsfeld played an important role in developing techniques to analyze and measure the effectiveness of war-related propaganda, in addition to providing a theory of propaganda that had considerable practical use during the postwar period.

In a little-known 1949 article co-authored with Robert Merton, entitled "Studies in Radio and Film Propaganda," Lazarsfeld and Merton referred to several war-related, domestic, propaganda operations in which they and Lazarsfeld's wife, Herta Herzog, were involved.[53] These operations included a series of radio programs and a series of documentary films created to raise the morale of the domestic population, as well as the construction of a "pamphlet concerning negroes," which aimed at convincing African Americans that the discrimination they would face under Hitler would be worse than the discrimination they faced in the United States. The article is of importance, however, not only because it indicates Lazarsfeld's involvement in these OWI projects, but because Lazarsfeld and Merton used this article as an opportunity to expound on the nature of propaganda. "Studies in Radio and Film Propaganda" contains Lazarsfeld and Merton's definition of *propaganda,* their formulation of "technological propaganda" (which they also refer to as "the propaganda of facts"), their understanding of the role social psychologists should play in the refinement of propaganda, and a clear statement of their belief in the necessary function to be served by propaganda in the postwar world.

In defining *propaganda,* Lazarsfeld and Merton drew heavily from Harold Lasswell, in that, like Lasswell, they held that only controversial issues could be the subject of propaganda: "We understand by propaganda any set of symbols which influence opinion, belief, or action on issues regarded by the community as controversial. These symbols may be written, printed, spoken, pictorial, or musical. If, however, the topic is regarded as beyond debate, it is not subject to propaganda."[54] Thus, issues in a particular community that are not under dispute, for instance, "the belief that 2 and 2 make 4" and "the moral conviction that mother–son incest is evil" cannot be the subject of propaganda. Lazarsfeld and Merton also tried to rescue the notion of propaganda from those who defined it as the communication of false or deceitful information. Propaganda could be false or deceitful, they argued, but it does not necessarily have to be so. According to Lazarsfeld and Merton, statements of fact could serve very well the cause of effective propaganda. "An authentic account of the sinking of American merchant ships in the time of war," they argued, "may prove to be effective propaganda inducing citizens to accept deprivations which they would not otherwise accept in good spirits."[55]

Lazarsfeld and Merton noted that the selective use of such "facts" proved to be effective tools of persuasion precisely because of the increased suspicion among population of attempts to persuade them. "One of the most conspicuous responses we observed in our tests," they wrote, "is the pervasive distrust of propaganda exhibited by many people. Propaganditis has reached epidemic proportions. Any statement of values is likely to be tagged as mere propaganda and at once discounted."[56] Lazarsfeld and Merton noticed that this distrust of propaganda was particularly acute against propaganda that "seeks to sway or stir people by general appeals to sentiment."[57] They realized, however, that these same individuals who rejected attempts to play on their emotions and sentiments were especially vulnerable to another kind of propaganda, which they labeled "technological propaganda" or "the propaganda of facts." The goal of this kind of propaganda, then, is the presentation of specially selected factual or technical information that is devoid of emotional appeals, yet aims at influencing opinions and behaviors about a chosen controversial issue. Such a "technological propaganda" was successful because people possess a natural interest in "detailed circumstantial facts," Lazarsfeld and Merton argued, and these facts could be selected in such a way as to serve as a model that helps orient people to the world in which they live. Describing a world remarkably Orwellian in character, and taking a position toward human rationality not unlike the position Walter Lippmann had taken in his *Public Opinion*, Lazarsfeld and Merton wrote:

> For large sections of the population, the historical events which they experience are wholly bewildering. Nations which are enemies one day are allies the next. The future seems dark with despair or bright with promise. Many have not the time or capacity to understanding the trends and the forces behind them, yet they sense how closely these are bound up with their lives. All this accentuates a powerful need for orientation. Concrete facts take on the role of models in terms of which more complicated events can be explained and understood.[58]

Lazarsfeld and Merton did not address the larger epistemological questions about what constitutes "facts," nor were they interested in raising the questions about how particular social or ideological vantage points color the selection of these facts. Instead, they took a much more pragmatic approach to understanding these facts, arguing that different kinds of facts could be selected to serve different kinds of propagandistic purposes. "Facts which integrate and 'explain' a general course of events," they wrote, "comprise one important component of the propaganda of facts."[59] In addition "startling facts"—facts of the "believe-it-or-not variety—have "attention-value" because they draw people's attention to the issue being promoted, they have "diffusion-value" because they "readily become part of the currency of communication and small talk," and they have "confidence-value" because as facts "they are not likely to elicit the distrust which is so widely latent in the population."[60]

It would be a mistake to assume, however, that because Lazarsfeld and Merton advocated a "propaganda of facts" they were interested in appealing to the rationality of their target audience. On the contrary, they were interested in bypassing this rationality while appearing to address it directly, as a way of getting their target audience to accept their conclusions. In addition to offering what they understood to be the parallels between "technological propaganda" and progressive education, Lazarsfeld and Merton made this point explicit when they wrote:

> In passing it might be remarked that the logic of the propaganda of facts is not far removed from the logic of progressive education. It is typical in progressive schools that the teacher does not indicate what children are to do and believe but rather creates situations which lead them to decide for themselves the conduct and beliefs which the teacher considers appropriate.[61]

Likewise, Lazarsfeld and Merton built this kind of subterfuge into the very interviewing methodology they employed in measuring the effectiveness of propaganda. Noting that there were two kinds of "respondents"—those who are articulate and those who are not—Lazarsfeld and Merton argued that they had most difficulty in extracting appropriate responses from more articulate individuals because these individuals often provide advice on how to make the propaganda more convincing and effective. "They seek to act as professional critics or consultants and this is precisely what we do not want," Lazarsfeld and Merton noted. "Interview tactics have had to be devised for the purpose of avoiding such consultant attitudes on the part of the interviewees and of making it possible for them to report their own immediate responses to the propaganda."[62]

Lazarsfeld and Merton did not believe that exhortative propaganda, which aimed at emotional appeals, would be completely replaced by their formulation of "technological propaganda." However, they felt that historical circumstances, as well as the critical character of the population, necessitated that this "technological propaganda" be utilized on a grand scale. "Widespread distrust and skepticism pushed to the extreme of cynicism are corrosive forces," they wrote. "But, since they are here, they must be considered. If propaganda is restricted wholly to exhortation, it runs the risk of intensifying distrust. The propaganda of facts can be utilized to supplant cynicism with common understandings."[63] Although not believing that they had offered the definitive approach to propaganda, Lazarsfeld and Merton realized that their formulation could have considerable application in the postwar world—a world they envisioned would require the systematic reorientation of public opinion. "Our observations may be useful to those of us who are concerned with a constructive post-war era," they wrote. "We should not wait until post-war problems press upon us before we recognize that a re-integration of societies must, to some extent, draw upon the instrument of propaganda."[64]

This instrument of propaganda was not left to chance, but instead required the careful application of the social science methodology that Lazarsfeld and Merton helped to develop and could train others to conduct. This methodology, including content analysis, response analysis, focussed interview, and opinion polling, greatly facilitated the work of the propagandist, because "in general, writers of propaganda cannot know how audiences will respond to their material merely by relying on intuition or by observing their own reactions."[65] Indeed, the propagandist, in order to be successful, required "a continuing flow of intelligence information concerning prevalent attitudes and sentiments in the population," and social scientists trained in this research methodology could provide this service.[66] Attempting to fuse the skills of the creative propagandist and the analytical social scientist, Lazarsfeld and Merton wrote:

> Creative ideas, whether expressed in words, sounds or pictures cannot be manufactured synthetically. But systematic research is needed to see whether propagandists have achieved their aims. Just as researchers cannot write acceptable scripts, so, we are convinced propagandists often cannot gauge the psychological effects of their products without using techniques such as we have described.[67]

As World War II ended, it must have occurred to many mass communication researchers that the future of their research was not entirely certain. Although great advances had been made in the development of persuasive techniques during the war, it was not clear whether or not sponsors would come forward to support mass communication research on the scale to which researchers had grown accustomed during the war. Faced with this situation, Lazarsfeld took the lead in arguing for the necessity of this research. In many ways, the growth of mass communications research in the postwar years was greatly aided by Lazarsfeld's work in emphasizing the important function that this kind of research could serve for national and international policymakers. At first, Lazarsfeld couched his plea for the utilization of mass communication research in terms of its ability to assist international organizations in securing peaceful relations among nations, although, as the Cold War started to heat up, his arguments for this research began to take a decisively pro-U.S. cast. In either case, the kind of research that Lazarsfeld's bureau could offer consisted essentially of providing propagandists with the information necessary for the effective creation and distribution of their propaganda.

For instance, at the end of the war Lazarsfeld wrote an article with Genevieve Knupfer in which they argued that the postwar world would require the construction of an "international authority" that would keep the peace by promoting "respect and sympathy among nations."[68] Lazarsfeld and Knupfer maintained that before such an international authority could be successful, however, it must have the support of people around the world. Noting that the mass media were particularly well suited in the "presentation and popularization of concrete symbols," Lazarsfeld and Knupfer asserted that "the media of mass communication can be used to build up something like an educational campaign, the purpose of which is to make the international authority accepted as part of everyday thinking, to give it prestige, to see that as many people as possible are intimately acquainted with its functions."[69] Yet, for such an "educational campaign" to be successful, it would require the expertise that a mass communications researcher could bring to bear. People who were interested in "fostering international cooperation" would need the kind of insight that Lazarsfeld and his colleagues could provide:

> To use the media of communications most effectively they must determine what avenues of access are open to them; they must remove the art of producing effective propaganda from the realms of instinct and guesswork; they must anticipate and recognize propaganda which is antagonistic to their own purposes. None of these problems can be solved except through systematic communications research. None of them can be approached except by a rigorous discipline. If the promoters of the IA [international authority] accept this challenge, if they attempt to control the media of communications through achieving a high degree of effectiveness, science will have become the tool of social progress.[70]

In 1946, Lazarsfeld, although continuing to argue for systematic communication research to aid international cooperation, made his pitch for this research in the Department of State's efforts to "sell America" abroad. "Research opportunities here are obvious," he wrote. "It will be necessary to poll public opinion in other countries in order to find out what misconceptions about America exist."[71] Thus, Lazarsfeld called for the careful study of the listening habits of people in others countries. Such a study would seek to answer such questions as "at what hours do most people listen? how different are the listening tastes in various social walks? what sponsorships would be favorably received in other countries and which should be avoided?"[72]

By 1950, Lazarsfeld had dropped the rhetoric about the need for mass communication research in the advancement of international cooperation, and argued straightforwardly about the necessity of this information in the conduct of the many propaganda activities of the U.S. government. The Cold War had taken concrete shape by 1950, and it was clear to all insiders that the preponderance of research money in mass communications would flow from the national security apparatus of the U.S. government, which had as a primary consideration the control and shaping of people's thoughts around the world. "In various ways the United States has to exercise a considerable influence in far-flung parts of the world," Lazarsfeld wrote; and although he thought it was "inappropriate to talk about an American Empire," Lazarsfeld asserted that it was "entirely in place to discuss the large and growing sphere of American influence."[73] This situation, he argued, would greatly facilitate the development of the mass communications discipline. Just as the field of anthropology, with its emphasis on face-to-face analysis, had developed out of the requirements for the colonial administration of the British Empire, the field of mass communications research developed out of the more remote means of control required by the U.S. situation. "It is not too far-fetched to say that the development of anthropology was a concomitant of the colonial problems existing at the beginning of this century," Lazarsfeld wrote in 1950. But because U.S. influence would be exercised primarily through the propaganda and information services of the mass media, he argued, "it can be predicted . . . that international communications research will be a natural concomitant of the current American situation in world politics."[74]

Lazarsfeld, of course, was perceptive to recognize that the United States' increasing domain of influence during the period of Cold War would present many research opportunities to him and his colleagues. The Cold War provided the climate in which Lazarsfeld's research interests could thrive, and it was during the Cold War that the bureau experienced its greatest period of growth. The bureau's revenue nearly tripled from its 1947–1948 level of $136,000, a year in which no government-sponsored research was reported, to its 1950–1951 level of $380,000 a year, in which 75% of the bureau's revenue was provided by government funds consisting primarily of large grants from the U.S. Air Force's Human Resources Research Institute and the Department of State's Voice of America program.[75]

By 1951–1952, when the Bureau's revenue jumped to $523,000, a full 83% was provided by governmental contracts. From 1948–1949, the first year for which government contracted research was reported, to 1954–1955, the government sponsored $1,602,390, or 58% of the bureau's revenue during this period. In addition to the HRRI and VOA contracted research, this government-sponsored research included a major study entitled "Negro Manpower Resources," which carried a "SECRET" classification and sought to analyze African American civilians' mobilization and African American soldiers' performance during the World Wars and the Cold War,[76] and a study of the methods of attitude measurement for the RAND Corporation.[77] In addition, "a large secret project" entitled "Interviewing Methodology" was conducted, which dealt ostensibly "with improving methods for interviewing German prisoners of war returning from the Soviet Union about the location of factories and the like," as well as a series of mass communication research projects concerning Europe and Asia that Lazarsfeld brought to the bureau.[78]

Although Lazarsfeld surrendered the title of Director of the Bureau of Applied Social Research to Kingsley Davis in 1949, when Lazarsfeld was named Chairperson of the Department of Sociology at Columbia, he remained active in the bureau as Associate Director and engaged extensively in many of the defense-related projects that were awarded to the bureau. For HRRI, the bureau engaged in a number of different research activities as early as 1951, the most significant being the "Urban Target Studies." These studies, which were to aid in the selection of military targets, sought "to identify and quantify sociological and psychological factors involved in strategic planning and in air attacks employing conventional and special weapons primarily in offensive air operations and secondly in defensive air operations."[79] The studies were broken down into several components, and the University of Michigan and the University of Chicago were also contracted for this project. The bureau's portion of the work consisted in the development of a "World Urban Resources Index," which HRRI described as "an intelligence tool, being designed for comparative, analytical studies of urban complexes on a world-wide basis. The results of these analyses are calculated to provide measures of similarities and differences among cities to show trends in growth and change, and to provide for estimates of conditions where psychological and sociological data are inaccessible."[80]

Kingsley Davis of the bureau was named principal investigator for this World Urban Resources Index; but the record indicates that Lazarsfeld assisted him with this project. In January 1951, Lazarsfeld was given security clearance through "SECRET" and he accompanied Davis on a trip to Germany and Austria for HRRI. The purpose of the trip, according to an HRRI memorandum, was "to monitor the research activities of a research team of professional experts presently engaged in the collection of research materials in Germany and Austria."[81] The World Urban Resources Index was considered by HRRI to hold "some promise for the development of a systematic theory of cities and the determination of socio-psychological strengths and

weakness through knowledge of the minimum essentials of urban functioning."[82] However, HRRI sponsorship of this project ended sometime during
the 1953–54 academic year, following an undisclosed congressional inquiry
of HRRI. Davis continued his research on this project under different sponsorship when he moved to the Institute for International Urban and Population Research at University of California, Berkeley.[83] As we see in the next
chapter, there is at least some circumstantial evidence that links HRRI-
funded research with later covertly funded CIA research.

The Department of State also established several substantial research
projects with the bureau through its Voice of America (VOA) program. Leo
Lowenthal, a former bureau researcher and Lazarsfeld's friend from the
Frankfurt Institute, was named Director of Research for the VOA in 1949,
and remained in that position until 1955.[84] Lowenthal's task at the VOA consisted of directing an office that evaluated the effectiveness of radio propaganda aimed at Eastern Bloc nations, and the effectiveness of radio, print,
and informal propaganda aimed at countries primarily in the Middle and
Far East.[85] Under Lowenthal's direction, the VOA maintained contracts
with many universities and commercial agencies that provided assistance in
this research. Yet, the close relationship between Lowenthal and Lazarsfeld,
who Lowenthal referred to as his "ever faithful friend," helped to foster a
particularly close relationship between the VOA and the bureau. The bureau conducted VOA-sponsored research in Greece and throughout Asia,
and, also in the late 1940s and early 1950s, in Iran, Turkey, Lebanon, Egypt,
and Syria, the results of which were later reported in Daniel Lerner's 1958
book *The Passing of Traditional Society: Modernizing the Middle East.*[86] Lazarsfeld was closely involved with much of this work, training interviewers, helping to devise questionnaires, assisting with the statistical analysis of data, and
hiring researchers for this project. His third wife, Patricia Kendall, supervised the data collection activities in Egypt.

Although the archival records of this research remain sparse, the general
purpose of this research remains clear: to provide the Department of State
"with a series of reports on the pattern of communications behavior in each
country which will serve as a framework around which policies with regard
to the Voice of America programming might be more effectively evaluated,
and where necessary, reformulated."[87] Recognizing the importance of the
two-step flow of communications as an effective propaganda device, one primary means of data collection consisted of a series of interviews with both
"formal" opinion leaders, "i.e., leading figures in the Government, in business, in labor, in education, and more specifically, the people who control
the media of communication," and with "informal" opinion leaders, "those
individuals in the community who because of their occupations become the
centers of word-of-mouth communication—doctors, lawyers, barbers, tav-
ern keepers, farmers, town clerks, club leaders and the like."[88] In each coun-

try, the researchers and their native assistants would "spend their time in strategic areas, observing and talking to people about the role and function of the various media in the life of the country."[89] Here again, however, the record indicates that the people being interviewed were not always cooperative, because they felt that some kind of underhanded purpose motivated the researchers. One researcher recalled that:

> I heard that after I had finished this interview rumors started to go around that I belong to the F.B.I. looking for Communists. Others said I want to take their sons to Korea. . . . Although I had explained the matter and purpose of the interview yet people were very skeptical about it. And any time the name of any big power or the name of their government used to be mentioned, you feel that they are not at ease and give short dry answers, this is the attitude I met with most of the non-educated class.[90]

Yet, despite being uneducated, these people were perceptive to be skeptical about the researchers' motives, because the information being gathered was used to control and shape their opinions in ways that were generally in the United States' interests, but not necessarily in their own best interests. The United States covertly intervened in the political affairs of some of these countries shortly before or after these interviews were conducted.

Here again, Lazarsfeld was able to provide researchers with useful techniques by which to gather the necessary information without raising the suspicion of the people being studied. "There is an increasing need to find out what people abroad believe, how these ideas are communicated over various strata of a population and how they can be influenced by American efforts," Lazarsfeld wrote in a May 1950 proposal to create a training manual for Foreign Service Officers.[91] Among the skills the manual would teach, Lazarsfeld listed: "Techniques of establishing a rapport with respondents and eliciting detailed information of specific experiences . . . the use of participant observation at points where communications take place, like coffee houses, town halls, public squares, and so on . . . ideas as to how to use specific situations like the showing of a film or the public reading of a newspaper or the listening to a narrator for the purpose of studying the flow of information . . . the role of opinion leaders and how they could be observed and studied . . . techniques by which distrust among desirable respondents against such types of inquiry can be overcome or reduced."[92]

Lazarsfeld's mass communication research for the Department of State, like his mass communication research for other governmental and commercial agencies, was carried out for the purpose of creating sophisticated techniques by which to control the opinions and behaviors of target audiences. The Bureau of Applied Social Research profited greatly from this research, and the mass communications "effects" tradition, as an important component of the propagandist's work, was firmly established as a result of this research. Lazarsfeld's personal relationships with important individuals who held the purse strings for research funding was a major factor in establishing the kind of research that was conducted in the bureau. Yet, he was more than merely a conduit for research money, and in fact played a significant role in defining which projects were worthy of attention. As his former student, James S. Coleman, wrote:

> Many of those around Paul Lazarsfeld felt extreme frustration, frustration because at times the problems [research problems under consideration] themselves appeared spurious, or unimportant. And frustration because Paul was not satisfied to see protégés and colleagues solve problems that others outside felt were important, but was only satisfied when a problem *he* saw as important was solved, and solved in a way that made sense to *him*.[93]

If colleagues and protégés felt frustrated, those who did not share Lazarsfeld's ideological or methodological perspective fared much worse. In the late 1930s, while the bureau was still the Office of Radio Research and located at Princeton, Lazarsfeld hired Theodor W. Adorno to conduct a study of music within U.S. culture. "I considered it a challenge," wrote Lazarsfeld, "to see whether I could induce Adorno to try to link his ideas with empirical research."[94] Adorno was not so easily taken in by Lazarsfeld nor his notion of "empirical" or "administrative" research, and the relationship ended soon after it began.[95] Although Lazarsfeld recalled later that the source of the disagreement was Adorno's ill temper, Adorno recognized probably more accurately that the source of the disagreement was the very ideological structure of the Office of Radio Research that Lazarsfeld directed. As Adorno wrote:

> There appeared to be little room for . . . critical social research in the framework of the Princeton Project. Its charter, which came from the Rockefeller Foundation, expressly stipulated that the investigations must be performed within the limits of the commercial radio system prevailing in the United States. It was thereby implied that the system itself, its cultural and sociological consequences and its social and economic presuppositions were not to be analyzed.[96]

Adorno's analysis was right on target. Although assuming the posture of the objective, value-free empiricist, Lazarsfeld had in fact surrendered any claim to objectivity by working only on those problems defined as such by the sources of his research funding.

Lazarsfeld's early involvement in the Vienna Socialist movement brought him into the study of propaganda, and his interest in this area both prepared him for and enhanced the market research that he was later paid to conduct in Vienna and in the United States. When World War II broke out, as head of the nation's only academic unit devoted solely to the study of the effectiveness of radio, Lazarsfeld was in a particularly advantageous position from which to serve as a leader in the evaluation and creation of wartime propaganda. As World War II ended and the Cold War began, Lazarsfeld was at the forefront of those individuals who argued for the necessity of mass communication research in the effective use of propaganda, and he was again able to profit from the huge, national, security-related contracts that were awarded to the bureau during this period. All of Lazarsfeld's work in mass communications bore the stamp of this operational view of the mass media for which he was paid, including his widely cited *Personal Influence*. Nevertheless, Lazarsfeld was sufficiently reserved with his ideological commitments to make it difficult to determine his position on important matters relating to the mass media. Thus, for instance, although he could agree with Bernard Berelson in 1952 that "a certain amount of apathy might be good for democracy," he was compelled to qualify his statement by adding "although too much of it certainly leads to exploitation."[97]

The question of the degree to which Lazarsfeld was concerned with the moral implications of his work is also not altogether clear. When Lazarsfeld's friend and colleague Leo Lowenthal, a man widely recognized for his critical scholarship, was asked about his own involvement with this propaganda research for the VOA, he sounded a common 20th-century refrain: "I was only the director of a certain department within the American propaganda apparatus that didn't make political decisions itself," Lowenthal said. "For practical reasons I was forced to find suitable employment. . . . I'd have to say that neither during the war, when I worked for the Office of War Information, nor in the post-war period did I ever have the feeling that I was working for an imperialist power."[98] Robert Merton, Lazarsfeld's colleague at Columbia, did briefly consider the moral dimensions of the mass communications research that he helped to develop. "The technician or practitioner in mass opinion and his academic counterpart, the social psychologist, cannot escape the moral issues which permeate propaganda as a means of social control," Merton wrote in 1946.[99] Merton understood well that "ends" can often only justify "means" by sacrificing the very constitution of those ends. For Merton, the moral dilemma facing the practitioner of propaganda was simply this: "He must choose between being a less than fully effective technician and a scrupulous human being or an effective technician and a less than scrupulous human being."[100] Merton's brief foray into the moral issues surrounding mass communications research were, nevertheless, short lived, and certainly not taken up seriously by those who were busy establishing this new applied field.

NOTES

1. Todd Gitlin, "Media Sociology: The Dominant Paradigm," *Theory and Society, 6* (September 1978), p. 207.

2. See, for instance, Robert K. Merton, James S. Coleman, and Peter H. Rossi, editors, *Qualitative and Quantitative Social Research: Papers in Honor of Paul F. Lazarsfeld* (New York: Free Press, 1979).

3. James S. Coleman, "Paul F. Lazarsfeld: The Substance and Style of His Work," in *Sociological Traditions From Generation to Generation: Glimpses of the American Experience*, edited by Robert K. Merton and Matilda White Riley (Norwood, NJ: Ablex, 1980), pp. 153–174.

4. David Morrison, "The Beginnings of Modern Mass Communication Research," *European Journal of Sociology, 19* (1978), p. 347.

5. As quoted in ibid., p. 349.

6. Herbert I. Schiller, *Culture, Inc.: The Corporate Takeover of Public Expression* (New York: Oxford University Press, 1989), p. 136.

7. One should also note that Daniel Lerner, who Schiller regarded as the leader of the group of researchers most involved in international propaganda, did much of his early work in this area within Lazarsfeld's Bureau of Applied Social Research.

8. Elihu Katz and Paul F. Lazarsfeld, *Personal Influence: The Part Played by People in the Flow of Mass Communications* (Glencoe, IL: Free Press, 1955).

9. Ibid., pp. 18–19.

10. Ibid., p. 19.

11. Ibid., p. 19.

12. The misinterpretation of Lazarsfeld and Katz's *Personal Influence* has led to a greatly skewed debate about the fields origins. One side of the debate has argued that, before the publication of *Personal Influence*, mass media scholars believed that the mass media had a "hypodermic" or direct and powerful effect on society, but the publication of *Personal Influence* provided evidence that the mass media had instead a limited or indirect effect on society. The other side of the debate has argued that mass media scholars always held that the mass media had a limited or indirect effect on society, and that Lazarsfeld offered a "theoretical foil" to draw attention to his own work. However, both sides of the debate fail to admit the propagandistic value of the two-step flow that is the central theme of *Personal Influence*. For a description of this debate — one that agrees with the basic assumptions of the debate — see Jeffery L. Bineham, "A Historical Account of the Hypodermic Model in Mass Communication," *Communication Monographs, 55* (September 1988), pp. 230–246.

13. David Sills, "Paul F. Lazarsfeld," in *International Encyclopedia of the Social Sciences, 18* (New York: Free Press, 1979), pp. 411–427.

14. Hans Zeisel, "The Vienna Years," in *Qualitative and Quantitative Social Research: Papers in Honor of Paul F. Lazarsfeld*, edited by Robert K. Merton, James S. Coleman, and Peter H. Rossi (New York: The Free Press, 1979), p. 11.

15. Ibid., p. 12.

16. Paul F. Lazarsfeld, "An Episode in the History of Social Research: A Memoir," in *The Varied Sociology of Paul F. Lazarsfeld*, edited by Patricia L. Kendall (New York: Columbia University Press, 1982), p. 13.

17. Sills, "Paul F. Lazarsfeld," p. 411.

18. Lazarsfeld, "An Episode in the History of Social Research," p. 13.

19. Sills, "Paul F. Lazarsfeld," p. 413.

20. Lazarsfeld, "An Episode in the History of Social Research," p. 20.

21. Ibid., p. 20.

22. Ibid., p. 25.

23. Zeisel, "The Vienna Years," pp. 13–14.

24. Sills, "Paul F. Lazarsfeld," p. 413.

25. Zeisel, "The Vienna Years," p. 13.

26. Marie Jahoda, Paul F. Lazarsfeld, and Hans Zeisel, *Marienthal: The Sociography of an Unemployed Community* (Chicago: Aldine-Atherton, 1971), p. 5. First published in 1933 as *Die Arbeitslosen von Marienthal*.

27. Ibid., p. 6.

28. Ibid., p. 6.

29. Ibid., p. 7.

30. Sills, "Paul F. Lazarsfeld," p. 413.

31. For a discussion of the impact of some of these émigrés, including Lazarsfeld, see Anthony Heilbut, *Exiled in Paradise: German Refugee Artists and Intellectuals in America from the 1930's to the Present* (Boston: Beacon, 1983).

32. Being Jewish and a former socialist were apparently issues to the Rockefeller Foundation when they were considering to grant Lazarsfeld an extension in his fellowship, although it appears that the foundation was able to look beyond these two "shortcomings." See John V. Van Sickle to Robert Lynd, April 27, 1934, Paul F. Lazarsfeld Papers, Box 27, Re—Rockefeller Fellowship (1), Folder: Rockefeller Foundation Fellowships, Columbia University Archives. In later years, Lazarsfeld said about Robert Lynd: "Lynd always was, without knowing it, an anti-Semite. There is not the slightest doubt." Paul F. Lazarsfeld Oral History Project, Columbia University, The William E. Weiner Oral History Library of the American Jewish Committee, February 21, 1975–April 19, 1975, p. 31.

33. The term *machine* was an expression Lazarsfeld himself used to describe his activity of founding and developing social science research institutes. See Dear Bob (no date given), Paul F. Lazarsfeld Papers, Box 2B: Correspondence, Lazarsfeld–Piaget, Folder: Correspondence Lynd, Robert, Columbia University Archives.

34. Lazarsfeld, "An Episode in the History of Social Research: A Memoir," p. 12.

35. Paul Felix Lazarsfeld to the President of the University of Newark, 3, Paul F. Lazarsfeld Papers, Columbia University Archives, Box 26: Princeton Radio Research Project (2)—Rand Project, File: Princeton Radio Research Project #10.

36. Ibid., p. 7.

37. Ibid., p. 6.

38. Lazarsfeld, "An Episode in the History of Social Research," pp. 41–42.

39. Princeton Radio Research Project, Plans and Problems, January 1, 1938, Paul F. Lazarsfeld Papers, Columbia University Archives, Box 26: Princeton Radio Research Project (2)—Rand Project, Folder: Princeton Radio Research Project #8. No author is cited on this particular document, although as director of the Office of Radio Research at that time Lazarsfeld no doubt had significant influence in the document's wording, if he did not write the entire document himself.

40. For a comprehensive listing of these studies see Judith S. Barton, *Guide to the Bureau of Applied Social Research* (New York: Clearwater, 1984).

41. Outline for the UNESCO study of the administrative structure and working methods of selected social science research institutes, 5, Paul F. Lazarsfeld Papers, Columbia University Archives, Box 29, Subject File: Television—University of Chicago, Folder: Unesco 2.

42. Paul F. Lazarsfeld to President Grayson Kirk, December 17, 1956, Paul F. Lazarsfeld Papers, Columbia University Archives, Box 15, Subject File: BSS-ch—Columbia University (1), Folder: Departmental.

43. Lazarsfeld, "An Episode in the History of Social Research," p. 52.

44. As quoted in ibid., p. 50.

45. See Allen H. Barton, "Paul Lazarsfeld and the Invention of the University Institute for Applied Social Research," in *Organizing for Social Research,* edited by Burkart Holzner and Jiri Nehnevajsa (Cambridge, MA: Shenkman, 1982), pp. 28–29.

46. Marjorie Fiske and Paul F. Lazarsfeld, "The Office of Radio Research: A Division of the Bureau of Applied Social Research, Columbia University," in *How to Conduct Consumer and Opinion Research,* edited by Albert B. Blankenship (New York: Harper & Brothers, 1946), pp. 141–146.

47. Gitlin, "Media Sociology: The Dominant Paradigm," pp. 234.

48. Paul F. Lazarsfeld, "Radio Research and Applied Psychology," *The Journal of Applied Psychology, 23* (1939), p. 1.

49. Paul F. Lazarsfeld, *Radio and the Printed Page* (New York: Duell Sloan and Pearce, 1940), p. XVII.

50. Lazarsfeld, "An Episode in the History of Social Research, " p. 66.

51. Lazarsfeld did receive U.S. citizenship during the war, which was very rare among Austrian immigrants to the United States. See Paul F. Lazarsfeld Oral History Project, Columbia University, The William E. Wiener Oral History Library of the American Jewish Committee, February 21, 1975–April 19, 1975.

52. James S. Coleman, "Lazarsfeld, Paul Felix," in *Encyclopedia of American Biography*, edited by John A. K. Garraty (New York: Harper & Row, 1974), pp. 646–647.

53. Paul F. Lazarsfeld and Robert Merton, "Studies in Radio and Film Propaganda," in Robert Merton, *Social Theory and Social Structure: Toward a Codification of Theory and Research* (Glencoe, IL: Free Press, 1949), pp. 265–285.

54. Ibid., p. 265.

55. Ibid., p. 265.

56. Ibid., p. 281.

57. Ibid., p. 281.

58. Ibid., p. 283.

59. Ibid., p. 283.

60. Ibid., p. 283.

61. Ibid., p. 284

62. Ibid., pp. 272–273.

63. Ibid. p. 274.

64. Ibid., p. 284.

65. Ibid. p. 267.

66. Ibid., p. 275.

67. Ibid., p. 299.

68. Paul F. Lazarsfeld and Genevieve Knupfer, "Communications Research and International Cooperation," in *The Science of Man in World Crisis*, edited by Ralph Linton (New York: Farrar, Straus, & Giroux, 1980), p. 466. Originally published in 1945.

69. Ibid., pp. 465–466.

70. Ibid., p. 495.

71. Paul F. Lazarsfeld, "Radio and International Co-operation as a Problem for Psychological Research," *Journal of Consulting Psychology, 10* (January–February 1946), p. 55.

72. Ibid., pp. 54–55.

73. Paul F. Lazarsfeld, "The Comparative Study of Communications Systems," Paul F. Lazarsfeld Papers, Columbia University Archives, Box 32, Subject File: Vera Institute of Justice (2) — State University, Folder: Voice of America (1).

74. Ibid., p. 3.

75. Apparently, no complete breakdown of the history of bureau funding exists, although from the bureau's estimated income and expenditures for 1950–1951 it is clear that the HRRI and VOA research funds were expected to make up well over half of the bureau's anticipated revenue, and these were the only governmental contracts listed. See "Exhibit 'B': Estimated Income and Expenditures, 1950–1951," Paul F. Lazarsfeld Papers, Columbia University Archives, Box 6: AR-Bureau of Applied Social Research, File: #14.

76. "Negro Manpower Resources" Paul F. Lazarsfeld Papers, Columbia University Archives, Box 11 — Bureau of Applied Social Research: Black Military, Folder: Bureau of Applied Social Research — Negro Manpower Resources.

77. Hans Speier (The RAND Corporation) to Dr. Raymond V. Bowers (HRRI), September 19, 1949, Paul F. Lazarsfeld Papers, Columbia University Archives, Box 7 — Bureau of Applied Social Research, Manpower (1), Folder: Bureau of Applied Social Research, Manpower (1).

78. Barton, "Paul F. Lazarsfeld and the Invention of the University Institute for Applied Social Research," p. 27.

79. "The Human Resources Research Institute, Strategic Intelligence Program In Urban Target Studies," 1, Paul F. Lazarsfeld Papers, Columbia University Archives, Box 10—Bureau of Applied Social Research (1), Folder: Bureau of Applied Social Research—Black Military #6.

80. Ibid., pp. 2–3.

81. "Subject: Invitational Travel, To: Person Concerned, 8 January 1951," 1, Paul F. Lazarsfeld Papers, Columbia University Archives, Box 2A—Correspondence H–L, Folder: Correspondence K.

82. "The Human Resources Research Institute, Strategic Intelligence Program in Urban Target Studies," pp. 5–6.

83. Raymond V. Bowers, "The Military Establishment," in *The Uses of Sociology,* edited by Paul F. Lazarsfeld, William H. Sewell, and Harold L. Wilensky (New York: Basic, 1967), pp. 241–242.

84. "Lowenthal, Leo, 1900– ," in *Contemporary Authors: New Revision Series, 5,* edited by Ann Evory (Detroit: Galesburg Research Co., 1982), p. 336.

85. Leo Lowenthal, *An Unmastered Past: The Autobiographical Reflections of Leo Lowenthal,* edited by Martin Jay (Berkeley: University of California Press, 1987), pp. 81–110.

86. Daniel Lerner, *The Passing of Traditional Society: Modernizing the Middle East* (Glencoe, IL: Free Press, 1958).

87. "Contract between U.S. Department of State and the Bureau of Applied Social Research," Paul F. Lazarsfeld Papers, Columbia University Archives, Box 32: Vera Institute of Justice (2)—Wayne State University, Folder: Voice of America (2).

88. Ibid., p. 4.

89. Ibid., p. 4.

90. As quoted in David Riesman, "Introduction," in Lerner, *The Passing of Traditional Society,* p. 1.

91. Paul F. Lazarsfeld, "A Training Manual for Fieldwork in *Comparative Communication Research,*" 1, Paul F. Lazarsfeld Papers, Columbia University Archives, Box 6: Ar—Bureau of Applied Social Research, File #13.

92. Ibid., pp. 2–3.

93. Coleman, "Paul F. Lazarsfeld: The Substance and Style of His Work," p. 170.

94. Lazarsfeld, "An Episode in the History of Social Research," p. 58.

95. For a discussion of the Adorno–Lazarsfeld affair, see David E. Morrison, "Kultur and Culture: The Case of Theodor W. Adorno and Paul F. Lazarsfeld," *Social Research, 45* (Summer 1978), pp. 331–355. See also Wayne M. Towers, "Lazarsfeld and Adorno in the United States: A Case Study in Theoretical Orientations," in *Communication Yearbook I,* edited by Brent D. Ruben (New Brunswick, NJ: Transaction, 1977), pp. 1933–1945.

96. As quoted in Willard J. Rowland, *The Politics of TV Violence: The Policy Uses of Communication Research* (Beverly Hills, CA: Sage, 1983), p. 61.

97. Paul F. Lazarfeld to Dr. Bernard Berelson, circa November 19, 1952, From "RE: Study of Political Behavior," Paul F. Lazarsfeld Papers, Columbia University Archives, Box 1A: Correspondence A–C, Folder: Correspondence—Berelson, Bernard, p. 26.

98. Lowenthal, *An Unmastered Past,* pp. 93–94.

99. Robert K. Merton, *Mass Persuasion: The Social Psychology of a War Bond Drive* (New York: Harper & Brothers, 1946), p. 185.

100. Ibid., p. 185.

Wilbur Schramm and the Founding of Communication Study

Wilbur Schramm was the founder of communication study, not only in America but in the world.
—Steven H. Chaffee and
Everett M. Rogers, 1997[1]

O N APRIL 21, 1947, University of Illinois President George Stoddard wrote a letter to Wilbur Schramm, who had recently accepted an offer to serve as the founder and first director of the Institute of Communications Research at the university. "I have a feeling," Stoddard wrote, acknowledging Schramm's acceptance, "that historians of education will someday take note of this particular event."[2] Stoddard was perceptive to recognize that the institutionalization of communication study would constitute a significant influence on U.S. educational thought, and that historians of education would eventually come around to examining its origins and implications, ultimately attempting to place the founding of mass communications research in historical context, and trying to understand the objectives and ideological perspectives that undergirded the development of the field.

Schramm's new Institute of Communications Research at the University of Illinois was one of the first such academic units of its kind in the United States, and Schramm became widely recognized as the founding architect of mass communication research. Yet, when Wilbur Schramm died 40 years later on December 27, 1987, his death was given only scant attention in the nation's periodicals that are predisposed to report such events. *The New York Times* ran a short obituary listing some of his major achievements in the field of mass communications research.[3] Likewise, the various academic institutions with which he was associated—University of Iowa,[4] University of Illinois,[5] and Stanford University[6]—took note of his death and cited the contributions he made to each respective institution. Still, Wilbur Schramm's death went largely unnoticed outside of these circles, despite the tremendous influence he exerted beyond their confines.

If the news of Schramm's death caused little stir among the information media, his life—perhaps more so than any other academic in the 20th century—helped to determine both the character of the information media and the way in which its social role was to be interpreted. In the 1930s, Schramm was the founder and first Director of University of Iowa's highly regarded Writers' Workshop. He served as Educational Director of the Office of War Information. He delegated authority as head of the University of Iowa's Department of Journalism from 1944 through 1947, and was instrumental in establishing the first doctoral program in mass communications in the nation. He became the first Director of the University of Illinois Institute of Communications Research in 1947, where he also served as University President George Stoddard's special assistant and as Director for University of Illinois Press.

During and after World War II, Schramm performed research on propaganda theory for the United States Information Agency and the United States military. He became highly influential in the development of the United States' educational broadcasting system from the late 1940s through the 1970s, both as the chief liaison between the Joint Committee on Educational Broadcasting (JCET) and the corporate foundations who were to fund this broadcasting system so heavily, and as the major communications researcher to assist the JCET. He directed research projects for the National Security Council. He established Stanford University's Institute for Communications Research in 1955, while holding an endowed chair in communications research and a joint appointment with the College of Education. He became a strong advocate for a single international broadcasting system, and argued at various times for the creation of "educational" broadcasting systems in such countries as Vietnam, El Salvador, and Iran. He was the preeminent defender of television as an educational medium, and became one of the nation's leading figures in communications theory and research, authoring or co-authoring over 100 books and articles, and training scores of researchers.[7]

Who was this man who won a national literary award for fiction; who penned at least some of President Franklin Roosevelt's fireside chats; who played baseball for a farm team of the Pittsburgh Pirates and flute for the Boston Pops; who often piloted an airplane to the various meetings and seminars he conducted; who became a much sought-after teacher and lecturer, despite having a severe stuttering problem that had plagued him since he was 5 years old; and who is widely considered to be the individual most responsible for the development of the field of mass communications research in the United States?[8] Who was this man, and what particular vision of the good society and the nature of human being did he bring to the study of mass communications? What particular ideological position did he engender in his students? And to what degree did his vision, itself in part historically conditioned, help to create the paradigm within which subsequent communications research was conducted?

To fully answer these questions would require an analysis of Schramm's entire life in historical context, as well as an extensive survey of the field of communications, taking note of the developments that could be attributed to Schramm. Such, however, is outside the scope of this chapter. On the other hand, one still can get a sense of Schramm as both a researcher and an organizer by examining the years he spent at the University of Illinois. It was at Illinois that Schramm began to establish the framework that characterized his life's work: his emphasis on the "effects" of mass communications, his advocacy of educational broadcasting, and his role as an advisor to the federal government and military. It was also at Illinois that Schramm — by reason of his appointment as University President George Stoddard's assistant, Director of the University Press, and Director of the Institute of Communications Research — was able to shape university policy in a decisive manner.

Schramm's tenure at the University of Illinois was a short one, spanning roughly between 1947 and 1955. But these were important years for the university, for broadcasting, and for the development of the field of communications. The university underwent tremendous expansion during this period. With the 1944 passing of the GI Bill (which provided educational and other benefits to veterans), thousands of returning GIs enrolled at colleges and universities throughout the United States.[9] The University of Illinois was no exception to this trend, increasing from 17,392 students during the prewar academic year of 1940–41 to 38,637 students in the postwar academic year of 1947–48 — an increase of over 120%.[10] This kind of expansion necessitated new and far-reaching policy decisions that facilitated the management of a student body markedly different in both size and character than the university was accustomed to managing. Schramm stepped into a leadership role in making and implementing these policy decisions, utilizing his immense personal and organizational talents in the interest of creating consensus for policy among the student body, faculty, and staff.

Broadcasting also experienced massive growth during this period. Although the technological requirements for television existed as early as 1928, it was not widely marketed until after World War II.[11] A year after the end of the war, in 1946, there were only 8,000 American homes equipped with television sets. By 1949, 940,000 American homes were so equipped. Three short years later, in 1952, over 15 million television sets were in operation in American homes. By 1960, over 90% of U.S. homes had television sets (a number approaching 46 million television sets), and U.S. residents were spending more and more of their time in front of the magical boxes that transported images across vast areas of space.[12] No one knew for certain, in the late 1940s and early 1950s, how television would change U.S. life, but thoughtful elites realized that they were unleashing the most powerful means of thought control and manipulation ever devised. In 1949, Wilbur Schramm saw things more clearly than most people when he wrote:

> *What is television doing to people?* We're a little too close to the experiment to an-swer that in any detail yet, but we do know, (a) that television is demanding much closer attention than does radio (b) that television is proving more at-tractive to children than radio, (c) that television is able to produce new social patterns very quickly—for example, the large number of new wrestling fans it has made among middle-aged women who, ten years ago, would just as soon have been caught in a house of ill-fame as at a wrestling match. The expecta-tion is, therefore, that television has the power to produce social changes of great magnitude.[13]

Schramm, however, did not limit himself to merely reflecting on the power of television to produce social change. He also set himself to the task of trying to produce social change through the development of the educa-tional, or public, television system in the United States. Here again, his per-sonal charisma and his organizational skills came in handy as he sought out corporate foundations to support this project. Equally important was his justification for such an educational broadcasting system, which suggested an educational philosophy as well as a theory of communication.

Finally, as we have seen, the growth of both communication theory and mass communications research must be understood in light of the Cold War, which dominated the political and cultural atmosphere in the post-World War II United States. The National Security Act of 1947 created the Central Intelligence Agency, and sought to integrate "policies and proce-dures for the departments, agencies, and functions of the government re-lating to national security."[14] Central among the concerns of those who drafted the National Security Act was the need to orchestrate and fund re-search deemed necessary for the maintenance of national security, which included the development of techniques by which foreign and domestic populations could be manipulated to achieve desired policy objectives. De-partments of psychology, sociology, political science, and education at major universities across the country were solicited to bring their expertise to bear in devising new methods of social control, and were paid handsomely for their efforts. Sometimes, this research was funded openly through military and other governmental agencies; at other times, the research was funded surreptitiously through foundations, some of which were established pre-cisely for these purposes.[15] In either case, the funding was instrumental in setting the agenda for the kind of research that was conducted in recipient departments and institutes. In addition, this research funding had implica-tions beyond the departments and institutes of origin to the larger disci-plines—establishing the dominant paradigms, granting legitimacy to cer-tain research questions and problems, emphasizing particular methods of inquiry with attendant ideological assumptions, and creating the social networks that determined who would and would not be regarded as authorities in these fields. The situation was accentuated in communications studies, because the field was just beginning to crystallize into a distinct discipline during this time period.

The Institute of Communications Research at the University of Illinois, founded by Wilbur Schramm in 1947 (who also served as its first director), was one such department that received enormous funding from military and intelligence sources. The institute received so much of this kind of funding that, by the early 1950s, faculty members and researchers were at work on matters primarily related to psychological warfare and propaganda. The institute was one of the nation's first academic institutions of its kind to treat the study of mass communications as a serious subject of study, and without a doubt the national security contracts that pervaded the institute influenced the framework with which many people, both inside and outside the institute, came to view and understand mass communications in their society. Wilbur Schramm's role in propagating this framework deserves a close examination.

THE EDUCATION OF A
MASS COMMUNICATIONS EXPERT

Wilbur Lang Schramm was born on August 5, 1907, in the small college town of Marietta, Ohio. It was the same year that Irving Babbitt wrote his book *Literature and the American College,* detailing the neohumanist principles under which Schramm was later educated.[16] It was also the year that the DeForest Radio Telephone Company began to broadcast a few short radio messages in New York City, heralding the arrival of the age of communications.[17]

What is known about Wilbur Schramm's early years indicates that they were rather uneventful. His father, a former schoolteacher, was a well-known local probate court judge when Wilbur was growing up. His mother ran the family household, and was an active member of the local Lutheran church. Both his mother and his father were musicians, and the regular evening concerts in the family parlor clearly inspired Wilbur's own interest in music.[18] His parents were able to provide Wilbur and his younger sister with a stable, middle-class home in Marietta, Ohio, free from both the yoke of rural poverty and the increasing alienation of the industrialized urban centers.

Perhaps Marietta, Ohio, in the early 20th century was not unlike the community described by Sherwood Anderson in his 1919 novel *Winesburg, Ohio.* In this novel, Anderson described a community of people in a small Ohio town who kept thinly veiled the fear and rigidity that made them "grotesque."[19] Yet, although Anderson's main character, the young George Willard, was able to understand the peculiar circumstances that made the towns-people grotesque, and consequently came to deepen his understanding of human life, Schramm recalled no such intellectual journey during his early years in Marietta. Instead, Schramm remembered the many games of sand-lot baseball, the numerous dips in the Muskingum and Ohio rivers, and the frequent trips to his Uncle Fred's farm where he herded sheep.[20] Still, all was not rosy for young Wilbur. Sometime around his fifth birthday he began to stutter, a condition that plagued him throughout his life. There is no basis from which to conjecture about the particular events or psychological fear that precipitated Wilbur's stuttering problem, but it remained a condition that influenced his later career decisions.[21] Moreover, Wilbur's stutter must have caused a self-conscious understanding of the complexity of human communication, which intensified his approach to the formal study of com-munication in later years.

Wilbur did not let his stutter sideline him during his time as a student at Marietta High School. He excelled in baseball and basketball for the school, and demonstrated his early interest in journalism by writing a column for a local daily newspaper. When he graduated from Marietta High in 1924, he enrolled at Marietta College, the small liberal arts college that was nearby. Still enjoying the comforts of living at home, Wilbur was able to further his interests in journalism and make $18 a week working for the *Marietta Regis-trar.* When that paper closed down during his senior year in college, Wilbur received invaluable experience for his future administrative positions by serving as assistant to the Public Relations Director of the college. He con-tinued to play basketball, baseball, and music throughout his years at Mari-etta College, and when he graduated at the top of his class in 1928, he re-ceived offers to play professional baseball and music, and to serve as the night editor for the local newspaper—all offers he considered, but de-clined. Wilbur's father wanted him to follow in his footsteps by enrolling in law school. But Schramm declined this option as well, deciding instead to enroll in Harvard University's Master of Arts program in literature.[22]

During the years immediately preceding the stock market crash, Boston offered many opportunities to a young man of Schramm's talents and back-ground, a White middle-class male, who was not an immigrant, and who had thoroughly internalized the Protestant work ethic. Schramm took full ad-vantage of the many opportunities available to him in Boston by writing for the *Boston Herald,* playing flute for the Boston Pops in a handful of concerts, and playing basketball for $5 a game, while pursuing his graduate degree at Harvard under such scholars as Alfred North Whitehead and Bliss Perry. When the stock market crashed in 1929, Schramm had $260 in his pocket, and as the Depression began to be felt even among Boston's upper middle classes, the opportunities that were once open to Schramm doubtlessly be-gan to diminish.[23] Nearly out of money and still stricken with his severe stuttering problem that could no longer be left untreated, Schramm decided to leave Boston. He finished his remaining requirements at Harvard University, received his A.M. degree, packed his belongings, and moved to Iowa City during the summer of 1930.

His decision to move to Iowa City and to enroll in the Ph.D. program in the Department of English at the University of Iowa was influenced by a number of factors. First, the University of Iowa was home of one of the finest speech pathology departments in the country, and Schramm saw this as an opportunity to receive professional treatment for his stuttering condition. He did participate in therapy sessions during his stay at Iowa, and apparently his stutter was alleviated somewhat, although it remained with him for the rest of his life.[24] Second, the Department of English was one of the strongest of its kind in the nation, as was the entire School of Letters, and Schramm was most likely aware of the innovative changes being initiated by Carl Seashore, then Dean of the Graduate College. As early as the 1922–23 academic year, Seashore set into motion the idea that creative work could be submitted as a Masters' thesis equivalent for some fields.[25] Finally, Schramm was aware of the intellectually stimulating atmosphere that he would find at Iowa, a university with a small budget but a quickly growing reputation. Over 50 years later he would recall the kind of university he encountered in the 1930s and 1940s:

> Iowa was a remarkable place in the 1930s and 40s, and chiefly because of the spirit of creativity that pervaded it. Other universities perhaps were more creative in science and invention, but no place that I have ever known did so much with so little to spread the creative flame in art and music, writing and drama, and some of the social sciences. Remember, this was Iowa in the middle of the depression, with a budget about one-eighth what I found when I went to Illinois in 1947.[26]

Yet, if Schramm had some indication of the kind of intellectual excitement that was fomenting at Iowa, he was probably not aware that his move to Iowa would bring him into contact with Norman Foerster, the one man who would be most responsible for shaping his perspective as well as helping him begin his academic career. Norman Foerster was Irving Babbitt's student at Harvard during the early years of the 20th century, and became the leading exponent of Babbitt's neohumanist movement.[27] A scholar of considerable stature, Foerster had just been appointed Director of the School of Arts and Letters at the University of Iowa. Resigning his professorship at the University of North Carolina, he moved to Iowa City in 1930, arriving approximately at the same time as Schramm.[28] As the two men began to acquaint themselves with the campus and grow accustomed to the expansive horizons of Iowa's farming country, they established a close professional relationship that significantly shaped the younger man's career. And although this relationship would eventually end as a result of university political tensions, and in his later years Schramm would emphatically deny any great intellectual debt to Foerster, no accurate portrait of Schramm would be possible without an analysis of Foerster's influence on him.[29] In addition, the relationship between Foerster and Schramm constitutes an important chapter in the history of the neohumanist movement, a small yet vocal protest against the dominant intellectual currents in the United States of the 20th century.

Like his mentor Irving Babbitt, Norman Foerster saw himself within the rhetorical humanist tradition that found its earliest expression in the teachings and writings of Isocrates, Cicero, and Erasmus. At the turn of the 20th century, Babbitt began to resurrect and reassert this tradition, although reworking some of the positions so that they would be applicable to the modern world. Yet, it would be a mistake to suggest that Babbitt's neohumanism departed significantly from the rhetorical humanist tradition of his intellectual progenitors. Indeed, it was locating the standards for conduct and taste of classical antiquity that was the neohumanists' primary concern. As Schramm himself recalled:

> Humanism to Babbitt and Foerster meant the intellectual dignity of man without the supernatural framework; in literature, it meant the ideas of a piece of writing, the ethos, as opposed to the aesthetics. Explication, as Foerster encouraged them, were therefore chiefly concerned with the ideas; and insofar as they dealt with characters they dealt not with the psychological qualities of the person or his surrounding society and its influences, but rather the decisions he made on a set of judgments usually referred back to those other "humanists—the Greeks of the great period."[30]

Thus, the major tenets of the rhetorical tradition were left intact by Babbitt's, and later Foerster's, neohumanism, and what remained was a fairly consistent vision about the nature of humans, the characteristics of a good society, and the role of the educated gentleman in an essentially aristocratic social order. Schramm inherited a significant part of this vision, both consciously and unconsciously, and one can detect part of this view underlying much of his subsequent work in mass communications.

From Isocrates onward, the rhetorical humanists saw a dualism residing in the heart of human existence, and the ability to develop a balance between this dualism was both the goal of the humanists' educational program as well as the mark of a virtuous man. Although this dualism included the distinction between passion and reason, it extended beyond this simple dichotomy to an overarching epistemology. For Isocrates, this was played out in his attack on both the Platonists, or disputers, who attempted to arrive at a logical and objective account of reality and moral conduct; and the Sophists, who typically proffered a relativistic account of phenomena and morality. Instead, Isocrates sought a middle position between these two epistemological extremes based not on absolute knowledge or subjective experience, but instead on intuition, practical judgment, and expertise in the realm of communication and rhetoric. As Frederick Beck wrote: "Wisdom, for Isocrates, was based on rhetoric. Without the power to speak well, and to persuade others, there could be no civic or political efficiency. For this reason higher education was for Isocrates training in the use of meaningful speech. The accumulation of knowledge was less important then the ability to understand one another."[31] Likewise, the 20th-century neohumanist attempted to balance between the two dominant, yet polemical, epistemological traditions—romanticism and scientific naturalism—both of which, according to Babbitt, distorted the perspective necessary for proper study. The neohumanists also saw in intuition and the art of communication the sole expressers of truth, and they fashioned their educational program accordingly. Babbitt formulated the "will to refrain" as the means by which a scholar could temper the extremes of both romanticism and scientific naturalism.[32]

The good society for the early rhetorical humanists, as it was for the 20th-century neohumanists, was that of an aristocratic social order. Arguing that the great mass of people were simply not capable of the kind of self-governance that a democratic social order required, the rhetorical humanists maintained that the best state was one that educated the privileged and talented few in the art of efficient and virtuous leadership. Perhaps Babbitt expressed this sentiment best when he wrote: "Some persons will remain spiritually anarchical in spite of educational opportunity, others will acquire at least the rudiments of ethical discipline, whereas still others, a small minority, if we are to judge by past experience, will show themselves capable of more difficult stages of self-conquest that will fit them for leadership."[33] The neohumanists did not object to vocational or other kinds of technical education being provided to the masses, but, for the most part, they resisted any widespread attempt to make the humanities available to those unprivileged many who were not destined to rule.[34] "Train an elite, cultivate excellence, and you will change the world"—this was the neohumanist educational and social credo, according to Ernest Becker.[35]

It should be noted, however, that there is a pragmatic strain that runs throughout one line of this rhetorical humanist tradition. Although they were not always very compromising in their educational ideals, these rhetorical humanists traditionally set out to educate political leaders, or political advisors, who would be able to compromise in the world of daily affairs. Specifically, the rhetorical humanist held up as an educational ideal the "Renaissance Man," a multitalented gentleman who would be conversant in a number of different disciplines and possess well-developed skills in the art of persuasion. In addition, this well-rounded gentleman would be a man of action, able to seek practical solutions to real and pressing problems of the state. Consequently, this man would be taught to compromise his principles when the efficient working of the aristocratic state was in jeopardy. Of course, the great danger of any philosophical position that permits its principles to be compromised in the interest of achieving desired political ends is that it will drift into a kind of sophistry without any defining principles. Still, even this kind of sophistry might be justified for the neohumanists if the larger aristocratic social order was left intact.

Perhaps it is this pragmatic strain in the rhetorical humanist tradition that permitted Norman Foerster to make some alterations in the neohumanist educational program, first by replacing the Latin and Greek language requirements with modern foreign languages, and second by coming out publicly in the late 1940s in favor of a democratization of the study of the humanities.[36] Although Irving Babbitt could not have condoned either of these changes, Foerster no doubt made them because it was culturally and politically expedient to do so. Foerster probably felt uneasy about making what he knew were real compromises in the neohumanist educational program. However, he must have been able to console himself with the knowledge that the rhetorical tradition itself vindicates such compromises when it is necessary. Perhaps it is also this pragmatic strain that explains why in 1944 Schramm, although adhering to many aspects of the neohumanists' worldview and clearly exemplifying their ideal of the well-rounded gentleman, would seek to disavow any association with the neohumanist movement and with Norman Foerster when it became politically and professionally expedient to do so. Schramm had learned his neohumanist principles well, although one might argue that he had drifted increasingly in the direction of the sophist by that time.

Schramm worked closely with Foerster from 1930 until about the beginning of 1944, and became fully enthralled with the neohumanist perspective. He completed his dissertation in 1932, entitled "Studies in the Longer Narrative Verse of America, 1775–1860," under Foerster's guidance.[37] And after completing a 2-year National Research Fellowship, which culminated in the publication of his short book *Approaches to a Science of English Verse,* Schramm became an assistant professor of English at Iowa, a position Foerster doubtlessly helped him to secure.[38] Foerster chose Schramm to revise Foerster's widely read anthology *American Poetry and Prose,* and when in 1935 Foerster established his journal *American Prefaces,* he asked Schramm to serve as its editor.[39] Then, in 1939, with the sudden death of Edwin Ford Piper (the English professor responsible for conducting the writing seminars at Iowa), Foerster saw the opportunity to establish a writers program at Iowa that would attempt to fuse the widening gap he observed between the writer and the literary scholar. Foerster chose Schramm to found this Writers' Workshop and serve as its first director.[40]

As mentioned earlier, the idea of permitting creative work to be submitted as a Master's thesis-equivalent in some fields was being considered at Iowa in the early 1920s, largely due to the efforts of Carl Seashore. True to neohumanist form, which rejects the German notion that the Ph.D. necessarily represents new knowledge, Foerster and Schramm extended Sea-shore's emphasis on creative work to the Ph.D. program in writing. In 1941, Foerster and Schramm published their book *Literary Scholarship: Its Aims and Methods* (with chapters by John C. McGalliard, Rene Wellek, and Austin Warren), and argued in defense of granting the creative writer legitimate academic status, as well as making their pitch for the adoption of the neohumanist curriculum.[41] If there remained any question as to the degree to which Schramm "bought" Foerster's neohumanism, these questions could have been laid to rest with the publication of Schramm's chapter, entitled "Imaginative Writing." In this chapter, Schramm argued entirely from the neohumanist position. As Babbitt had done in his *Literature and the American College* and Foerster had done in his *The American Scholar*, Schramm maintained that literary scholarship was being run amok by the two-headed beast of romanticism and scientific naturalism.[42] On the one hand, the writer, motivated by the romantic "cult of experience," had completely rejected the world of academic scholarship. Schramm argued:

> The writer has learned to use as his most damning adjective, *academic*, which is to say, *dead*. He has been accustomed to prefer the company of unlearned men to that of learned; to regard the university as an antithesis of life, rather than a place for living; and in his own education to substitute "real life" for thought-upon-life enriched by knowledge of the other humanities and the mind of the past. On the whole, the harvest of a month on the road was considered by a typical young realist of the nineteen twenties to be greater than the harvest of a semester with Plato and Whitehead.[43]

On the other hand, scientific naturalism had created an emphasis, in literary studies, on the accumulation of the most obscure historical facts that had little bearing on the world of the practicing writer and critic. Thus developed a schism between the literary scholar and the literary artists, in which the artists were banished to the streets and the scholars recoiled into the archives. Schramm wrote:

> The university has become the scholar's fortress. As a man of letters, the scholar busies himself in the past, rather than the present; prefers the example and company of the scientist and social scientist to the company of the artist. In administration, the scholar assigns the teaching of "composition" to the young assistants; relegates contemporary literature to an incidental "luxury" or "popular" course, in either case rather frivolous. . . . The official viewpoint, Max Eastman said, has come to be that a poet in history is divine, but a poet in the next room is a joke.[44]

Schramm and Foerster envisioned the Writers' Workshop as a means by which the writer and the literary scholar could be brought together again. Granting a Ph.D. for creative work would both legitimize the writer's activity as well as keep him or her within the university fold, surrounded by learned people, and thus raise the standard of his or her work. Apparently, Schramm and Foerster's rationale was convincing. With the establishment of the Writers' Workshop at Iowa, students were able to submit original fiction, poetry, and drama in lieu of the traditional dissertation for the Ph.D.[45]

The Writers' Workshop was an innovation new not only to Iowa, but to the rest of the country as well, and the workshop received a great deal of national attention from writers, critics, and scholars alike. Schramm, as its first director, was elevated to a position of considerable status, and consequently came into contact with a number of nationally prominent writers, such as Robert Frost, Archibald MacLeish, and Robert Penn Warren, some of whom stayed at Schramm's home while they served as visiting lecturers.[46]

As director of the workshop, Schramm was now in a position to think more seriously about the role of the writer in contemporary society. It was not surprising that, in defining that role, as he was also defining the role of the mass communicator in society, Schramm relied largely on the neohumanist perspective within which he was trained. The writer, like the Greek orator, was primarily concerned with persuading people to accept particular arguments and to adopt particular attitudes. This could be accomplished by a writer well trained in the skills of creating certain effects. In this regard, teaching creative writing could be seen as a process of imparting the practical knowledge of how to create particular effects. Thus, Schramm described the writer's vocation in this way:

> The writer's problem with literary form is somewhat like the business man's problem with his advertising. Each has something to sell. The merchant has toothpaste or furniture or automobiles; the writer has a theme, a character, or a series of incidents. The merchant knows that no single advertising formula will always fit his needs. He can't sell toothpaste with the same advertising that sells automobiles. He can't sell venetian blinds in the same way he sells coal ranges. And the writer, too, realizes that there is no "right" form, no single kind of plot. Each different article he has to sell requires somewhat different advertising.[47]

In making this statement, Schramm was reflecting the larger cultural trend toward the emphasis of technique over content. In addition, one can detect in this passage the germination of the basic approach to the study of communications that he used so fruitfully in later years. Just as he was concerned with the "effects" of the advertiser's message and the "effects" of the writer's story, it was the "effects" of mass communication messages that would be his primary concern as a communications researcher. How the message persuaded a population to think or to behave in a certain manner, or the emotional response elicited by the message, were to remain more important considerations for Schramm than did the truth or falsity of the message.

Although Schramm was greatly influenced by Foerster's neohumanism, and although Foerster saw Schramm as his protégé and heir to the neohu-

manist movement, it would be a mistake to suggest that Schramm had simply embraced the entire neohumanist orthodoxy. "As graduate students,"
Schramm's roommate at Iowa, Wallace Stegner, wrote, "we pretty much all
disparaged it [neohumanism] and laughed at some of its assumptions behind Foerster's back. But it turns out that there was much in it that we consciously believed, and still do. The new humanism was merely an academic
retouching of the whole humanist tradition in which we were trained."[48]

As participants in a protest movement, the neohumanists were at fundamental odds with the prevailing cultural and political currents of the time,
and as such they often appeared to be anachronistic and rather rigid in their
positions. Although, as mentioned earlier, Foerster was able to compromise
on some positions, he would not budge on others, and this caused numerous political confrontations within the School of Arts and Letters at Iowa.
When the chips were falling Foerster's way, it was beneficial for Schramm to
remain sided with him. But as the tide began to change and Foerster fell increasingly out of favor with the university faculty, Schramm began to distance himself from Foerster and the neohumanist movement. In addition,
Schramm was aware that any open acknowledgment of his adherence to
neohumanism, which was both expressly undemocratic and decisively un-
scientific, would not be in his political or professional best interest. The
1930s and 1940s, after all, was a period marked by a spirit of democracy in
the United States, and that—coupled with the rise of the scientific manager
in all fields—must have made neohumanism exceedingly unpopular. Of all
Schramm's talents, perhaps his most thoroughly developed was his ability
to play whatever role, and to attach himself to whatever philosophical position, that would take him the farthest. On the eve of the outbreak of World
War II, it must have been very clear to Schramm that public adherence to
neohumanism would no longer serve that purpose.

On December 15, 1941, eight days after the bombing of Pearl Harbor,
Schramm wrote a letter to Archibald MacLeish, recently appointed head of
the Office of Facts and Figures (the organizational precursor to the Office
of War Information). Since 1939, MacLeish had been on the stump alerting
people to the dangers of European fascism, and his literary background
made him a natural selection to head the United States' wartime propaganda machine. In his letter to MacLeish, Schramm volunteered his services, as well as those of other professors at Iowa, to the war effort. Schramm
astutely observed that:

> Perhaps more than any previous war this is likely to be a war of communica-
> tion. On the home front it will be important to maintain the morale and unity
> we seem at last to have achieved. They are most likely to be maintained, we be-
> lieve, neither by keeping silent nor by allowing false rumors to dominate men
> by excoriating the "Beast of Berlin," but rather by imparting enthusiasm and a
> rational, informed view. In the case of students and teachers, this problem of

communication can be best handled by persons accustomed to deal with students and teachers.[49]

In addition to offering his and his colleagues' services to the war efforts, Schramm began to sketch out ways in which the University of Iowa could contribute to a governmental propaganda operation directed at Midwest educational institutions, including using Iowa's Writers' Workshop; the educational radio station; and the departments of journalism, art, psychology, and others. "We are equipped to furnish a continuous supply of trained men to handle these problems of communication," Schramm wrote, "and our laboratories are geared to research ways and means and effectiveness of communication. I may say that we have discussed these matters with administrative officials and have been assured that they are as anxious as we to find how the university can now be of most service."[50] MacLeish must have been favorably impressed with Schramm's insight and organizational talents. Before the end of December 1941, Schramm took a leave of absence from Iowa and was in Washington, D.C., serving with the Office of Facts and Figures.

During his appointment to the Office of Facts and Figures (a position that would lead to Schramm being named Educational Director of the Office of War Information), Schramm wrote a memorandum to his colleagues, dated January 31, 1942, regarding his "First recommendations toward an informational program for universities, colleges, school and affiliated groups."[51] This 19-page memorandum is a significant historical document, revealing some of Schramm's earliest plans for educational broadcasting—many of which would take concrete form in the early 1950s. In this memorandum Schramm began to envision a comprehensive propaganda network aimed at universities and schools across the country, utilizing not only educational broadcasting but also school-based print media (including textbooks and university newspapers), and calling for the organization of faculty and student groups to both disseminate information and monitor public opinion. Although much of the hyperbole that runs throughout the document can be attributed to the climate created by the war, Schramm made it clear that the program he was devising would not end with the war but instead continue well after armistice.

In this memorandum, Schramm provided several explanations as to why educational institutions would make viable and worthwhile targets for a governmental "information" or propaganda campaign. First, Schramm recognized the importance of influencing the opinions of the educated class (long before the notion of the "opinion leader" and the "two-step flow" became popular in the literature of mass communications research), and he realized the best place to reach this audience was at the institutions where they were being educated. "The educational institutions are an important part of the national mind," he wrote, "a part which accumulates force and potency with the years. Any salutary direction of the school mind will pay off at compound interest for sixty years. Furthermore, by means of an effective and subtle kind of re-communication, the school mind has considerable effect on the minds around it."[52] Second, educational institutions by themselves offered a large target audience, with over 30 million teachers and students. In addition, educational institutions represented important communication vehicles in their own right, publishing books, periodicals, and newspapers, and often creating radio programming and other instructional aids. Finally, Schramm was aware of the newly developed techniques for measuring opinions and attitudes that were appearing at many universities. By directing a propaganda campaign at educational institutions and their surrounding communities, Schramm reasoned, these universities could use their new opinion- and attitude-polling techniques to measure the effectiveness of the propaganda. He wrote:

> They [universities] have become vastly interested in the techniques of measuring attitudes and shifts in attitudes, the sampling method of polling, the testing of information, many have set up courses and laboratories in these areas. Thus, they are ready not only to provide the avenues of communication to a vast and influential audience, and the communicators and the materials, but also the means to determine the effectiveness of any given communication.[53]

Schramm envisioned establishing an entire network of student and faculty groups at universities across the country, to facilitate the dissemination of carefully selected government information and also monitor public opinion. He realized that "no man, no agency in Washington, is big enough to navigate for twenty million students and forty million of their relatives and friends, without the most expert and informed advice."[54] Therefore, he planned for an intricate bureaucratic network that would pass information from a central governmental agency, to five regional directors, and then on to campus committees. This network would be overseen by a "brain trust" who would be aided by a group of "experts in each field of educational communications: the best men in college radio, visual extensions, college newspapers, departments of speech, etc."[55] At the local level, the campus committees would become a listening-post service, but would gradually develop into a system in which "the listeners are more than mere reporters—until they can cooperate in treating the ills that they discover."[56]

The ills that these campus committees would discover, of course, were dissenting opinions, and one can only imagine the types of methods that might have been employed to eradicate such dissenting opinions. Nevertheless, Schramm saw in these campus committees an important link in reducing the diversity of national opinion and sentiment concerning the war effort and the postwar plans. He hoped to approach a corporate foundation about the possibility of establishing a summer program to train these college leaders. These college leaders, then, "would be expected to go back to their campuses and be focal points for realistic thinking about the international situation and the problems of living in the world today. Also, these college leaders might be expected to become civic leaders after graduation."[57] Schramm hoped to stimulate enthusiasm for these campus organizations by providing the kind of regalia that he thought would attract members. "The academic mind likes pomp, grades, uniforms, titles," he wrote not very highly of his academic colleagues. "I suggest that we give a lapel button or an arm insignia (perhaps one chevron) to every teacher or student (e.g., the editor of the newspaper) who participates in any important way in this program."[58] He envisioned organizing these campus committees into a single national unit, and together with the organization of educational broadcasting, the revision of textbooks, and the widespread use of newly developed opinion and attitude measurement techniques, Schramm was seeking to eliminate the variety and freedom of opinion necessary for the maintenance of democracy, and in its place establish the means by which a single consenting voice on U.S. policy could be achieved. "The job that is really the purpose of all these others," he wrote without reservation or qualification, is "bringing the mind of the colleges and universities into closer contact with the mind of which they are a part—the mind of the state."[59]

It is difficult to ascertain the degree to which Schramm's recommendations were implemented. Presumably, the idea of providing arm bands and similar symbols of membership in the campus committees was not something that found wide acceptance. After all, these arm insignias smacked too much of the symbolism associated with German Nazism to be of much effectiveness. Yet, the specific observations and recommendations Schramm made concerning educational broadcasting, and his particular shrewdness in conceptualizing various approaches to manipulating the educated individuals who would attend to educational broadcasting, would have likely found a receptive audience among national security planners during the Cold War.[60] After coming to the University of Illinois in 1947, Schramm became perhaps the most tireless worker in the educational broadcasting movement, and a much sought-after expert on educational broadcasting issues.[61]

In his 1942 memorandum, Schramm observed that, although reaching a small but influential audience, the educational broadcasting stations across the United States did not have a central organization that distributed programming to these stations. Instead, individual educational radio stations often produced programs that were heard only within their own domain of origin. For someone who was concerned with manufacturing a national consensus, the idea of isolated educational radio stations creating programming that might depart from the state's official line must have caused considerable anxiety. Schramm did not foresee the likelihood of establishing an educational broadcasting network at that time. However, he did conceive of a central transcription service in which programming could be passed from one station to another. "The educational stations probably never will be able to afford an educational network," he wrote in this 1942 memo, "but the passing around of transcriptions is a natural substitute for that, and one that will doubtless be resorted to in the future."[62] It took passage of the Public Broadcasting Act of 1967 before anything approaching a national educational broadcasting network came to take shape. Yet, Schramm was instrumental in establishing a central program transcription service at the University of Illinois in 1951, when the National Association of Educational Broadcaster's headquarters were moved to the Champaign-Urbana campus.[63]

It is clear from this 1942 memorandum that Schramm envisioned this propaganda network, aimed at educational institutions, continuing in operation long after the end of the war; and it is this particular point of view that should cause us to question Schramm's motives in working to establish educational broadcasting in the late 1940s and early 1950s. "Of all the audiences available for government information this is perhaps the one best adapted to a long view and a long term program," Schramm wrote. He continued:

> Therefore, let us try to make this program one that will have use and implication far beyond the immediate present. If schools and colleges need to pay more attention to political and social realities, they will need to pay just as much attention to them when the war is over. . . . If it is necessary to define our national attitudes now, it will be equally necessary after the war.[64]

Like many of his contemporaries in 1942, Schramm looked at a world that, to him, appeared to be running completely out of control. It would require new and extraordinary measures to regain order. Schramm realized that controlling the opinions of the mass society meant first controlling the opinions of that society's educated members, and that this educated class was not easily taken in by the usual pap offered over the airwaves. Indeed, controlling the opinions of the educated class required a distinctly sophisticated and subtle approach, yet such an approach would pay off in great dividends. "Let us recognize," he wrote, "that this audience has a psychological tempo somewhat slower than that of many other audiences, that it is poorly adapted to high-pressure treatment and well adapted to long-range planning, and that it can indeed make a great solid contribution to the war effort, but that its greatest contribution—to the reservoir now being built up for the *post-war* effort—may be on a level too deep to be spectacular"[65] (emphasis in original).

The full story of Schramm's organizational planning for a wartime propaganda campaign directed at U.S. educational institutions remains incomplete. Yet, it is important to note here that his appointment to the Office of Facts and Figures (and later to the Office of War Information, when the OFF was subsumed under the OWI in June 1942) drastically changed his life—it altered the direction of his intellectual pursuits, thrust him into a circle of national decision making elites, and prompted him to refer to himself as a social scientist rather than as a literary humanist. His new group of colleagues included Carl Hovland, Paul Lazarsfeld, Harold Lasswell, Margaret Mead, and others inclined to a more positivist approach to the study of human being and society than Schramm had previously displayed. Having had little academic training in either the physical or social sciences, aside from the brief period of his National Research Fellowship when he analyzed the objective qualities of English metered verse, Schramm was soon directing large research projects for the federal government and offering his advice as to the best direction of national policy.

His transition from playing the role of literary scholar to that of social scientist was not completed overnight. The wartime propaganda effort required not only organizational men and women who could construct informational channels and measure public opinion, but also creative men and women who could manipulate the symbols and create the myths by which other people would willingly rally around the flag. Schramm played this role as well, by writing the texts for some of Roosevelt's fireside chats, and writing several short stories, published during the war in such popular magazines as the *Atlantic Monthly* and the *Saturday Evening Post,* that were aimed at getting the reading audience behind the war.[66] Much like the many propaganda films created by the cooperative effort of the Office of War Information and the Hollywood movie moguls, which sought to shape the image of a virtuous and just United States not torn by great inequities and racial hatred, Schramm's short stories aimed at reaching deep into the United States' mythic past to create an image of the country that was at once brave, superior, and virtuous.[67]

Some of his stories, for instance "The Flying Coffin" and "The Story of Wilbur the Jeep," attempted to convince the reader of the United States' superiority in military technology by personifying this technology and envisioning it being able to withstand tremendous enemy and natural environmental pressures.[68] Yet perhaps his most effective story was "Boone over the Pacific," which recalled the U.S. frontier myths as a way of explaining to U.S. citizens their war in the South Pacific.[69] In this story, three U.S. soldiers—a Tennessean, a Texan, and a Swede from Minnesota—have been separated from their company and are in a foxhole stranded behind enemy lines. With "Swede" wounded, the three are unable to move and must simply wait for their company to rescue them. Days pass without any sign of rescue, and they each begin to consider the question: "If you could bring in one man to help you out of this . . . how would you answer that?" True to mythic form, the Tennessean chooses Daniel Boone, the Texan chooses Davy Crockett, and the Swede chooses Paul Bunyan. Each soldier explains how his respective hero would go about whipping the "Nips" or "Japs" in this situation. All myths must necessarily conclude with "good" overtaking "evil," and in Schramm's story this is no exception. The soldiers begin to act, as their heroes would act and effectively outsmart those "Japs." To be sure, Schramm's stories are not examples of high literature, and their low quality suggests that perhaps Schramm was correct in understanding that his real talents did not reside in the area of creative writing. Still, Schramm's short stories were no doubt effective in helping to build consensus for the war by both idealizing the actual fighting of the war and demonstrating the mythological link this war had with previous U.S. wars. At least one panel of critics found value in Schramm's short stories, and he was given the O. Henry literary award in 1942 for his short story "Windwagon Smith," which was published after the war with a collection of other stories under the title *Windwagon Smith and Other Yarns.*[70]

When Schramm returned to Iowa in the fall of 1943, Norman Foerster was involved in a fierce debate with other faculty members in the School of Arts and Letters over proposed curriculum changes. Foerster refused to compromise, even though most of the faculty did not side with his position. Schramm, who was already well on his way out of the literary area, did not come to Foerster's defense, and it was this particular dispute that severed any remaining formal ties Schramm had with Foerster and neohumanism. Wallace Stegner, two-time Pulitzer Prize winner and Schramm's lifelong friend, recalled that:

> There was a continuing strain in the English Department, where Norman Foerster's innovations were not universally popular. Wilbur had been an assistant to Foerster, had pretty much revised Foerster's book on American Literature, and had been Foerster's handpicked candidate to run the writing program when it was established on a formal basis. Wilbur also edited the program's magazine, *American Prefaces.* So he was seen in the department as Foerster's man, and that could have been uncomfortable—more uncomfortable all the time as the department and Foerster drew further apart. . . . Foerster eventually resigned. . . . And Wilbur, when he came back from Washington in 1943, came back as head of the Journalism School, not as director of creative writing.[71]

The particular circumstances surrounding Foerster's resignation and Schramm's transition from literature to journalism are difficult to construct, although it is clear the Foerster felt betrayed by Schramm. Foerster came to believe that Schramm had engaged in several machinations in order to ensure his own professional well-being. After resigning his position in the spring of 1944, Foerster wrote to Schramm:

> You know how pleased I am with myself that I had faith in you from the beginning—how I recognized your great and diverse talents and did all I could to get your career started, especially your teaching career. You know how pleased

I have been with you as you have developed your capabilities and made good in a worldly sense. These things I shall never be able to forget, despite my sadness in the perception that our relationship has apparently changed in the past year. I have formed my impressions on the basis of your actions, what you did or didn't do. To a lesser extent I considered reports when they seemed to be authentic. I tried to close my ears to malicious comments and unsupported suspicions as to your motives. The net result, I am sorry to say, was disquieting.[72]

There was, then, a definite break between Foerster and Schramm in 1944, although Schramm would downplay the personal aspects of this break in later years.[73] Perhaps Schramm's conscience began to trouble him over his treatment of Foerster during this crisis at Iowa. In any event, Foerster returned to North Carolina, most likely feeling that his neohumanist movement had been severely diminished. Schramm would begin his career as Director of the School of Journalism, a position that served as a stepping stone to his founding the Institute of Communications Research at the University of Illinois.

If Foerster felt betrayed by Schramm on a personal level, he could not have been justified in thinking that Schramm led to the further dissolution of the neohumanist movement. Indeed, in many regards, Schramm had come to personify the neohumanist's ideal of the well-rounded person of action, and his subsequent success in the field of mass communication theory and research could only be seen as further vindication of the neohumanist educational program. To be sure, Schramm refused to call himself a neohumanist, and presumably he did not consciously look back to the classical Greeks for his standards of moral conduct. In addition, there were many policy positions that Schramm supported in later years that both Babbitt and Foerster would have found quite reprehensible. In more important ways, however, Schramm carried the neohumanist legacy into the germinating field of mass communication research. The neohumanist ideal of a hierarchical, aristocratic social order; the conceptualization of mass communications as a process of persuading people to adopt a certain mode of thinking and behaving; and the emphasis on an educated elite masterminding this communication process were central to Schramm's thinking throughout his career.

As for Schramm, his ability to play whatever role, and to adhere to whatever theoretical position most expedient at the time, was a trait he appeared to have learned well from his neohumanist past. He had no substantial training in either the physical or social sciences and, in fact, was educated in a tradition that possessed an inherent distrust of science, yet he was to become a leading figure in the field of mass communications research by advocating a more or less positivistic approach. In one regard, this characterizes Schramm as a sophist, it gives us some indication of his diverse talents, and it sheds light on his ability to be a convincing impostor. This point did not escape the notice of his friend and colleague Lyle Nelson, who wrote in 1977:

> The record would not be complete, if it did not note that in one major respect—known only to a few of his closest friends and colleagues—Wilbur Schramm was one of the academic world's most successful impostors. He posed as a social scientist who applied the rigorous intellectual discipline of the hard sciences to inquiry into a new field. And he did it with great success. But at heart he was, and is, a humanist.[74]

In another important regard, however, Schramm's ability to be a successful impostor supports those who point to the fundamental normative nature of the social sciences. Although it is almost a truism to suggest that all social science is conducted from a particular interpretive vantage point with implicit assumptions about the nature of human life, what constitutes a good society, and so on, Schramm's career as a social scientist offers an interesting historical example of this truism in the context of the Cold War. Much of the rest of this chapter is concerned with illuminating the perspective that undergirded Schramm's research in mass communications.

Schramm continued to direct the School of Journalism at Iowa from 1944 to 1947, and he continued to deepen his understanding of how the print media could be manipulated to produce certain desired social effects. Yet, he became increasingly fascinated with all forms of communication, particularly television, which was still waiting in the wings at this time. He realized that the postwar years would witness vast changes in communication networks as well as changes in communication technology, and that these changes, in turn, would foster deep changes in human consciousness. "It will be no small responsibility to work with communications in the post-war years," Schramm wrote in 1945. "We approach it like a boy with his first rifle, keenly aware of the power of the weapon for good or evil, cognizant of the unfamiliar weight on his shoulder, fingering the new gun a little gingerly as he goes out hunting with his people looking worried and hopefully after him."[75]

When Schramm's former colleague at Iowa, George Stoddard, was named president of the University of Illinois in the spring of 1947, he invited Schramm to establish the Institute of Communications Research.

The boy gladly accepted the loaded gun.

FOCUSING THE INSTITUTE'S FORCES

During the week of November 6, 1977, it became known to the public that the Central Intelligence Agency had funneled $193,000 through their front organization, the Society for the Investigation of Human Ecology, to the Institute of Communications Research at the University of Illinois from 1960 to 1963, while the Institute was under the directorship of Professor Charles Osgood.[76] The money, a part of the CIA's extensive MKULTRA research program initiated to develop methods of mind control, was used to finance Osgood's research on the "semantic differential," a propaganda technique that would enable the propagandist to select words that could convey particular kinds of meanings to people of various cultures. The revelation of the covert CIA funding of both research at the institute and drug research at the University of Illinois Medical Center caused considerable consternation among the university community. Editorials were written to the campus and local papers expressing grief about the situation, and reminding the community of the implications of researchers not being fully informed of either who was funding their research or the eventual uses to which their research would be put. Nevertheless, within a couple of weeks, the issue of clandestine CIA funding of university research was no longer considered to be newsworthy by those who controlled the media outlets, and the issue was dropped from their newspapers.

While the story of the covert CIA funding was still receiving press coverage, however, there was a deliberate attempt by the university administration and the principal researchers involved to downplay the significance of the covert funding — to make the covertly funded research seem like an isolated incident or an aberration that deviated from the normal course of activities at the university and within the institute. Osgood maintained he was unaware that the CIA was funding his research through their front organization, although he did admit that he approached the CIA in 1959 with the interest of receiving their financial support but was turned down at that time.[77] Furthermore, he argued that he really didn't begin to collect data on other cultures until after the CIA funding had ended, implying that the CIA, therefore, did not fund the major part of his research. University President John E. Corbally said that the university would have permitted the CIA to sponsor the research, so the covert funding was unnecessary. Yet Corbally was quick to make it appear that the CIA funding of university research projects was not widespread — that it did not extend beyond the propaganda research conducted by Osgood from 1960 to 1963 within the institute and the drug research carried out by the University Medical Center. "As far as we're concerned," Corbally stated, "if the documents [CIA documents released through the Freedom of Information Act] sent to us are all the documents that there are, *and we must assume this,* then we must simply rule out University projects other than the two described"[78] (emphasis added). The reason why Corbally felt compelled to make such an ill-founded assumption is clear: To assume otherwise would be to cast a shadow over other university research projects and to permit the avenue by which questions could be raised about the purpose and legitimacy of these projects.

Although it is uncertain as to what Corbally knew about the history of Osgood's project, he may have had good reasons for wanting to control the discussion around the issue of CIA funding of university research. It now appears likely that the Central Intelligence Agency covertly funded research projects within the Institute of Communications Research at least as early as 1951, when the institute was under the directorship of Wilbur Schramm. The evidence for the early CIA funding of research within the institute remains circumstantial—evidence that is made apparent later in this chapter. Yet, the evidence for the early covert CIA funding of research at the institute, as well as the more easily documented evidence of extensive overt military and State Department funding of research conducted at the institute during the late 1940s and early 1950s, clearly raises important questions about the Cold War influences on both the institute and the origins of mass communications research.

With a single motion in the spring of 1947, University of Illinois President George Stoddard created a multifaceted position for Wilbur Schramm, which both tapped Schramm's diverse talents and placed him squarely at the center of the university's information activities. In addition to being appointed the first Director of the Institute of Communications Research, Schramm was also appointed to the position of Director of the University Press, and Assistant to President Stoddard. As Stoddard's assistant, Schramm was largely responsible for the public relations operations of the university, including acting as a liaison between the news media and the university, and overseeing the functions of the university media outlets such as the university newspaper, *The Daily Illini*, and the University radio station, WILL. Then, in 1950, Stoddard and Schramm went a step further in unifying the modern university's information operations by creating a Division of Communications, which brought together the Speech Department, the School of Journalism and Communications, the Library School and the University Libraries, University Broadcasting, Athletic Department Publicity, the Alumni Office, University Extensions, University Publicity, Agricultural Information, the Allerton House Conference Center, the Institute of Communications Research, and other teaching and service units within the university, all under a single division. Schramm was made Dean of the entire division in June of 1950, and thereby sat at the controls through which most people learned of the university's activities.[79]

Although Schramm's other duties exhausted much of his time, his primary focus remained the Institute of Communications Research. Here he steadily constructed a highly regarded interdisciplinary research department that was the base of several faculty members who were near the top of their respective disciplines. In 1948, Schramm brought notable visiting professors to the institute, such as Paul F. Lazarsfeld from Columbia University's Bureau of Applied Social Research, and Clyde W. Hart, the Director of the

National Opinion Research Center. In 1948, Schramm also hired Dallas W. Smythe, an economist from the Federal Communications Commission, and a young educational psychologist named Harry Grace. Additionally in 1948, Schramm transferred resident journalism professors F. S. Siebert and C. H. Sandage, and sociology professor J. W. Albig, from various departments within the university to the institute. In 1949, Schramm brought psychologist Charles Osgood and broadcaster Robert Hudson to the Institute. Osgood was later to become President of the American Psychological Association. Hudson, who had formerly been employed by the Office of War Information and served as the Director of Education and Opinion Broadcast for CBS, ran the university radio station WILL and eventually became Vice President of National Educational Television. Finally, Charles Swanson, a sociologist from Minnesota, and Joseph Bachelder, a political scientist from Washington State University, were brought to the institute in 1951 to round out the group, and to provide extra support for work on the large military contracts that were awarded to the institute in the early 1950s.[80]

At the time of the 1947 founding of the Institute of Communications Research, Schramm envisioned that "the central object of the research [at the institute] should be to help communications realize as fully as possible their potential for the good of man in a democratic society."[81] In written plans for the institute, Schramm sought to limit the amount of research financed by outside agencies that would be conducted within the institute. "Research projects assigned to the Institute by outside agencies," Schramm wrote, "should be undertaken only when time and manpower are available, when the results are to be public, and when the research will contribute in an important way to general knowledge as distinguished from commercial use."[82] Yet, before Schramm had even completed his written plans for the institute, he was actively seeking to conduct research for "outside agencies" that would have results that would not be public property and that would contribute not to general knowledge or to the "good of man in a democratic society," but instead to highly specific knowledge that could be only dubiously regarded as being for the good of "men" in a democratic society. Despite written plans to the contrary, a significant amount of research conducted within the institute during Schramm's tenure as director was funded by military agencies for the expressed purpose of creating psychological warfare techniques.[83] Did Schramm have a change of heart about limiting the amount of institute research to be funded by outside agencies? Or did he plan from the very beginning to solicit these massive military contracts, and simply wrote the provision that limited outside funding into his plans for the institute as a way of ensuring that the plans would be favorably received? The gross inconsistency between Schramm's stated plans for the institute and its actual activities make these questions difficult to ignore.

As early as November 15, 1947, a research proposal was written at the institute entitled "Communication and Inter-Continental Warfare," requesting $255,000 for developing various propaganda techniques to psychologically prepare people for an intercontinental war, and to find the means by which to persuade people to adopt a certain course of action should such a war come about. "The battle for the minds of men is already underway on an inter-continental scale," the proposal stated in Schramm's familiar style.

> What happens in the minds of civilians in the next five or ten years will determine whether there is such a war. What happens in the minds of civilians if war comes will determine how effectively we fight. This is especially true in countries like this [the United States] where civilians will never be fully regimented. They will have to be persuaded, rather than ordered. They must understand: They will never obey without question. They will have to be prepared by mass communications and directed by whatever communication remains available to them when war comes.[84]

The proposal was broken down into six subsections consisting of various research projects, including those for developing methods of countering propaganda, gauging American public opinion on war, studying the comparative effects of different media in influencing people's opinions and behaviors, analyzing the reactions of civilians to warlike situations, and examining and interpreting Russian propaganda. As preliminary research projects, much of the proposed work centered around reviewing existing literature and examining the records of the Office of War Information and the Office of Strategic Services to ascertain the effectiveness of their propaganda techniques during the war; however, the use of controlled experiments on jails and community homes was also proposed as a way of measuring the effectiveness of various propaganda techniques, particularly the use of rumors. The proposed research was to be situated within the institute, but several visiting professors were hired to carry out the work, including Carl Hovland and Bernard Berelson. It was proposed that Jerome Bruner would direct the research for two of the six projects. Of course, Bruner became one of the leading educational psychologists during the 1960s and 1970s, and it is interesting to speculate on how his early involvement with propaganda research would influence his later work on human learning, and what kind of enduring impact this involvement and influence may have had. To what agency this proposal was directed, and whether the proposal was actually accepted, is not clear from what remains in the institute's files. Nevertheless, the proposal clearly indicates the extent to which Schramm was willing to utilize the institute for research matters relating to propaganda as early as 1947.

In April 1948, the United States Department of State asked Schramm and University of Illinois psychology professors Donald Brown and Thomas Harrell "to conduct a study to determine how many stories should be carried in news broadcasts."[85] The research, obviously pursued for its value in aiding propaganda campaigns, consisted of controlled experiments on subjects largely drawn from the U.S. Air Force and from the ranks of nonacademic employees at the University of Illinois. Six newscasts were constructed with varying degrees of complexity, and the subjects were asked to recall certain aspects of them. Although the public was not informed that the State Department was funding the research, a version of it was published in the June 1949 issue of the *Journal of Applied Psychology,* under the title "Memory in Radio Listening."[86] The goal of this research should have been obvious to anyone who perused the article, yet the authors tried to conceal the true objectives of the research by never mentioning the words *propaganda* or *psychological warfare* in the description about the purpose of the research.[87] The results of the experiment would have been helpful to the State Department in creating newscasts for both foreign and domestic audiences. As one might expect, Schramm, Harrell, and Brown concluded that "an audience remembers a proportionally smaller percentage of the items in a 15-minute newscast as the number of items is increased from 20 to 30 to 40." In addition, the results of the research indicated:

> that human interest and spectacular events are remembered by the mass audience, whereas such serious subject matter as public affairs is remembered less well by the part of the population which is not gifted with good memories. Nearby events are more likely to be remembered by the mass audience than events of distant origin. Details and names do not make for mass remembrance, and details of political events and foreign names in a public affairs story are especially hard to remember. "Index words" of a sensational or familiar nature are also helpful in penetrating the memories of the mass audience.[88]

Even if the conclusions drawn from this research seem a bit obvious, it would have been useful to the State Department and raised additional research questions. Some of these research questions also found willing support within the institute. If, for instance, as the research results maintain, "index words" are capable of "penetrating the memories of the mass audience," then it would be fruitful for the propagandist to develop a list of such index words. As we see later in this text, much of the work of Charles Osgood, who was hired by Schramm in 1949, was concentrated in locating this list of "index words."

With the onset of the Korean war on June 25, 1950, the military apparatus began an accelerated attempt to secure psychological warfare research, and Schramm began an accelerated attempt to secure these research contracts for the institute. After spending the summer in Europe "working on a survey of international communications"—a trip for which the full purpose remains a mystery—Schramm wrote a letter to Assistant Secretary of State Edward W. Barrett volunteering the institute's services to the State Department.[89] Barrett, formerly the editorial director of *Newsweek,* had directed the

overseas operations for the Office of War Information and, in many respects, had a career that paralleled Schramm's.[90] There is no doubt that Barrett found Schramm's proposal for research assistance worthy of additional
consideration. In his letter to Barrett, dated September 7, 1950, Schramm
both declared his commitment to the cause of developing propaganda techniques and sketched out two particular research areas in which the institute
could offer research assistance. Schramm wrote that he had "a deep respect
for the effectiveness of Russian propaganda," and "a deep conviction that,
no matter how fast we mobilize on the shooting front, we had better mobilize on the propaganda and information front now."[91] The institute could
help in this mobilization, Schramm argued, by acting as a "press intelligence
service" for gathering information about what "is being carried in papers
and journals in key countries," and by gathering information "concerning
reading, listening and viewing habits, tastes, and times in key countries."[92]
Schramm knew that having this kind of information was essential to the
propagandist. And, as a propagandist of long standing on the U.S. scene,
Schramm was aware that "the United States is the only country for which
such information exists in detail."[93]

About 6 weeks later, Schramm followed up with a proposal to Barrett providing more specific recommendations on how the institute could help the
State Department in its propaganda efforts. In this comprehensive proposal
(which was also sent to James H. Ennis of the State Department), Schramm
contended that the United States should develop propaganda efforts "in the
friendly countries of Western Europe and in the doubtful countries of the
Arab region and of Southern Asia," as strong as the propaganda efforts then
being directed at those countries "behind the Iron Curtain."[94] To help ac-
complish this goal, Schramm offered three recommendations:

1. A strengthening of intelligence reports on this subject [communication
   and opinion-forming patterns of particular countries] from our embassies, perhaps by attaching to the embassies a specialist in this field.
2. A two or three-man investigating team to be sent to Europe for an inten-
   sive study of this subject, lasting perhaps three months. (Similar arrangements would have to be made for other areas.)
3. A series of fellowships, of the general nature of the Fulbright study fellowships to be given [to] civilian specialists in this field to study communication and opinion-forming patterns in selected countries, for periods of six
   months to one year.[95]

Of these three recommendations, it was the last one concerning the use
of fellowship-receiving civilian scholars to gather information—that received Schramm's most vigorous endorsement. These study fellowships,
Schramm proposed, would not only be "of the general nature of the Fulbright" program, but would actually be part of the Fulbright Fellowship
program. One would not locate these scholars, however, "by scanning the

Fulbright applications," Schramm reasoned. "You will have to make out a list (with the best advice you can get), go out and sell the candidates on the idea, then have them apply through whatever channels you think best."[96] Although he recognized that there were some negative aspects to the recommendation—that it would be costly and was better suited to long-term programs rather than to situations in which immediate information was needed—Schramm argued that the recommendation would lead to more comprehensive results, it would provide more expert information, and that, by recruiting and sending these scholars into foreign countries to collect information on the communication and opinion-forming patterns, the State Department would be developing "a cadre of trained and expert advisers on communication to these countries."[97] In addition, Schramm observed that "this will look more like a scholarly inquiry; these fellows will be civilian scholars; they will be free of the taint of 'spying' from the embassies and can talk more freely both to the scholars and to the general public."[98] Yet it is precisely the activity of "spying" in which Schramm proposed these civilian Fulbright scholars engage. The scholars were to bring "their families, which will make the mission look less official (and will give them additional contacts and listening posts)."[99] While they are stationed in their host country they are to study the ways in which people come to hold certain opinions by surreptitiously interviewing citizens of the country, by working with media specialists within the country, and by attending closely to the content of the mediums of mass communications within the country. Specifically, the Fulbright scholars would try to find answers to such questions as:

> What are the reading and listening and general leisure time habits of various groups?
>
> What do different groups tend to trust among media? . . .
>
> What seems to be the relation, among different groups and in different situations, of personal and mediated information?
>
> What are the distinctive interests of different groups—youth, labor, the intelligentsia, the church party—to which an information campaign should try to appeal?
>
> In general, how do these various groups make up their minds? Where are the predispositions relatively solid and fixed? Where are they open to change?
>
> What should a communicator know about the pattern of anxieties, tensions, needs and wants?[100]

Schramm, however, was not content with simply having the scholars collect information in their host countries. He was also interested in having the scholars test hypotheses about the opinion formation habits of people within a country. "I see no reason why a fellow, when he gains a fairly good grasp of opinion and information within his country," Schramm wrote, "should not be able to test out one hypothesis he has derived."

Suppose, for example, he decides that the way to approach the youth of a given country is through library circulation of a given kind of material. With the cooperation of State, he could see that a library at a given center is adequately stocked with that material and the fact publicized. Or suppose he decides that labor is drastically misinformed on a certain point, and that they will believe an American labor leader and listen to the radio. State can arrange that kind of situation on the VOA [Voice of America]. And it will be relatively easy to get a before-and-after measure of attitude.[101]

For Schramm, as for many of his contemporaries, developing the means by which people of other countries could be manipulated was a necessary component in the sustenance and expansion of the U.S. empire. Masking espionage and intelligence gathering as scholarship and legitimate inquiry was a useful way in which the influences of the United States on the internal affairs of other nations could remain opaque and not easily detected. Schramm's comments in this proposal clearly demonstrate the low regard he had for democracy, the autonomy of people from other countries, and the ideal of scholarship as an open and honest exchange of ideas and information. In addition, Schramm's recommendation of testing hypotheses on people who are not aware that they are the subjects of experiments raises serious ethical questions. Having demonstrated such a low regard for both inquiry and the object of his inquiry when that inquiry was to be situated on foreign soil, the natural question to raise is whether Schramm would behave more ethically when his inquiry was situated in U.S. communities and when the objects of his inquiry would be U.S. citizens.

It is doubtful that Schramm offered the State Department anything new to the kind of intelligence-gathering activities then being employed by the State Department and other agencies of the U.S. government. It does not appear that the State Department took any immediate action on Schramm's proposal at that time. However, in June 1952, the State Department offered the institute $65,000 to conduct research on the effectiveness of some of their foreign propaganda efforts. From Schramm's description of this contract to C. C. DeLong, the university bursar, it seems likely that the State Department offer was in part a response to Schramm's proposal from 2 years earlier:

The State Department called me to Washington Wednesday and urged me to accept a contract for about $65,000 to develop a way in which they can begin to measure the effectiveness of their information program in foreign countries. This refers to information excluding the Voice of America. It isn't generally known that the lion's share of State Department propaganda funds do not go into the Voice but into information posts which they maintain in 80 countries. These posts are the centers for our activity in local radio, news dissemination, motion pictures, publications of all kinds, and exchange of persons.[102]

Presumably, the contract was accepted by the university because Schramm was in favor of taking it on. However, like much of the other propaganda-related research conducted by the institute, the details surrounding the research are no longer in the archival records.

In November 1950, Schramm was asked by the Human Resources Research Institute, a division of the United States Air Force Air University program, to take part in a small research team being sent to Korea. The team's mission, ostensibly to measure the performance of Air Force personnel, was actually to gauge the morale among the troops and study the effectiveness of both the North Korean and United States' psychological warfare campaigns.[103] His 2-month Korean mission, lasting from November 25, 1950, to about February 1, 1951, was significant in establishing Schramm's image as a psychological warfare expert, and apparently it was also his first contact with the Human Resource Research Institute (HRRI). HRRI became a most generous provider of funds for psychological warfare research to the Institute of Communications Research in the early 1950s, and it was a generous provider of funds to similar departments at many to other universities as well. In addition, there would be some interesting connections among HRRI, the CIA, and the CIA's MKULTRA program (which was found to have funded Charles Osgood's propaganda research during the early 1960s).

Schramm's actual activities while stationed in Korea are sketchy at best. It is clear, however, that he interrogated North Korean prisoners and interviewed South Koreans who were interned during the North Korean occupation of Seoul. He also offered his advice as to the best direction of U.S. propaganda in the region. Like much of Schramm's work, this advice was more often based on Schramm's own intuitive approach to propaganda and manipulation rather than being based on anything approaching a quantifiable science.

Schramm's mission to Korea led to the publication of *The Reds Take a City: The Communist Occupation of Seoul,* written with John W. Riley, a Rutgers University sociologist; as well as two journal articles written with Riley and HRRI psychological warfare chief, Dr. Fred W. Williams.[104] Although *The Reds Take a City* was touted by the Air Force for its "useful insights" into the workings of communist propaganda, the book was obviously a skillful propaganda tool in its own right that was aimed chiefly at the U.S. public. [105]Schramm's skill and experience as a creative writer no doubt was useful in writing *The Reds Take a City.* The book is largely a collection of stories about the hardships and repression faced by various people during the North Korean occupation of Seoul, presumably based on interviews with these people. The selection of the people whose stories are included in the book is itself an interesting issue. The people chosen all come from professional occupations whose positions mark them as important opinion leaders, and who consequently retain important positions in influencing the opinions of others.

The chapter titles indicate this: "The Escape of a Physician," "The Escape of a Public Prosecutor," "What Happened to a Teacher," "What Happened to a Newspaper Man," "What Happened to an Actress," "What Happened to a Clergyman," and "What Happened to a Congresswoman." The reason why these particular people were chosen as worthy subjects is that Schramm and Riley assumed that important U.S. opinion leaders in these same or similar occupations could identify with these stories, and would thus develop more vigorous anticommunist sentiments. The State Department must have found value in Schramm and Riley's approach — they ordered 10,000 copies of the book and distributed them throughout their areas of influence.[106]

The Korean mission was the very first mission conducted by the Air Force's HRRI, and it began an important relationship between HRRI and the Institute of Communications Research. Established in July 1949 by Air University at Maxwell Air Force Base in Alabama, HRRI's stated objective was to orchestrate research in the social sciences for the Air Force. Consisting of a professional staff of more than 50 people (most of whom were military officers), HRRI was directed by a civilian, Dr. Raymond V. Bowers, during its first 2 years of existence. Other people of note during the early years of HRRI were Colonel George W. Croker, who served as Deputy Director; Dr. Fred W. Williams, who served in the CIA from 1949 to 1950 before being assigned to HRRI in April 1950 and who, as chief of psychological warfare research, served as the primary contact person for Schramm and the Institute of Communications Research; and Major James L. Monroe, who on leaving HRRI in 1957 became the director of the CIA front organization, the Society for the Investigation of Human Ecology. HRRI was overseen by an advisory board that included Charles Dollard, the President of the Carnegie Corporation, who served as the chairman of the advisory board; Dr. Leland C. DeVinney of the Rockefeller Foundation; and Dr. William C. Menninger of the Menninger Foundation. Among the many institutions that received research contracts from HRRI from 1949 through 1951 were the University of Chicago, Columbia University, Harvard University, University of Michigan, University of North Carolina, University of Southern California, University of Indiana, Educational Testing Service, and the University of Washington.[107]

Although the story surrounding the HRRI contracts at most of these and other universities has yet to be told, that concerning HRRI-sponsored research at the University of Washington has been told in part, even if it was related by someone who would rather forget about HRRI's involvement in the research. During the early 1950s, Melvin DeFleur was a doctoral student in sociology at the University of Washington. In 1951, he was assigned to assist in conducting research for a highly secretive research project financed by a quarter of a million dollars from HRRI, which was referred to by the name "Project Revere."[108] In 1958, DeFleur and Professor Otto N. Larsen published the major findings of the Project Revere research in their *The Flow of Information: An Experiment in Mass Communications*.[109] Regardless of who was actually funding the research, Project Revere raises some serious ethical questions, because in most cases the people in the communities who received leaflet drops were unwitting participants in the study. Also, there are important questions to be asked concerning the legitimacy of the research aims of such a study. Nevertheless, when DeFleur re-released his book *The Flow of Information* in 1987, although still arguing for the importance and legitimacy of the work, he acknowledged in a new forward that it was highly likely that the CIA had actually been behind the funding and organization of Project Revere. Several decades after the Project Revere research was conducted, DeFleur wrote:

> A curious reporter in Washington D.C. was poking through previously classified CIA documents. He discovered a link between that agency and Project Revere. The Air Force officer who provided the liaison between that military service and the University of Washington research team turned out to have been an agent of the CIA. The "major" with whom the team worked continuously had, at the close of the project, suddenly transformed himself into the (civilian) director of the "Human Ecology Fund." Supposedly a private foundation which was revealed in the previously classified documents as a front for the CIA, the fund had been set up covertly to supply financial support for various university research projects in the social and biological sciences. The recipients of the grants did not know the true source of their funds. The CIA referred to these studies as the MKULTRA Mind Control Project. One of their projects of concern was how the mass media played a part in shaping the beliefs, attitudes, and behavior of populations. It came as quite a surprise in 1977 for one of the authors of *The Flow of Information* to learn nearly twenty years after its publication that he had probably been employed by the CIA during his Project Revere days, and that some of his later research had secretly been funded by that agency![110]

"In retrospect," DeFleur cynically added, "all the cloak and dagger considerations now seem more humorous than insidious."[111]

The major to whom DeFleur referred in this passage was Major James Monroe. After working with HRRI, Monroe went on to direct the CIA front organization, the Society for the Investigation of Human Ecology, from 1958 up until at least the early 1960s.[112] DeFleur did not cite the documents that led him to believe that Monroe worked for the CIA during the early 1950s while he was assigned to HRRI, but it is clear that DeFleur believed that Monroe was in fact working for the CIA while supervising HRRI's contracted research. If DeFleur was correct in his beliefs, then there is reason to call into question the full gamut of research conducted for HRRI, research that included massive amounts of research money and many of the most prominent academic institutions in the United States. One should also note that Albert Biderman's study *March to Calumny: The Story of American POW's in the Korean War* was initially sponsored by HRRI and then later supported by the Society for the Investigation of Human Ecology, largely through Monroe's administrative actions.[113]

Although James Monroe was responsible for overseeing the HRRI Project Revere research at the University of Washington, Dr. Fred Williams was responsible for overseeing the HRRI psychological warfare research that was conducted at the University of Illinois. Williams, one may recall, was himself a CIA agent from 1949 through 1950, when he was reassigned to HRRI. It is certainly not too far afield to suggest that he continued to work for the CIA while serving in his administrative capacity at HRRI. Obviously, to substantiate such claims would require fuller access to CIA files, which does not appear likely. Nevertheless, if the circumstantial case for covert CIA funding of research through HRRI turns out to be accurate, then the story of covert CIA funding of research at the University of Illinois, as well as the covert CIA funding of research at many other universities, is much more widespread than had been originally known.[114]

Schramm developed a close working relationship with Williams and HRRI from late 1950 up until at least the end of 1953. After returning from Korea in February 1951, Schramm was offered a permanent position with HRRI, which he considered but declined. Throughout the spring and summer of 1951, Schramm was at work on several psychological warfare training manuals for HRRI. His ability to pilot a plane made his frequent trips to Maxwell Air Force Base in Alabama a matter of minimal inconvenience. He was a tireless worker for HRRI throughout this period, advising HRRI on personnel for various projects, helping to develop psychological warfare training programs, and assisting in the assessment of those training programs. So committed to the cause for which HRRI was devoted, Schramm wrote the following message to HRRI director Ray Bowers: "If I am to do my war job at Illinois I want it to be (a) a substantial and important job, (b) answering some of your real needs, (c) in areas where we [the institute] are strongest. If we can't work that out at Illinois, then obviously I've got to work somewhere else, and I shall."[115]

In March 1951, Schramm wrote a memorandum to Fred Williams and Ray Bowers at their request, regarding "Research pertinent to psychological warfare and intelligence now in the planning stage at the University of Illinois."[116] On Schramm's list of psychological warfare work being planned at Illinois were Charles Osgood's work on developing measures of the "implicit content" of communication messages; also on his list were a study of the nature of a satellite state and the most efficient means by which the nucleus state can control the satellite state, a plan to develop a censorship policy in the event of an "atomic war," an analysis of the communications systems of other countries, an analysis of Soviet propaganda techniques, and the establishment of community laboratories in which to conduct various mass communication experiments. Of the six projects Schramm listed in this memorandum, it was the plan for the establishment of the community laboratories for which he offered the most detail:

> Beginning this summer we are creating three community laboratories, ranging from a rural community to a segment of a city. Bachelder from Washington State is coming to be chief technician for this operation. We aren't going to study public opinion in the polling sense. We are going to begin by learning all we can about the personal histories, intellectual histories, communication patterns, personality patterns, and attitude clusters of the persons with whom we shall be dealing. We want to know that as a basis for studying the decision function, the formation of attitudes, the pattern of authority, the passage of rumor, and all the other basic questions which you can study in a semi-controlled laboratory like these. We plan to use each of these laboratories until they show signs of wearing out. We shall take on a number of projects related to them. For example, we can feed material into them and watch the passage through. We can start with a decision and follow it backward through its components. We can tell, not so well the overall reaction of American public opinion to an event or a policy, but *why* certain groups and kinds of Americans reacted as they did. We hope to have about as near a precision tool as you can get in this business.[117]

Precisely where these community laboratories would be located remained undisclosed, although one assumes that close proximity to the University of Illinois would be an important criteria in selecting the communities. In a memorandum to the staff of the institute, Schramm contributed the following suggestions about the community laboratories:

> It is proposed that three types of publics be organized: 1) a public consisting of all the families of a community of not more than 2,500 population with samples from the surrounding farm population (Monticello, or Paxton, or a similar community); 2) a representative sample of the individuals and families of a city from 5,000 to 10,000 population; and 3) a city of 100,000 or more where television is already established.[118]

Williams wrote back to Schramm that of the six projects listed, the proposals concerning Osgood's measure of "implicit content," the analysis of Soviet propaganda techniques, and the establishment of community laboratories were of most interest to HRRI at that time. Williams asked Schramm to submit a more detailed proposal to HRRI regarding these and other research areas. Schramm's response to Williams' request, written on October 30, 1951, asked for over $167,000 to conduct research in the following four broad areas:

> (a) for a program of research and consultation on the utilization of social science research findings by the Air Force; (b) for a study of the implicit content

of communication; (c) for the provision and supervision of task forces to attack problems of importance to the Air Force in the field of communication,
notably in the areas of psychological warfare, military intelligence, and human relations. In addition, because field laboratories will be needed as soon as
possible for experimental and testing purposes, the contract also (d) provides
for the establishment of a few such laboratories where continuing research
can be conducted.[119]

Schramm listed himself as the proposed principal investigator for these
projects, although he planned to delegate authority for specific aspects of
these research projects to other staff members, particularly the study of the
"implicit content" of mass media messages (which would fall chiefly under
Osgood's direction). The community laboratories would continue to be
supervised by Joseph Bachelder, who was recruited from Washington State
University. The description of the community laboratories in this proposal
shares a remarkably close resemblance to the description of the community
laboratories utilized in the Project Revere experiments, in terms of the necessity of receiving cooperation, in both projects, from media outlets in the
communities:

> For many communication problems, ranging from rumor studies to leaflet ex-
> periments, community laboratories will be needed. In order to conduct exper-
> iments in communities with precision at all comparable to laboratory experi-
> ments, a great deal must be known about the community and *control must be
> possible over some of the community's communication.* We have felt the need of such
> field laboratories and in the last year have made a start at preparing three of
> them. Now it is proposed that HRRI join us in expediting the preparation of
> these communities so that by sometime in 1952 we can be putting experiments
> through them. Details on the planning for these laboratory communities have
> already been given. It should be said here that this part of the work will be
> under the direction of Dr. Joseph Bachelder, that the communities, when
> ready, will be available with a field staff for a variety of experiments of impor-
> tance to the Air Force and especially to the general orientation of this con-
> tract, and that approximately $10,000 will be required.[120] (emphasis added)

It is impossible to determine definitively, from what remains in the university records, whether or not HRRI accepted Schramm's proposal and if
the proposed research was actually conducted. There is no record of a single Air Force contract for $167,000 having been awarded to the institute
during 1951 or 1952. Nevertheless, three untitled Air Force contracts were
awarded to the Division of Communications during the spring of 1952 [AF
18(600)-321, AF 18(600)-335, and AF 18(600)-336] at a total of $147,991.[121]
Osgood and Schramm's work on the "implicit content" of mass media messages was funded by the Department of State (SCC-21437) and came to be
known as the "Illinois Associational Code for Content Analysis," a method of
determining the meaning of particular messages by ascribing special status

to a group of referent words and concepts. By locating these referent words and concepts, Osgood and Schramm hoped to develop a "semantic dictionary" that would permit the propagandist to select words and concepts that would convey particular meanings. The Illinois Associational Code received only mixed reviews when it was sent to researchers at other universities. However, HRRI seemed generally pleased with Osgood and Schramm's approach, and HRRI's comments suggested that HRRI found the Code worthy of additional consideration:

> The focus of attention upon the linkages of meanings in propaganda content, which is the basis of the *Code,* is certainly a very significant step forward in the propaganda analysis field. Extensive application of this new development will not only be of great value to propaganda operations but will also forward significantly our understanding of communication processes. It makes possible much more effective application of psychological theory to problems of content analysis.[122]

It appears likely that the Illinois Associational Code for Content Analysis was the early spade work for Osgood's work on the "semantic differential" that the CIA covertly funded during the early 1960s through the Society for the Investigation of Human Ecology.

The issue of the community laboratories that were planned to be developed under the HRRI contract is even more mysterious, and perhaps even more disturbing. It is clear from Schramm's comments that the laboratories would be located in U.S. communities, and that two communities in close proximity to the University of Illinois—Paxton and Monticello—were being considered as possible sites. It is also clear that Schramm thought it necessary for the research team to be able to control at least some of the media outlets within the community. One of the arguments put forward for the adoption of educational broadcasting by Schramm and his colleagues at the 1949 Allerton House Seminar on educational broadcasting was that educational broadcasting stations could serve as "pilot plants" in which research would be conducted for the entire broadcasting industry, and it is reasonable to assume that these educational broadcasting stations were considered for use in this HRRI-sponsored propaganda research.[123] Finally, Schramm had no apparent ethical qualms about subjecting communities of unwitting people to experimentation, as evidenced by his endorsement of such experimentation by Fulbright scholars who were to study communications patterns in other countries. Whether or not the information obtained through the experiments conducted in these community laboratories was transferable to U.S. propaganda operations in foreign countries is a debatable issue. Yet, it is clear that such experimentation on U.S. communities would have provided useful information to those agencies interested in finding the means by which to manipulate the people of this country. Unfortunately, the questions raised by these community laboratories are impossible to answer definitively with the information currently available. Still, the issues surrounding these community laboratories remain important considerations when examining the nature of the early research conducted by the institute.

Schramm realized that the massive contract with HRRI amounted "to establishing a kind of annex of HRRI" at Illinois.[124] Yet, Schramm continued to make himself and the institute available to other governmental agencies interested in sharpening their psychological warfare and propaganda skills. In November 1951, the U.S. Army, through their Operations Research Office, asked Schramm to make a second trip to Korea. This Korean mission lasted only 2 weeks, from November 16 to December 5, and was apparently concerned with psychological warfare research similar to that he conducted the year before.[125] The United States Information Agency (USIA) signed a contract with the Institute (Contract 1A-W-362), which culminated in Schramm and Hideya Kumata's *Four Working Papers on Propaganda Theory* in 1955.[126] Also, Schramm wrote his 1954 text *The Process and Effects of Mass Communications* for the USIA, although the precise contractual arrangements between Schramm and the USIA are uncertain.[127] An unspecified amount of contract money was also provided to the institute by the Department of Defense, through its Working Group on Human Behavior of the Research and Development Board, for unspecified research concerning an "analysis of communication principles and data."[128] Like so much of the psychological warfare research Schramm conducted for the State Department and HRRI, the records of the research conducted for the U.S. Army, the United States Information Agency, and the Defense Department remain so fragmented and so sparse that it is impossible to get a complete understanding of just what these research projects entailed and just how much revenue they brought into the institute. Indeed, such incomplete information makes it impossible to be certain that this survey represents a complete list of all such psychological warfare and propaganda research conducted within the institute. Nevertheless, even a partial list, such as this, gives an indication of how pervasive this kind of research was within the institute during its early years.

In late 1977, shortly after the revelation of covert CIA funding of Charles Osgood's research during the early 1960s, UCLA Psychology Professor Patricia Greenfield interviewed Osgood and other professors about the CIA-funded research. Osgood held firm to his position that he was unaware the CIA was behind the "human ecology" funding, and that the CIA did not shape or interfere with his research in any manner. Attempting to trace Osgood's original connection to the Society for the Investigation of Human Ecology, Greenfield wrote:

> Osgood said that he hit upon Human Ecology from a psychologist at Stanford who had been his boss at Illinois; Osgood was then visiting the Center for Advanced Studies in Palo Alto. This person suggested Human Ecology as a source

of funding for cross-cultural research. Osgood learned on seeing the CIA document from his project [CIA document released through the Freedom of Information Act] that the CIA had made a decision to fund his project four to five months before he had submitted a formal proposal or made any contact with Human Ecology.[129]

Had Greenfield or her brother John Marks, author of *The Search for the "Manchurian Candidate,"* been curious enough to find out who this Stanford "psychologist" was, they would have concluded with a minimal amount of research that he was no other than Wilbur Schramm. Having made this discovery, Greenfield and Marks may have been inclined to look into the kind of research that was conducted at the Institute of Communications Research at Illinois while Schramm was Osgood's "boss." What they would have found at that point was an academic department whose early research projects were chiefly in the area of psychological warfare and propaganda. Although they may have been unable to prove definitively that the CIA was responsible for funding the research within the institute during the early 1950s, they would have been able to conclude that the research aims of the institute were in many ways parallel with the social control aspirations of the CIA's MKULTRA program. If nothing else, Greenfield and Marks would have been able to conclude that it was no great mystery why the CIA was interested in the institute's work.

It should be stated again that the case for CIA funding of research at the institute during the early 1950s remains circumstantial. A Freedom of Information Act Request to the Air Force for information concerning the HRRI-contracted research has been denied, on the basis that this information "is no longer a matter of record."[130] Unfortunately, there is no avenue under the Freedom of Information Act by which to appeal a "no finding" decision. Until this information is released, some of the more important questions surrounding the community laboratories, the Illinois Associational Code, and other aspects of this project must continue to remain unanswered. Still, the available evidence strongly suggests that the CIA was behind this research, and that covertly funded CIA research was conducted within the Institute of Communications Research almost 10 years earlier than had been generally known.

The issue of covert CIA funding of research at the institute and at other universities remains an interesting and important consideration. Yet, beyond the issue of CIA funding of research lies the equally compelling consideration of overt military and State Department research. This research, too, went a long way in shaping the paradigm in which so much of the early research in mass communications was carried out. That it was accepted so readily by the University of Illinois and other universities across the United States seems to have confirmed Norman Foerster's fear about the character of the university in the postwar world when he wrote in 1944:

When our young men—and young women—return from the wars, many of them will return to the university. What kind of university will it be then? Will it be a university they remember, unchanged by the most violent storm in human history? Will it be a meaningless prolongation of the wartime university, a university focusing its forces upon the destruction of human beings?[131]

That Foerster's protégé, Wilbur Schramm, could be seen 45 years later as a central figure in establishing "a university focusing its forces upon the destruction of human beings" is a matter of considerable, yet disturbing, irony.

University of Illinois President George Stoddard was forced to resign during the summer of 1953, following a controversy concerning some fraudulent medical research conducted at the university.[132] Wilbur Schramm, who had been brought to the university by Stoddard and who had served as Stoddard's assistant, took a 2-year leave of absence. The National Security Council hired Schramm to direct some undisclosed research projects during 1954, while he was on this leave of absence. Then, in 1955, Schramm was invited to establish the Institute for Communications Research at Stanford University and to serve as its first director, a position he held until his mandatory retirement in 1973.

Although Schramm's tenure at the University of Illinois ended prematurely, his influence on the field of mass communications research was significant during this period. A preliminary analysis such as this one raises important issues relating to the founding of the field. Schramm's early adherence to neohumanism prepared him practically and ideologically for a leadership role in this new research field. Exemplifying the neohumanist ideal of the well-rounded man of action, Schramm was conversant in a number of different disciplines and possessed the ability to communicate with a wide variety of people, making him the natural person to synthesize the diverse elements impacting on mass communications research at mid-century. One can also see how the neohumanist ideal of the hierarchical, aristocratic social order, the emphasis on persuasion, and the belief in an educated elite shaping the opinions of the mass society was reflected in Schramm's research work at Illinois during this period of Cold War.

NOTES

1. Steven H. Chaffee and Everett M. Rogers, "The Establishment of Communication Study in America" in Wilbur Schramm, *The Beginnings of Communication Study in America: A Personal Memoir*, edited by Steven H. Chaffee and Everett M. Rogers (Thousand Oaks, CA: Sage, 1997).

2. George Stoddard to Wilbur Schramm, April 21, 1947, University of Illinois Archives, Institute of Communications Research, Files of the Director, 13/5/1, Box 4, File: Wilbur Schramm Personal, 1947–1949.

3. "Wilbur Schramm, Wrote Many Works on Communications," *The New York Times* (1 January 1988), p. A-10.

4. Martha Miller, "Writers' Workshop Founder Dies at 80," *The Iowa City Press-Citizen* (30 December 1987), p. 12.

5. "Wilbur Schramm," *Illiniweek, 7* (12 January 1988), p. 5.

6. Bob Beyers, "Media Pro Wilbur Schramm Dead at 80," *The Stanford University Campus Report* (6 January 1988), p. 3.

7. Steven H. Chaffee, editor, *Contributions of Wilbur Schramm to Mass Communication Research* (Lexington, KY: Association for Education in Journalism, 1974).

8. Daniel Lerner and Lyle M. Nelson, editors, *Communication Research—A Half-Century Appraisal* (Honolulu: University of Hawaii Press, 1977).

9. See Clarence J. Karier, *Individual, Society and Education: A History of American Educational Ideas* (Urbana: University of Illinois Press, 1986), pp. 301–307.

10. "Registrar's Report—Comparative Summary of Students: Year 1939–40 and Year 1940–41" and "Office of Admissions and Records—Comparative Summary of Students: Years 1947–48 and 1948–49," University of Illinois Archives, Admissions and Records, Statistics, Enrollment Tables 1936–1952, Record 25/3/0/10, Box #2.

11. Erik Barnouw, *A Tower in Babel: A History of Broadcasting in the United States, Volume I—1933* (New York: Oxford University Press, 1966), p. 210.

12. U.S. Bureau of the Census, *Historical Statistics of the United States: Colonial Times to 1970—Part II* (Washington, DC: U.S. Department of Commerce, 1975), p. 796.

13. Memo to (University) President and Provost from Wilbur Schramm, December 20, 1949, University of Illinois Archives, Institute for Communication Research 1947–1952, Files of the Director, Record 13/5/1, Box #7, File: President.

14. U.S. Congress, *National Security Act of 1947—Public Law 253,* 80th Cong., July 26, 1947 (Washington, DC: U.S. Government Printing Office, 1966), p. 1.

15. See, for instance, John Marks, *The Search for the "Manchurian Candidate": The CIA and Mind Control* (New York: New York Times Books, 1979).

16. Irving Babbitt, *Literature and the American College* (New York: Augustus M. Kelley, 1972).

17. Erik Barnouw, *A Tower Babel: A History of Broadcasting in the United States, Volume I—1933* (New York: Oxford University Press, 1966), p. 287.

18. Elizabeth Schramm, "Early Years," in *Communication Research—A Half-Century Appraisal,* edited by Daniel Lerner and Lyle M. Nelson (Honolulu: University of Hawaii Press, 1977).

19. Sherwood Anderson, *Winesburg, Ohio* (New York: Penguin, 1976).

20. Elizabeth Schramm, "Early Years," p. 298.

21. Miller, "Writers' Workshop Founder Dies at 80." Jacqueline Marie Cartier claimed that Schramm's stutter was the consequence of a botched tonsillectomy. Jacqueline Marie Cartier, "Wilbur Schramm and the Beginnings of American Communication Theory: A History of Ideas," (Ph.D. Dissertation: University of Iowa, 1988), p. 59.

22. "A Confidential and Shameless Biography of Wilbur Schramm," University of Iowa Archives, Wilbur Schramm Vertical File.

23. Charles Calmer, "The Many Sides of Wilbur Schramm," *Playbill, 66* (April 1987), p. 18.

24. Miller, "Writers' Workshop Founder Dies at 80."

25. Steve Wilbers, *The Iowa Writers' Workshop: Origins, Emergence & Growth* (Iowa City: University of Iowa Press, 1980).

26. *There were Giants in the Earth in Those Days,* speech given by Wilbur Schramm at the University of Iowa on April 14, 1981. University of Iowa Archives, Wilbur Schramm Vertical File.

27. For an insightful discussion of this movement, see Clarence J. Karier, *Individual, Society and Education: A History of American Educational Ideas* (Urbana: University of Illinois Press, 1986).

28. J. David Hoeveler, Jr., *The New Humanism: A Critique of Modern America 1900–1940* (Charlottesville: University of Virginia, 1977).

29. In 1977, Schramm was still trying to disassociate himself from Foerster. He wrote: "I never bought Foerster's ideas. My mentor at Harvard had been Whitehead, not Babbitt. I had

grown up studying too much science and social science on the one hand, and with too much interest in the anatomy of self-expression of art on the other." Where and when Schramm studied so much science and social science remains a mystery, because his record indicates no such study in the sciences. Wilbur Schramm to Steve Wilbers, March 10, 1977, University of Iowa Archives, Workshop Correspondence with Steve Wilbers.

30. As quoted in Wilbers, *The Iowa Writers' Workshop*, p. 72.

31. Frederick A. G. Beck, *Greek Education: 450–350 B.C.* (New York: Barnes and Nobel, 1964), p. 257.

32. Karier, *The Individual, Society and Education*, p. 188.

33. As quoted in Karier, *The Individual, Society and Education*, p. 189.

34. Ibid., pp. 189–193.

35. Ernest Becker, *Beyond Alienation: A Philosophy of Education for the Crisis of Democracy* (New York: George Braziller, 1967), p. 11.

36. Ibid., p. 203.

37. Wilbur L. Schramm, *Studies in the Longer Narrative Verse of America, 1775–1860* (Ph.D. dissertation, University of Iowa, 1932).

38. Wilbur L. Schramm, *Approaches to a Science of English Verse* (Iowa City: University of Iowa, 1935).

39. Norman Foerster, *American Poetry and Prose* (Boston: Houghton Mifflin, 1934).

40. Wilbers, *The Iowa Writers' Workshop*.

41. Norman Foerster et al., editors, *Literary Scholarship: Its Aims and Methods* (Chapel Hill: University of North Carolina Press, 1941).

42. Babbitt, *Literature and the American College*, and Norman Foerster, *The American Scholar* (Port Washington, NY: Kennikat, 1929).

43. Foerster et al., *Literary Scholarship*, pp. 179–180.

44. Ibid., pp. 177–178.

45. Wilbers, *The Iowa Writers Workshop*, p. 73

46. Wilbur Schramm, "There Were Giants in the Earth Those Days," p. 5.

47. Wilbur L. Schramm, *The Story Workshop* (Boston: Little, Brown, 1938), p. 159.

48. Wallace Stegner to the author, March 9, 1988.

49. Wilbur Schramm to Archibald MacLeish, December 15, 1941, University of Iowa Archives, Wilbur Schramm Vertical File.

50. Ibid., p. 3.

51. Wilbur Schramm, "Memorandum to Mr. Rich, Mr. Bell, others interested," Date 1/31/42, Subject: First recommendations toward an informational program for universities, colleges, schools and affiliated groups." The National Archives, Record Group 208, OWI, OFF, Subject File, 1942 (E-7) Box 45, Wilbur p. Schramm.

52. Ibid., p. 1.

53. Ibid., p. 3.

54. Ibid., p. 6.

55. Ibid., p. 7.

56. Ibid., p. 17.

57. Ibid., p. 16.

58. Ibid., p. 9.

59. Ibid., p. 17.

60. It is important to note that educational institutions were to become primary targets for CIA infiltration and control throughout the 1950s and 1960s. Indeed, the CIA was the major source of funding for the National Student Association throughout this period, and the CIA has covertly funded the activities of the National Educational Association, The Congress for Cultural Freedom, and other organizations. Also, the recruitment of university faculty has been, and continues to be, a routine CIA practice. See, for instance, Sol Stern, "A Short Ac-

count of International Student Politics & the Cold War with Particular Reference to the NSA, CIA, Etc.," *Ramparts, 5* (March 1967), pp. 29–39; "CIA Secret Financing of Private Groups Disclosed," *Congressional Quarterly Almanac,* 1967, 90th Cong., 1st Session, Vol. 23 (Washington, DC: Congressional Quarterly Service, 1967), p. 358. And the U.S. Congress, Senate, Select Committee to Study Governmental Operations with respect to Intelligence Activities, *Foreign and Military Intelligence—Book I,* 94th Cong. (Washington, DC: U.S. Government Printing Office, 1976), pp. 179–203.

61. Schramm's influence on the development of educational broadcasting in the United States was significant. In 1949 and 1950, he organized the Allerton House Seminars on educational broadcasting, which brought together those individuals who would be responsible for the development of educational broadcasting in the 1950s, and which led to the Federal Communication Commission reserving 209 television stations for educational broadcasting in 1951. For a discussion of Schramm's influence during this period, see Timothy Glander, "The Battle for the Minds of Men: Wilbur Schramm at the University of Illinois, 1947–1953," Archibald O. Anderson Library, University of Illinois, 1988. It is also important to note that Schramm retained an interest in educational broadcasting throughout his career by publishing, among others, the following works: Wilbur Schramm, editor, *The Impact of Educational Television* (Urbana: University of Illinois Press, 1960); Wilbur Schramm, editor, *Educational Television: The Next Ten Years* (Stanford, CA: Institute for Communications Research, Stanford University, 1962); Wilbur Schramm, Jack Lyle, and Ithiel de Sola Pool, *The People Look at Educational Television* (Stanford, CA: Stanford University Press, 1963); Wilbur Schramm, *The Audiences of Educational Television: A Report to NET* (Stanford, CA: Institute for Communications Research, Stanford University, 1967); Wilbur Schramm and Lyle M. Nelson, *The Financing of Public Television* (Aspen, CO: Institute for Humanistic Studies and the Academy for Educational Development, 1972).

62. Schramm, "Memorandum to Mr. Rich, Mr. Bell, others interested . . . ," p. 12.

63. Robert J. Blakely, *To Serve the Public Interest: Educational Television in the United States* (Syracuse, NY: Syracuse University Press, 1974), pp. 9–10.

64. Schramm, "Memorandum to Mr. Rich, Mr. Bell, others interested . . . ," p. 18.

65. Ibid., p. 19.

66. Calmer, "The Many Sides of Wilbur Schramm," p. 20.

67. For a discussion of some of these movies, see Clayton R. Koppes and Gregory D. Black, *Hollywood Goes to War: How Politics, Profits and Propaganda Shaped World War II Movies* (New York: Free Press, 1987).

68. These stories were also published after the war in Schramm's anthology of short stories. See "The Flying Coffin" and "The Story of Wilbur the Jeep" in Wilbur Schramm, *Windwagon Smith and Other Yarns* (New York: Harcourt, Brace, 1947).

69. Ibid., p. 96.

70. Chaffee, editor, *Contributions of Wilbur Schramm.*

71. Wallace Stegner to the author, March 9, 1988.

72. Norman Foerster to Wilbur Schramm, July 30, 1944, University of Iowa Archives, Norman Foerster Papers.

73. Schramm wrote in 1977: "I should not like to think that there was a break between Norman Foerster and me, although it may have looked that way from the outside. The evidence is against it, because I bought his house—bought at it—when he left Iowa City." Wilbur Schramm to Steve Wilbers, March 10, 1977, University of Iowa Archives, Workshop Correspondence with Steve Wilbers.

74. Lyle M. Nelson, "The Stanford Years," in *Communication Research,* edited by Lerner and Nelson, p. 323.

75. Wilbur Schramm, "Communication After the War," 1945, University of Iowa Archives, Wilbur Schramm Vertical File.

76. Charles Stone, "UI Wouldn't Have Objected to CIA-Sponsored Projects," in *The Daily Illini* (11 November 1977), p. 3.

77. Ibid.

78. Ibid.

79. Robert B. Hudson, "The Illinois Years," in *Communication Research*, edited by Lerner and Nelson, pp. 311–316.

80. Wilbur Schramm, "Annual Report of the Institute of Communications Research" University of Illinois Archives, Institute of Communication Research, Files of the Director, 13/5/1, Box 3, File: Institute of Communications Research, Annual Reports.

81. Wilbur Schramm, "A Plan for the Institute of Communications Research at the University of Illinois," 1, University of Illinois Archives, Institute of Communications Research, Files of the Director, 13/5/1, Box 3, File: Institute of Communications Research Plans, 1947.

82. Ibid., p. 9.

83. The documentation listing all research revenues at the institute during Schramm's tenure has not been located. Nevertheless, it is clear that the military-related contracts provided a substantial source of institute income. In 1952, Schramm wrote that he was in charge of "a quarter million dollars annually of government research." See Wilbur Schramm to Hugh B. Masters and Dr. Robert G. Van Dyn, August 15, 1952, University of Illinois Archives, Institute of Communications Research, Files of the Director, 13/5/1, Box 8, Vertical File: K–1952. Yet, the total expenses for all the subdivisions of the College of Communications, including the library school, Allerton house, the school of journalism, and others, were only $807,220. University of Illinois, *Transactions of the Board of Trustees, 1952–1954* (Urbana: University of Illinois, 1954), p. 1001.

84. "Communications and Inter-Continental Warfare," University of Illinois Archives, Institute of Communications Research, Files of the Director, 13/5/1 Box 1, File: Inter-Continental Warfare.

85. Wilbur Schramm to Donald E. Dickenson, April 21, 1948, University of Illinois Archives, Institute of Communications Research, Files of the Director, 13/5/1, Box 4, File Research Project Radio News Broadcasts, 1948.

86. Thomas W. Harrell, Donald E. Brown, and Wilbur Schramm, "Memory in Radio Listening," *Journal of Applied Psychology, 33* (June 1949), pp. 265–273.

87. Ibid., p. 265. Harrell, Brown, and Schramm wrote:

Questions of practical importance have arisen in the field of radio involving the extent to which a listener is able to remember what he hears on a newscast. The newscaster is anxious to know how tightly he can "pack" his newscasts—how many stories he can put into a given time without giving his audience more than they can absorb. Beyond that, he wants to know the effect on memory of repetition within the newscast. He is interested in what kinds of subject matter and what treatments of those are remembered better than others. He would like to know whether his audience listens for "index words," whether it remembers names and details, whether it remembers items far removed in locale as well as it remembers items originating nearby. Finally, he would like to know, if possible, what kinds of items discriminate least between good memories and poor memories, and therefore, so far as the factor of memory is concerned, are mass materials for a mass medium.

88. Ibid., p. 274.

89. Wilbur Schramm to Edward Barrett, September 7, 1950, University of Illinois Archives, Institute of Communications Research, Files of the Director, 13/5/1, Box 1, File B.

90. See "Edward Barrett Named to Succeed George Allen as Assistant Secretary for Secretary for Public Affairs," in *UNESCO National Commission News, 3* (February 1950), pp. 1, 6. For a discussion of Barrett's involvement in domestic propaganda, see Bob Spiegleman, "A Tale of Two Memos," *Covert Action Information Bulletin, 31* (Winter 1989), pp. 71–74.

91. Wilbur Schramm to Edward Barrett, September 7, 1950.

92. Ibid.

93. Ibid.

94. Wilbur Schramm to Edward Barrett, November 28, 1950, University of Illinois Archives, Institute of Communications Research, Files of the Director, 13/5/1, Box 8, File B., p. 1.

95. Ibid., p. 1.

96. Ibid., p. 3.

97. Ibid., p. 2.

98. Ibid., p. 2.

99. Ibid., p. 3.

100. Ibid., p. 5.

101. Ibid., p. 6.

102. Wilbur Schramm to C. C. DeLong, June 12, 1952, University of Illinois Archives, Institute of Communications Research, Files of the Director, 13/5/1, Box 8, File, D.

103. General George C. Kenny to General Hoyt S. Vandenberg, October 16, 1950, University of Illinois Archives, Institute of Communications Research, Files of the Director, 13/5/1, Box 5, File: Air Force * Korean Mission Business.

104. John W. Riley and Wilbur Schramm, *The Reds Take a City: The Communist Occupation of Seoul* (New Brunswick, NJ: Rutgers University Press, 1951); J. W. Riley and Wilbur Schramm, "Communication in the Sovietized State, as Demonstrated in Korea," *American Sociological Review, 16* (December 1951), pp. 757–766; J. W. Riley, Wilbur Schramm, and F. W. Williams, "Flight from Communism: A Report on Korean Refugees," *Public Opinion Quarterly, 15* (Summer 1951), pp. 274–284.

105. In his foreword to the book, Fred Williams dramatically wrote:

This is not a book to be read through at one sitting, extraordinary as such advice may sound for the story is too provocative. Put it down after each chapter and think of the three months capsuled here. Think of three days in the life of any of these Korea men and women — or their compatriots whose life they represent for you. Put this book down occasionally and think of three minutes, the three seconds, which meant life to the one who is telling the story and, so often, death to others. Reflect well upon the bitterness, the indignity, and the inhumanity of the communist leaders of aggression and their misled followers.

Riley and Schramm, *Reds Take A City,* pp. VII–VIII.

106. "The Human Resources Research Institute: A Brief Statement of Status at the End of the Second Year," prepared for the Fourth Meeting of the Advisory Research Council 6–8 December 1951," University of Illinois Archives, Institute of Communications Research, Files of the Director, 13/5/1, Box 5, File: Air Force Correspondence, 1950–1951.

107. Ibid.

108. For a discussion of Project Revere, see Chapter 3 in this volume.

109. Melvin L. DeFleur and Otto N. Larsen, *The Flow of Information: An Experiment in Mass Communications* (New Brunswick, NJ: Transaction, 1987).

110. DeFleur and Larsen, *The Flow of Information,* pp. IX–X.

111. Ibid., p. X.

112. See John Marks, *The Search for the "Manchurian Candidate."*

113. Albert D. Biderman, *March To Calumny: The Story of American POW's in the Korean War* (New York: Macmillan, 1963), pp. 274–275.

114. The best-known work on the topic of covert CIA funding of biological and behavioral research is John Marks' popular *The Search for the "Manchurian Candidate": The CIA and Mind Control.* This ex-Foreign Service agent wrote a highly readable book that includes many revelations concerning the CIA's MKULTRA program and its relationship to the CIA front organization the Society for the Investigation of Human Ecology. However, Marks failed to consider Monroe's activities prior to his becoming director of the Society for Investigation of Human

Ecology; therefore, Marks failed to scrutinize the research programs Monroe supervised through HRRI.

115. Wilbur Schramm to Ray V. Bowers and Colonel George W. Croker, October 11, 1951, University of Illinois Archives, Institute of Communications Research, Files of the Director, 13/5/1, Box 5, File: Air Force Correspondence, 1950–1951.

116. Wilbur Schramm to Ray Bowers and Fred Williams, March 11, 1951, University of Illinois, Institute of Communications Research, Files of the Director, 13/5/1, Box 5, File: Air Force Correspondence.

117. Ibid., p. 1.

118. Wilbur Schramm to J. W. Albig, Grant Fairbanks, T. W. Harrell, et al., July 19, 1950, University of Illinois Archives, Institute of Communications Research, Files of the Director, 13/5/1, Box 6, File: Institute of Communications Research, 1951–1952.

119. "A Research Proposal to the Human Resources Research Institute—United States Air Force," University of Illinois, October 30, 1951. University of Illinois Archives, Institute of Communication Research, Files of the Director, 13/5/1, Box 5, File: Air Force Correspondence.

120. Ibid., p. 2.

121. University of Illinois, *Transactions of the Board of Trustees, 1952–1954* (Urbana: University of Illinois Press, 1954), pp. 515–516.

122. "HRRI Comments on Illinois Associational Code," University of Illinois Archives, Institute of Communications Research, Files of the Director, 13/5/1, Box 8, File: Illinois Associational Code.

123. One might reasonably suspect that WILL, the educational broadcasting station at the University of Illinois, would have been one station where the research team would have had certain control, because Schramm had handpicked Robert Hudson, his colleague from the Office of War Information, to serve as director of the station.

124. Wilbur Schramm to Ray Bowers and George Croker, October 11, 1951, University of Illinois Archives, Institute of Communications Research, Files of the Director, 13/5/1, Box 5, File: Air Force Correspondence.

125. Wilbur Schramm to George Stoddard, November 12, 1951, University of Illinois Archives, Institute of Communications Research, Files of the Director, 13/5/1, Box 7, File: Operations Research Office.

126. Wilbur Schramm and Hideya Kumata, *Four Working Papers on Propaganda Theory*, written in part with the help of the United States Information Agency, under contract 1A-W-362, between USIA and the Institute of Communications Research (University of Illinois, 1955).

127. Wilbur Schramm, editor, *The Process and Effects of Mass Communications* (Urbana: University of Illinois Press, 1954).

128. Institute of Communications Research Biennial Report, 1949–1950, 1950–1951. University of Illinois Archives, Institute of Communications Research, Files of the Director, 13/5/1, Box 6: File Institute of Communications Research Biennial Report.

129. Patricia Greenfield, "CIA's Behavior Caper," *American Psychological Association Monitor,* 8 (December 1977), p. 11.

130. Robert A. Burlton (Management Analyst, Records Management Branch, Randolph Air Force Base) to the author, November 9, 1988.

131. Norman Foerster, "A University Prepared for Victory," in *The Humanities After the War,* edited by Norman Foerster (Freeport, NY: Books for Libraries Press, 1944), p. 26.

132. For Stoddard's account of this scandal, see George D. Stoddard, *The Pursuit of Education: An Autobiography* (New York: Vantage, 1981).

CHAPTER SIX

The Universe of Discourse
in Which We Grew Up

In contemporary America children must be trained to insatiable
consumption of impulsive *choice and* infinite *variety. These
attributes, once instilled, are converted into cash by advertising
directed at children. It works on the assumption that the claim
that gets into the child's brain box first is most likely to stay there,
and that since in contemporary America children manage parents,
the former's brain box is the antechamber to the brain box of the latter.*
—Jules Henry, 1963[1]

THE TITLE FOR this chapter is borrowed from a 1962 essay by Paul
Goodman (1911–1972), and reworked slightly to identify a crucial intersection of historical and personal meanings. Goodman was speaking in
the present tense about the "general culture as a climate of communication," and frankly asked: "What happens to the language and thought of
young Americans as they grow up toward and through adolescence?"[2] His
prescient response to this question echoed the urgency with which many dissident scholars came to regard the individual and social implications of the
emerging mass society in the postwar period, and his response remains
highly relevant today. Embodied here was not only a sharp critique of the
prevailing "universe of discourse," but also the exceedingly narrow, and ultimately dehumanizing, definition of communication proffered by most
experts in this new field. "Communication" came to be regarded, both in
theory and practice, as the simple transfer and exchange of processed information; increasingly lost, in both the actual operations of the existing
culture and in the dominant academic interpretations, was the view that
genuine communication was a necessary precondition for authentic selfhood and public transcendence.

Although Goodman never wrote a book that focused exclusively on the
mass media, like other critical commentators during this period, the impact
of the media on U.S. cultural life was a constant and recurring theme in
much of his work. Goodman even briefly served as the television critic of *The*

179

New Republic from January through June 1963, although he rarely wrote about the television programming directly, attending instead to the medium's larger social impact.[3] As Taylor Stoehr put it, Goodman "thought the condition of popular arts and news services in America so desperate that by 1964 he was calling it a 'constitutional crisis'—by which he meant that our democracy could no longer claim to be based in the public mores or have its justification in the public good, because of the usurpation of every forum by centralized media overseers."[4] In many ways, Goodman's critique of formal schooling in the United States was based on the schools' inability to act as a countervail to the crushing effects of the mass media. Schools in the 20th-century United States had increasingly become another form of mass communications, standardizing thought and behavior and making it difficult to advance meaning that challenged the monolithic culture: "As our children grow up, the articulate interpretation of their experience, the language and style in which everything is communicated, and the commodities they use, increasingly converge to one interconnected world-view; there are fewer meaningful alternatives."[5]

During the 1950s and early 1960s, Goodman mapped out much of the communication environment that has become commonplace today. He noted the homogenized and standardized worldview that issues from the various mass media that, although swamping in its output, offers little that could be understood to reflect alternative or rival perspectives. Goodman realized that fewer and fewer corporations were owning and controlling the dominant forms of communication in American society.[6] Political thought had been reduced to the administrative details put forth by the two major political parties that essentially agree on all matters of social consequence. Uniform values concerning what is considered successful, respectable, and normal were replicated ad nauseam in the interlocking world of advertising and entertainment. Schools, for Goodman, given their compulsory character in the 20th century, played an especially serious role in this march toward social conformity. The widespread use and acceptance of standardized testing, television, programmed instruction, and machine teaching in schools were merely "formal statements that *everybody apperceives in the same way, with no need for dialogue*."[7] The youth culture fads manufactured by advertisers, although often utilizing expressions of rebellion and freedom from the adult world, actually exerted a pervasive pressure to conform by the accompanying fear of social ostracism for those who are not up on the latest fad. The sheer ubiquity of the mass media, and the unceasing avalanche of images they provided, made it nearly impossible to find the solitude needed to sort things out or the belief in the legitimacy of one's own personal experience, which in turn might make such solitude worthwhile. For children and adolescents, Goodman argued, this represents nothing less than a form of "brainwashing," the components of which are: "(a) a uniform world-view, (b) the absence of any viable alternative, (c) confusion about the relevance of one's own experience and feelings, and (d) a chronic anxiety, so that one clings to the one world-view as the only security."[8]

At the moment when adolescents should be struggling to create a self-identity and to name the world from their unique vantage point and in their own way, they are met with a culture that accepts only the repetition of previously repeated clichés. Embarrassed by the inability to express to others what one is feeling, the adolescent becomes silent and frequently hostile, eventually denying even the existence of these feelings. Such defeated adolescents, wrote Goodman, begin to "identify with what has conquered them, in order to fill the gap with some meaning or other. Once they have made this identification, they feel strong in it, they defend it by every rationalization."[9] Once this introjection is complete, it becomes reasonable to deny the complexity of communication itself and the need for genuine forms of it. Communication is taken to mean little more than the transfer of prepackaged meanings and ideas—sound bites that can be replicated ad infinitum, because everyone knows exactly what they are supposed to mean. "In my opinion," Goodman wrote, "the speech defined in most contemporary communication theory is very like the speech of the defeated adolescents I have been describing. It is not pragmatic, communal, poetic, or heuristic. Its function is largely to report in a processed *lingua franca*."[10] On a mass scale, and in scholarly approaches too, U.S. culture had turned away from an exalted view of language and communication and had settled for a one-dimensional format of discourse that lessened anxiety while encouraging empty speech.[11] This necessarily translated into dangerously superficial purposes for education and literacy: "Society is increasingly taken to be a kind of machine directed by a central will, and in this structure the teaching of English is turned into social engineering. The purpose of learning to read is no longer political freedom, clarification, appreciation, and community, but 'functional literacy,' the ability to follow directions and be employable."[12]

Goodman was quite concerned with what was lost when communication was conceptualized in such a narrow and reductionist way. First, this definition of communication did not recognize the crucial function of speech whereby preverbal thoughts and experiences are given shape; authentic speech is the process by which "a speaker first discovers *what* he is thinking."[13] For Goodman, speaking was essentially the means by which one comes to develop an understanding of oneself and the world; communication needed to be defined to entail this critical pedagogical function. This kind of communication requires a trust of others, but it does not depend on a consensus with others. In fact, such a consensus would presumably obviate the need for speaking, because where consensus exists there is no need to engage in the arduous and meaningful task of making oneself clear to others. Thus, for Goodman, a second important function for authentic speech, which was lost on most postwar communication experts, is to "personally initiat(e) something by launching into an environment that is *unlike* oneself." Finally, Goodman argued that communication needed to be understood as dialogue, in which growth and change are necessary consequences of serious engagement with a subject matter or with others who are "committed to the conversation."[14] Communication could not be appropriately understood, as the new experts maintained, merely as providing information or propaganda in a one-way direction to a generally compliant audience; rather, the very essence of communication required a sense of mutuality and equality not typically found in the bureaucratic and technological dynamics of the mass media.

Of course, Goodman's notion of authentic communication required that certain social and cultural conditions be extant. And it was the loss of these conditions that precipitated the demise of genuine public discourse, as well as the emergence of a reductionist conceptualization of communication, which itself served to legitimate these conditions. Expressing himself in a manner that seemed to belie his argument, Goodman wrote:

> Speech cannot be personal and poetic when there is embarrassment of self-revelation, including revelation to oneself, nor when there is animal diffidence and communal suspicion, shame of exhibition and eccentricity, clinging to social norms. Speech cannot be initiating when the chief social institutions are bureaucratized and pre-determine all procedures and decisions, so that in fact individuals have no power anyway that is useful to express. Speech cannot be exploratory and heuristic when pervasive chronic anxiety keeps people from risking losing themselves in temporary confusion and from relying for help precisely *on* communication, even if the communication is Babel.[15]

Implicit in Goodman's analysis, however, is the recognition that genuine communication could serve to ameliorate the very social conditions that constricted its expression. A full and unfettered inquiry into the meaning and practice of communication might provide the possibility to reconstitute a genuine public discourse, with all the transformative potential such a discourse would entail. Of course, any such inquiry would necessitate a critical examination of those social forces that gave rise to the new field of communications, with its barren and reductionist orientation to human being. Goodman understood that this tendency toward reductionism in academic communication study was "reinforced by government grants and academic appointments, and it controls the pedagogy in primary schools."[16] He wrote, "Speech is increasingly reduced to a code to transfer information for increasingly narrow purposes. Conversely, the expressive part of speech, emptied of meaning and any relation to telling the truth is reduced to ornament or shallow entertainment. . . . Or much worse, it is something to manipulate politically, to create thoughtless collective solidarity. . . . I do not think this situation is the result of a conspiracy, although those who profit by the tide go along with the tide and have a vested interest in it."[17]

Had Goodman the benefit of historical distance with which to examine the rise of communication study, however, he would have been able to extend and deepen his criticism of the dominant perspective of the communications experts during this period. He would have been able to get a more accurate bearing on the funding sources for such study and on the objectives such study sought to achieve. He would have been able to have a greater understanding of how the work of these experts was actively used to stave off a thorough inquiry into communication and deny the effects of the mass media. As I have argued, communication study on university campuses grew essentially out of needs envisioned by national security planners during the Cold War, and its primary objective was to develop the theoretical justifications and practical techniques needed to manage an emerging mass society. There should be no mystery as to why Goodman found the dominant perspective on communication during this period so contracted and oppressive.

Of course, Goodman was not alone in urging a critical analysis of the prevalent conceptualizations of communication during this period, nor was he alone in recognizing the important influence the new mass media had in creating a mass society. Many intellectuals, from a variety of theoretical, disciplinary, and ideological perspectives, voiced their opposition to this mass media and the social and psychological characteristics the media tended to foster.[18] The concern about the emerging mass society was ubiquitous and multifarious, and it could be found in the work of many critical scholars and artists during this time period: Jules Henry, Herbert Marcuse, Erich Fromm, Lewis Mumford, to name just a few.[19] It could also be found in the work of such conservative and liberal scholars such as Dwight MacDonald, Thomas Molnar, T. S. Eliot, Hannah Arendt, and many others.[20] Regardless of ideological perspective, these thinkers shared common concerns about the increasing homogenization, standardization, and bureaucratization of social life; the centralization of power and the rise of a new managerial elite equipped with increasingly sophisticated means of social control; the advent of new technologies that seemed to mesmerize and marginalize human beings; the folding of political debate and metaphysical speculation into administration and technocratic efficiency; the widespread feeling of alienation, powerlessness, and anomie; and the essential irrationality and contradictions that seemed to be at the center of Western culture. Drawing connections between emerging character and psychological patterns with observed transformation in social structure, these thinkers anticipated radically transformed persons, possessed of dangerously ill-considered values, and lacking the critical capacity to understand themselves or their world. Educational ideas and practices were centrally implicated, because from various perspectives education was seen as both furthering and possibly counteracting the development of a mass society.

Historically situated to witness firsthand the vast changes wrought by technological innovation, military expediency, and capitalist values, many writers could find resonance in Lewis Mumford's 1951 image of the new "mass man" who was:

> incapable of choice, incapable of spontaneous, self-directed activities: at best patient, docile, disciplined to monotonous work to an almost pathetic degree, but increasingly irresponsible as his choices become fewer and fewer: finally, a creature governed mainly by his conditioned reflexes—the ideal type desired, if never quite achieved, by the advertising agency and the sales organization of modern business, or by the propaganda office and the planning bureaus of totalitarian and quasi-totalitarian governments.[21]

These writers placed considerable emphasis on the centrality of communication in this development, and several advocated various pedagogical practices to stem this ominous trend. Erich Fromm, in his 1955 text *The Sane Society*, called into question the notion of "consensual validation," which legitimated the dominant view of reality in a mass society. In order for such "consensual validation" to be authentic, it would need to be the outgrowth of discussion by people not alienated from the realities of their world: "The facts, however, are that the modern, alienated individuals has opinions and prejudices but no convictions, has likes and dislikes, but no will. His opinions and prejudices, likes and dislikes, are manipulated in the same way as his taste is, by powerful propaganda machines—which might not be effective were he not already conditioned to such influences by advertising and by his whole alienated way of life."[22] For Fromm, the remedy was to be found in returning to small group discussion and genuine community life:

> In such small groups the issues at stake can be discussed thoroughly, each member can express his ideas, can listen to, and discuss reasonably other arguments. People have personal contact with each other, which makes it more difficult for demagogic and irrational influences to work on their minds. . . . Through the discussion and voting in small face-to-face groups, a good deal of the irrational and abstract character of decision making would disappear, and political problems would become in reality a concern for the citizen.[23]

The factors that fed into the concerns about a mass society during the 1950s and early 1960s were great, and these thinkers pulled from deep and varied intellectual traditions. Classical theory in sociology and social psychology had provided evidence for the emergence of a masslike society whether one consulted Gustav LeBon's *The Crowd*, Ferdinand Tönnies's notion of a shift from a personal and closely knitted *Gemeinschaften* to an increasingly impersonal and industrialized *Gesellschaft*, or Freud's *Group Psychology and the Analysis of the Ego*.[24] Durkheim's notion of anomie increasing during periods of economic prosperity, Weber's articulation of the process of bureaucratization leading to a social order characterized as an "iron cage," Marx's references to alienation and the contradictions inherent in capitalism—all provided theoretical explanations to account for the social and cultural changes observed in the 1950s. In 1959, William Kornhauser argued that two major and disparate intellectual traditions accounted for the fact that the theory of a mass society cut across ideological lines. One view, which Kornhauser referred to as "the aristocratic criticism of mass society," identified a loss of authority in mass society and was premised on "the intellectual defense of elite values against the rise of mass participation." The other view, referred to as "the democratic criticism of mass society," lamented the loss of community and was based on the "intellectual defense of democratic values against the rise of elites bent on total domination." Kornhauser regarded these two views as complementary and sought to pull them together to construct a more general conception: "Mass society is a social system in which elites are readily accessible to influence by non-elites and non-elites are readily available for mobilization by elites."[25]

Early 20th-century community studies also suggested empirical support to the idea of an emerging mass society. As Maurice R. Stein demonstrated in his insightful 1960s study *The Eclipse of the Community*, U.S. community studies—including Robert Park's study of urbanization in Chicago, Helen and Robert Lynd's "Middletown" study of industrialization in Muncie, Indiana, and Lloyd Warner's "Yankee City" study of bureaucratization in Newburyport, Massachusetts—had already displayed that the conditions were present for the formation of a mass society.[26] By 1958, Arthur J. Vidich and Joseph Bensman revealed that the U.S. small town was not, despite the protestations of its inhabitants, isolated from the cultural values of the larger society, but rather was deeply shaped by the centralized organizations and institutions of the mass society.[27]

Writers and artists of all sorts were expressing these views during the postwar period, anxious to draw attention to the increasing centralization and homogenization of the social order and the alienation (and the eventual loss of autonomy) that resulted. Herbert Marcuse spoke of the social forces that attacked the very "inner dimension" of the mind and reduced people to a form of single dimensionality, disarming people of even the awareness of possible alternatives to the status quo.[28] Many people found compelling Vance Packard's critical exposé on advertising technique, *The Hidden Persuaders*, which remained on *The New York Times* best-seller list for a year.[29] Jules Henry noted how the contradictions inherent in U.S. capitalism were manifest in an omnipresent advertising system that promoted values antithetical to human life, especially with respect to the education and enculturation of children. By 1964, Betty Friedan critically examined the dominant mass-media stereotype of women as "happy housewife heroine," which had deleterious effects on selfhood and cut deeply into the social and economic advances women had made earlier in the century.[30] Even such a hopeful observer of media change as Marshall McLuhan wrote darkly of the new "Mass Man": "When man lives in an electric environment his nature is transformed and his private identity is merged with a corporate whole."[31] In various ways, these intellectuals were arguing that the mass media had a significant social and psychological impact, and that, taken as a whole, this was leading to the creation of a mass society.

C. WRIGHT MILLS, THE MASS SOCIETY, AND THE RISE OF PSYCHOLOGICAL ILLITERACY

Perhaps the strongest articulation of the theory of an emerging mass society, resulting from the historical transformation of communication, can be found in the work of C. Wright Mills (1916–1962). Mills argued that the transformation of a community of publics to a mass society was "one of the keys to the social and psychological meaning of modern life in America."[32] Mills offered his most thorough analysis of this in chapter 13 of *The Power Elite*, entitled "The Mass Society."[33] This pivotal chapter is a slight reworking of a 1954 essay entitled "Mass Society and Liberal Education," which Mills wrote for the Center for the Study of Liberal Education for Adults, and it expresses a clear purpose for education given the kind of social and psychological changes Mills described.[34] Here, Mills detailed the rise of "psychological illiteracy," which he thought was increasingly manifest as U.S. society shifted from a community of publics to a mass society.

In Deweyan fashion, Mills pointed out that human experience is essentially problematic: All human beings face personal troubles and problems. We learn when we confront these problems, understand the true meaning and source of these problems, and endeavor to solve these problems. However, this is possible only when social organization provides the avenues by which these problems can be clearly identified and solved. When social organization does not allow for the articulation and examination of real problems, a kind of psychological illiteracy develops; people are frustrated by problems but find no means to clarify the meaning of those problems or understand their origins. For Mills, then, a psychologically illiterate person lacks the ability to understand the problems in which he or she is engulfed; psychological illiterate people do not have a clear view of themselves or the social world in which they live.[35]

According to Mills, the primary factor in the transformation of the community of publics to the mass society, and the rise of psychological illiteracy, is the mass media of communication:

In a community of publics, discussion is the ascendant means of communication, and the mass media, if they exist, simply enlarge and animate discussion, linking one primary public with the discussions of another. In a mass society, the dominant type of communication is the formal media, and the publics become mere media markets: all those exposed to the contents of the mass media.[36]

Although we continue to talk about public opinion being the outgrowth of autonomous discussion, as "the result of each man's having thought things out for himself and contributing his voice to the great chorus," in reality public opinion is manufactured by people in power, through the use of increasingly sophisticated persuasion and propaganda techniques, as well as newer communication technologies that invade privacy and "encroach upon the small-scale discussion, and destroy the chance for the reasonable and leisurely human interchange of opinion."[37] Mills referred to four central dimensions which distinguish a democratic community of publics from a mass society:

1. In a community of publics, there are as many people who speak as there are those who listen; people are more or less able to formulate opinions based on their own personal experience and to share and debate these opinions with others, many of whom are personally known. In a mass society, a few people are in a position to speak to many million nameless and faceless people and to legitimate a certain view of reality.

2. In a community of publics, people have the opportunity to "immediately and effectively . . . answer back any opinion expressed in public." In a mass society, on the other hand, there is virtually no way for people to respond immediately and effectively to the opinions provided through the dominant communication outlets.

3. In a community of publics, effective action follows from discussion and debate, whereas in a mass society, "the realization of opinion in action is controlled by authorities who organize and control the channels of such action."

4. In a community of publics, no instituted authority infiltrates and aims to control public discussion and debate. In a mass society, secret police, agent provocateurs, and informers are used to harass, blackball, and intimidate people who might otherwise consider speaking out.[38]

Mills acknowledged that the decline of the public and the rise of the mass society was, to a considerable extent, the consequence of forces largely beyond anyone's control. Nevertheless, the mass media has enabled the power elite to increasingly control, manipulate, and manage public opinion, fostering psychological illiteracy and shaping, among other things, our standards of reality, our self-identity, and diminishing our sense of political belongingness. This occurs because the mass media is "organized around stereotypes" by the power elite, and these stereotypes displace direct, personal events of experience as being the most significant way in which people encounter the world. Therefore, the mass media, with the power elite at the controls, works to entrench a psychological disposition in mass society that "is not attuned to the development of the human being. It is the formula of a pseudo-world which the media invent and sustain."[39] The stereotypes embodied in the mass media instill in people a predisposition or bias toward that content to which they are exposed: "People tend strongly to select those media with which they already agree. There is a kind of selection of new opinions on the basis of prior opinions."[40] Because there is no genuine competition among different media, all mass media seem to embody the same general content, with only slight variation. The only hope of resisting the homogenizing effects of the mass media, and the psychological illiteracy that they foster, is through an interpretation of the "experience of meanings"—the process of uprooting stereotypes so "that an individual sees things freshly in an unstereotyped manner."[41]

Mills' conceptualizations of the community of publics and the mass society are, of course, Weberian "ideal types"; they have not existed anywhere at any time in pure form. Nevertheless, they provide a valuable means of understanding the major social and psychological changes that have transpired in the United States. Yet, it is clearly the case that Mills was no relativist or neutral observer in his analysis here; the democratic ideal of the community of publics is more conducive to the positive development of human beings than the mass society. The community of publics is premised on the belief that people can understand their worlds with sufficient reason to actually address the problems with which they are confronted. Mills wrote:

> The knowledgeable man in the genuine public is able to turn his personal troubles into social issues, to see their relevance for his community and his community's relevance for them. He understands that what he thinks and feels as personal troubles are very often not only that but problems shared by others and indeed not subject to solution by any one individual but only by modifications of the structure of the groups in which he lives and sometimes the structure of the entire society.[42]

This, however, is precisely what a psychologically illiterate person in a mass society is unable to do. As a passive consumer of television or radio fare, such a person in the mass society is not in a position either to articulate clearly the source of his or her troubles and anxieties, nor to determine whether these troubles are shared by others and perhaps have structural relevancy. Although the mass media provide a glut of information and news about the world:

They do not often enable the listener or the viewer truly to connect his daily life with these larger realities. They do not connect the information they provide on public issues with the troubles felt by the individual. They do not increase rational insight into tensions, either those in the individual or those of the society which are reflected in the individual. On the contrary, they distract him and obscure his chance to understand himself or his world, by fastening his attention upon artificial frenzies that are resolved within the program framework, usually by violent action or by what is called humor.[43]

Psychologically illiterate persons cannot transcend their personal milieu; they are unable to get a view of the larger structure of society, nor to understand how this structure shapes their life experiences. The ultimate consequence of the rise of psychological illiteracy in a mass society is that people will continue to be mired in problems for which they have little hope for resolution.

Educational institutions, from Mills' perspective, were subordinate institutions that, in the 20th century, have been used primarily to provide vocational training and indoctrinate nationalist loyalties. Understood as such, educational institutions were best regarded as simply another mass medium. However, Mills did not preclude the possibility that educational institutions could be "hospitable frameworks" for political debate. As such, "the task of liberal education would be: to keep the public from being overwhelmed; to help produce the disciplined and informed mind that cannot be overwhelmed; to help develop the bold and sensible individual that cannot be sunk by the burdens of mass life."[44] Mills was not optimistic about the likelihood of educational institutions averting this trend toward psychological illiteracy and the mass society, although he continued to sound a warning up until his death in 1962. "Above all," he wrote in 1956, "we must recognize that 'the common sense' of our children is going to be less the result of any firm social tradition than of the stereotypes carried by the mass media to which they are now so fully exposed. They are the first generation to be so exposed."[45]

It is interesting to note that Mills' concept of psychological illiteracy closely paralleled his views of mainstream U.S. sociology, which from his perspective was largely reductionistic, ahistorical, and pedantic. Like the "knowledgeable man in the genuine public," the systematic social scientist must possess a transcendent view of the social order. As such, the social scientist must recognize the absolute centrality of history in social inquiry. In a fundamental statement on the importance of history in understanding human being, Mills wrote:

Social science deals with problems of biography, of history, and of their interactions within social structures. . . . The problems of our time—which now include the problem of man's very nature—cannot be stated adequately without consistent practice of the view that history is the shank of social study, and

recognition of the need to develop further a psychology of man that is socio-
logically grounded and historically relevant. Without use of history and without an historical sense of psychological matters, the social scientist cannot adequately state the kinds of problems that ought now to be the orienting points
of his studies.[46]

This is a central and recurring theme in Mills' work; it is at the very cornerstone of what he defined as the sociological imagination, and it provides
the basis by which he began to explicate this notion of the mass society and
"psychological illiteracy." Human beings cannot be adequately understood
independent of the social roles they play within modulating institutions and
social structures. Historical forces of great magnitude transform these institutions and social structures and, in turn, transform the external biographies and internal psychological characteristics of human beings. The pe-
rennial objective for the social scientist, as it is for the truly *human* human
being, is to have a deepened awareness of this relationship, and, as far as
possible, to guide it in a rational and purposeful way.

However, it is clear that Mills thought that many social scientists were not
up to this task. Moreover, Mills was aware that mainstream U.S. social scientists were increasingly becoming servants to the power elite by developing
the propaganda techniques and theoretical justifications necessary to control the mass society. These social scientists, interestingly and predictably
enough, also disputed the claims relative to an emerging mass society.

WILLIAM W. BIDDLE AND THE
PROGRAM OF COMMUNITY DYNAMICS

There were other voices in the land, however, and one can observe an alternative purpose for sociological and educational inquiry in the work of William W. Biddle (1900–1971). Biddle established the Program of Community Dynamics (PCD) in 1947 at tiny Earlham College in Indiana to specifically address some of the conditions that Mills and others were describing.
Framed as a reaction to the social disintegration, alienation, and apathy accompanying the transformation of a community of publics to a mass society,
among the purposes of the PCD was to encourage community development
and to reinvigorate civic participation by engaging students in the confrontation of genuine problems in their communities. Through this problem-
posing approach, Biddle sought to connect liberal education with a thoroughly democratic sociology, which, in addition to providing the means by
which real human problems might be solved, aimed to offer "a realistic way
both for developing better citizens and for teaching teachers of citizenship."[47] Moreover, one of the apparent consequences of the PCD was that it
fostered better citizenship among participating college faculty by compel-

ling them to translate their theoretical knowledge into forms that were bound closely to authentic human needs.

Although the PCD ended in 1960, Biddle wrote vigorously on what he had learned as a participant, including such books as *The Cultivation of Community Leaders: Up From the Grass Roots* (1953), *Growth Toward Freedom: A Challenge for Campus and Community* (1957), *The Community Development Process: The Rediscovery of Local Initiative* (1965), and *Encouraging Community Development: A Training Guide for Local Workers* (1968). In addition, Biddle wrote and published extensive "Annual Reports" for each year of the PCD's 13-year existence.[48] Biddle's program was strongly endorsed by Paul Goodman, who saw it as a "really experimental approach." Goodman explained that the PCD's method was "for the professor and students to go into a problem area, to study with the people involved; they irradiate the problem from within, with such science and understanding as they have, and, in reported cases, solutions have emerged from their participation. Clearly this is both classical progressive education and classical pragmatic sociology."[49]

It was certainly no accident that Biddle's work in democratic community development (or "fundamental education," as he sometimes referred to it) stood in sharp contrast to the more heavily financed research and authoritarian approaches that were dominant at large public and private universities during the Cold War. Educated at Columbia University Teachers College under William Heard Kilpatrick and Goodwin Watson, throughout the 1930s Biddle was a thoughtful and vocal critic of the increasing attempts to manipulate the public through the use of the emerging mass media. In many ways, this criticism of the mass media seems to be a logical precursor to the kinds of activities Biddle promoted in the PCD, and it reveals the significant early influence that progressive social and educational thought had on his thinking. It also appears likely that his lifelong critical approach ensured his marginalization from mainstream U.S. academic life. Indeed, there are strong parallels between Biddle's career and that of Alfred McClung Lee (1906–1992), the Executive Director of the critical Institute for Propaganda Analysis, who shared Biddle's view of the transformative potential of a necessarily normative (and engaged) sociological enterprise, and who was similarly relegated to obscure academic posts and has largely been ignored by historians. Interestingly, like Alfred McClung Lee, who worked very closely with his wife Elizabeth Briant Lee, Biddle often co-authored essays and books with his wife Loureide J. Biddle. Given the legacy of U.S. sexism, however, both women faced even greater discrimination and restricted professional opportunities than did their already marginalized spouses.[50]

Biddle shared with Mills and Dewey a rejection of the authoritarian/top-down approaches to education and communication dominant in both their time and ours, and an endorsement of an educational philosophy that placed high value on the ability to see the relationship between individual experience and the larger social structure. Indeed, as we have seen, it was precisely the inability to discern this relationship that precipitated the confusion, apathy, and lethargy that Dewey and Mills noted. Biddle's PCD at Earlham College in the late 1940s and 1950s was an attempt to construct an educational program that would respond to the educational and social conditions described by Dewey and Mills. Moreover, Biddle's PCD was an effort to reclaim a traditional view of communication and community that was being submerged by both the onslaught of 20th-century electronic communications and an academic and business culture during the Cold War that legitimated (indeed, promoted) this onslaught. Biddle's work in this area was longstanding, and it anticipated his work in the PCD. In his 1932 text *Propaganda and Education* (as we noted in chap. 1), Biddle advocated an educational program that taught students to resist attempts to get them to conform to the values and interests of those in power.

Biddle had spent 15 years developing these ideas (ideas that would become increasingly unpopular during World War II and the Cold War), before fellow Teachers College alumnus and Earlham College President Thomas E. Jones invited him to create the Program of Community Dynamics in 1947.[51] Funded largely by existing college funds and later with a small grant from the Lilly Endowment, Inc., Biddle sought to utilize the PCD to put into practice those progressive educational and social ideas that would address the larger structural forces curtailing the democratic impulse.[52] In his 1953 book *The Cultivation of Community Leaders,* Biddle wrote:

> The technical devices of communication provided by modern invention make broadcasting possible to ever larger audiences of passive recipients. The rediscovery and development of individuals strong enough to mature democracy call for invention of social devices and skills to match the technical gadgets. As long as we deal with huge masses of people in attempting to influence change, the persuasive efforts will tend to reduce men and women to a passive and irresponsible role. The persuadee will develop more and more that characteristic frustration which grows from the feeling of being a pawn in a game played by others, who make the real decisions. The social devices which can rediscover the individual must be found in the smaller group. Hence the importance of perfecting the face-to-face meeting in community, in industry, in situations of conflict, as an instrument for promoting growth of personality.[53]

In keeping with this progressive/pragmatic temper, Biddle refused to establish in advance the likely activities and procedures of the PCD, wishing instead for the PCD to be a natural outgrowth of the learning provided by the circumstances in the communities in which the students and faculty were engaged. Likewise, Biddle consistently rejected any practice that even hinted at absolutism, authoritarianism, or elitism. Nevertheless, Biddle did attempt to prioritize the educational objectives to be sought by the PCD, allowing this list of priorities to expand and to be further shaped by the PCD participants.

   Biddle initially sought to situate the PCD within the liberal arts tradition of Earlham College, and to play off the strengths that a small liberal arts college could provide. "Earlham College is a liberal arts institution," he declared in his first annual report. "Any program it develops should fit into that function."[54] Biddle, therefore, made it clear that the first priority for the PCD would be to meet the educational needs of the Earlham students as they were envisioned within the liberal arts tradition understood to be operative at Earlham.[55] Biddle chose to emphasize the integrative nature of the liberal arts and the potential "liberating" character of these studies when they are realistically applied to the needs of citizens. "The primary purpose of the Community Program therefore, is to provide a better all-round education for students," he wrote. "More specifically, it seeks to develop socially-aware, concerned citizens who have learned some skills in solving the problems in the communities in which they live."[56] However, it became obvious within its second year that the PCD represented educational innovations that raised questions about the very core of the liberal arts at Earlham, and seemed to suggest to Biddle the need to entertain a fundamental revision of the college's curriculum. By the second year, the PCD aimed to be seen as a model by which liberal arts education might be reconceptualized and improved.[57] "Would it be possible," Biddle asked, "to revise a curriculum by calling upon a college to step out of the ivory tower and face the real problems of real people? Would not students be well trained as future citizens in such a process? The experience, though at times disturbing, might prove beneficial also for professors."[58] By the sixth year of the PCD's existence, Biddle thought the experience gleaned might actually suggest a radically new role for small liberal arts colleges in an era of expanding mega-universities. The small liberal arts institutions could actually be seen as bulwarks against the increasing fragmentation of knowledge and experience, although fundamental changes in organization would need to be made.[59]

   If Biddle understood that the primary objective of the PCD was to meet the educational needs of Earlham students, he made clear that an important corollary objective would be to assist communities in solving some of the real problems they faced. In the first annual report of the PCD, Biddle addressed these concerns and indicated the larger contextual circumstances that necessitated such a program:

> Many observers of American life have concluded that democratic participation is diminishing, especially at its point of origin, the small town or neighborhood. Citizens have been depending more upon the lobbying of special interest groups with distant and centralized authority. They have been progressively losing that cooperative self-reliance which is the strength of democracy. A major purpose of the Program of Community Dynamics has been to rediscover the sources of self-reliant democratic action in the daily lives of people, where they live, in communities.[60]

The PCD never asked to be involved in a community or impose itself where it was not wanted. Nor did the PCD identify the problems to be addressed. Once invited, the PCD attempted to act as catalyst for dialogue and to assist in broadening the base of participation and enlarging the range of perspectives on the problems. The goal was to stimulate local responsibility and initiative and then withdraw when it was deemed that a community had made substantial progress toward democratically responding to its circumstances. "Communities should grow as a result of our efforts," Biddle wrote. "We do not pose as experts to be called in to solve people's problems for them. We offer rather those activities of students and faculty which will help a community help itself."[61]

Work with actual communities in the confrontation of real problems itself raised perplexing questions about how people learn (or do not learn) to develop positive social relationships and responsive social institutions. Therefore, a third essential objective of the PCD was to conduct continuous "action research" in human relations, develop and refine the methodology for this type of research, and deepen the PCD participants' awareness of the factors impacting and the principles underlying social practice. "We do not propose to publish monographs on communities or surveys with findings and recommendations," Biddle wrote. "Rather it is our purpose to observe and record human reactions as people (including ourselves) struggle with real-life problems in their natural habitat, the community."[62] Biddle's hope here was for the democratization of social research: "When social research is democratized the scientist comes down from his pedestal of learned aloofness; his subject rises from his abject role of material-under-observation. Together they observe, record, and experiment on the situation that affects both. Both become simultaneously experimenter and guinea pig."[63]

It is important to recognize how sharply Biddle's objectives for the PCD differed from the dominant forms of social science research and education occurring at major research universities (e.g., Schramm's Institute of Communications Research at Illinois or Lazarsfeld's Bureau of Applied Social Research at Columbia) during this period. Here, increasing specialization led to narrowing of interests and the development of a professional bureaucracy in the social sciences that tended to move away from focusing on the problems of real people. Attempting to mimic the quantitative analysis of their colleagues in the physical sciences, these social scientists were inclined to adopt research methodology that was both inaccessible to the public at large and tended to reduce human beings to the level of objects to be manipulated and controlled. This mystification of social phenomena helped to support the elitist assumption that only experts could be relied on to decide the delicate issues of social policy. In order to make certain that expert decisions were heeded, great effort went into developing the techniques by which the critical capacities that might be present in the population could be circumvented. As we have seen, the historical circumstances associated with the Cold War seemed to warrant such an approach, and the widespread funding of the social sciences by the agencies of the national security state made it all possible.

However, beneath the historical context giving form to distinctive social science research paradigms was a pervasive pessimism about the future and a widely held view that people were essentially irrational. The reasons for this are diverse and many (creation of atomic weaponry, psychological "discoveries" about the human condition, demonstrable historical record of rapacious human behavior, etc.), and it is not important to rehearse these reasons here. It *is* important to recognize that Biddle explicitly premised his work on the contradiction of these assumptions, which is to say that Biddle's work with the PCD was animated by a deliberate (but not naive) utopian spirit, and that he argued incessantly in favor of the view that human beings were essentially good and in possession of the creative capacities to solve their problems. A guiding theme of Biddle's PCD was that anyone who assumed the role of community educator must be able to muster this faith in human beings and in the possibility of creating a better world.[64]

Biddle's PCD relied on harnessing the idealism that young people often exhibit during their college years, when many discover that the world does not quite square with the "Pollyanna"-style rhetoric of much of their earlier schooling. This idealism draws students to community service, and compels them to approach the solving of problems with energy and integrity. Biddle realized that it was essential to find ways to sustain this idealism once the initial shock of awareness of injustice was over, and once the arduous and frustrating actual work began. He argued against making enrollment in the PCD compulsory, understanding that such coercion undercut the very civic responsibility and freedom that the PCD was trying to encourage. "The educator who relies upon required learnings or experience to produce the initiative and responsibility, the self-choosing generosity of a free citizen, is foredoomed to failure," he wrote in seventh annual report of the program.[65] The interdepartmental seminar in community dynamics that juniors and seniors took in conjunction with the PCD's community work also followed this noncoercive path. Examinations were not given, and texts were not used. The seminar was oriented around the open discussion of community problems, which in turn determined the resources to be consulted and the disciplinary perspectives to be employed.[66]

The PCD worked on over 25 different community development projects during its 13 years of operation. Some of these projects were short term, existing for only a single school year, whereas others developed a variety of components over several years. These included the creation of a recreation center for adolescents in Williamsburg, Indiana; the organization of a community council that tried to address racism in North Richmond, Indiana; the development of a variety of different kinds of community-motivated surveys in several different Indiana communities; and environmental, housing, and transportation projects in both rural and urban areas in Indiana and Kentucky.[67] Biddle received many more requests for assistance from communities than the PCD was able to accommodate. The PCD also had a hand in initiating community development projects in Jamaica, Cuba, and Puerto Rico. The Tanama, Puerto Rico, project began in 1952 and lasted with PCD involvement until 1956, during which time the PCD engaged in substantial work.[68] "The project began with construction of a road," Biddle recalled in 1960. "It was followed by the building of a school, two churches (Catholic and Protestant), improvement in farming practices, and in health and nutrition and in family life, the construction of two community centers, and the formation of a permanent community council which continues active."[69] The educational workcamp was a favorite method of working with both domestic and international communities. In that setting, students, faculty, and community members shared living quarters, and sought to develop dialogue and shared effort around the problems at hand. As Biddle defined it, "the essence of good educational workcamping is neither work nor camping. It is the willingness to share ways of living, to merge their own with dissimilar streams of learning, for a time."[70]

The Program of Community Dynamics faced many challenges during its short years of operation. The communities themselves were unpredictable and fluid, and these realities made long-range planning difficult. Moreover, attempting to tackle systemic, deeply rooted community problems frequently made the PCD unpopular among certain segments of various communities. College politics were a constant source of friction. The interdisciplinary nature of the PCD, as well as its practical orientation, did not provide for an easy fit with a traditional liberal arts college, even one as progressively minded as Earlham. Biddle sensed significant resentment among certain parts of the faculty for the attention the PCD received following its successes. Program evaluation was always a point of contention, too. As well, Biddle worked hard to develop a means of program evaluation that would not undercut the nonquantifiable goals that were the basis of the PCD.[71] Although students absorbed much of the costs associated with their travel and living expenses during educational workcamping, budgetary constraints always needed to be faced. When Landrum Bolling, an Earlham College political scientist, was appointed President of the College in 1959, he decided to discontinue the PCD's activities. Although the official reason given for the program's termination was that Bolling "wished the College to move in other directions," there is some evidence to suggest that personal differences between Biddle and Bolling played a role in ending the PCD.[72] Biddle left Earlham shortly thereafter, although he continued to write, work in community development projects, and serve as a visiting professor at various institutions until his death in 1971.

Biddle's PCD can hardly be seen as a dominant force in shaping recent U.S. educational and social history. The PCD operated on a very small scale by design, and although it attracted some recognition during its years of operation, as with many other progressive educational ventures the memory of its activities soon faded. During its years of operation, the PCD reflected well many of the concerns of those who observed an emerging mass society, and Biddle advocated a practical educational program that many of these observers would have been able to endorse. The curtailment of his program must be understood in light of the critique of the notion of the mass society provided by those more entrenched in mainstream academic sociology and the communication field.

Central to nearly all conceptualizations of the mass society at mid-century, including Biddle's, was recognition of the significance of the new electronic mass media in promoting conformity in thought, values, and behavior. The readily observable success of various advertising campaigns suggested that human experience would become more standard and flat as the content and means of communication became more uniform. Yet, even this basic observation began to wane as the public became more comfortable with these new mass media and were simultaneously reminded of their benefits. The concern about the emerging mass society also began to gradually diminish. And, despite Hannah Arendt's observation in 1960 that the "mass society, whether we like it or not, is going to stay with us into the foreseeable future," within the next 2 decades the critical notion of an emerging mass society increasingly fell out of favor among social observers.[73]

NOTES

1. Jules Henry, *Culture Against Man* (New York: Vintage, 1963), p. 70.

2. Paul Goodman, "The Universe of Discourse in Which they Grow Up," in *Compulsory Mis-Education and the Community of Scholars* (New York: Vintage Books, 1964—originally published in 1962), p. 64.

3. Goodman's view of the medium justified this approach:

Inevitably . . . most serious writing about TV has concerned itself not with what is on the screen, as image or thought, but with the relation of what is so peculiarly on the screen with the forces that act behind the screen and in front of the screen. Criticism exists not in the intellect but in the ratings, and the ratings are of course as unauthentic as the rest of the process. But the institution itself is not unauthentic, it is an historical fact. Thus, writing about TV is not criticism but sociology, economic analysis and political rage.

Paul Goodman, "Sick Beside the Screen," *The New Republic* (8 June 1963), pp. 29–30.

4. Taylor Stoehr, *Format and Anxiety: Paul Goodman Critiques the Mass Media* (Brooklyn, NY: Autonomedia, 1995), p. 13.

5. Paul Goodman, "Don't Disturb the Children," *The New Republic* (16 March 1963), p. 28.

6. This is a trend that has accelerated in recent years, of course, without much coverage in the corporate media obliged to report such news. See Ben H. Bagdikian, *The Media Monopoly*, second edition (Boston, MA: Beacon, 1987).

7. Goodman, "The Universe of Discourse in Which They Grow Up," p. 66. Emphasis in the original.

8. Ibid., p. 67.

9. Ibid., p. 76.

10. Ibid., p. 79.

11. See especially Paul Goodman, *Speaking and Language: Defence of Poetry* (London: Willwood House, 1971), pp. 200–223.

12. Paul Goodman, "The Present Plight of a Man of Letters," in *Criticism and Culture: Papers of the Midwest Modern Language Association*, edited by Sherman Paul (Iowa City: Midwest Modern Language Association, 1972), p. 8. See also Paul Goodman, *New Reformation: Notes of a Neolithic Conservative* (New York: Random House, 1970), p. 120.

13. Goodman, "The Universe of Discourse in Which They Grow Up," p. 78.

14. Ibid., p. 78.

15. Ibid., p. 79.

16. Goodman, "The Present Plight of a Man of Letters," p. 7.

17. Ibid., p. 8.

18. "The sense of radical dehumanization of life which has accompanied events of the past few decades has given rise to the theory of 'mass society,'" Daniel Bell wrote in 1955. "One can say that, Marxism apart, it is probably the most influential social theory in the Western world today." Daniel Bell, "America as a Mass Society: A Critique" in *The End of Ideology: On the Exhaustion of Political Ideas in the Fifties* (Glencoe, IL: Free Press, 1964), p. 21. Bell's essay was originally written for the Congress for Cultural Freedom conference in Milan, Italy, September 1955.

19. See, for instance, Jules Henry, *Culture Against Man* (New York: Vintage, 1963); Erich Fromm, *The Sane Society* (Greenwich, CT: Fawcett, 1955); Herbert Marcuse, *One-Dimensional Man: Studies in the Ideology of Advanced Industrial Society* (Boston: Beacon, 1964); Lewis Mumford, *The Conduct of Life* (New York: Harcourt, Brace, 1951). Anthologies that focused on the implications of the mass society included Maurice R. Stein, Arthur J. Vidich, and David Manning White, editors, *Identity and Anxiety: Survival of the Person in Mass Society* (Glencoe, IL: Free Press, 1960); Bernard Rosenberg and David Manning White, editors, *Mass Culture: The Popular Arts in America* (New York: Free Press, 1956); Philip Olson, editor, *America as a Mass Society: Changing Community and Identity* (New York: Free Press, 1963).

20. See, for instance, Dwight MacDonald, *Against the American Grain: Essays on the Effects of Mass Culture* (New York: Random House, 1962); Thomas Molnar, *The Decline of the Intellectual* (Cleveland: World Publishing Company, 1961); Christopher Brookeman, "T. S. Eliot and Mass Society," in *American Culture and Society Since the 1930s* (New York: Schocken, 1984); Hannah Arendt, *The Origins of Totalitarianism* (New York: Harcourt, Brace, 1951).

21. Mumford, *The Conduct of Life*, p. 16.

22. Fromm, *The Sane Society*, pp. 294–295.

23. Ibid., pp. 296–298.

24. For an excellent treatment of the history of some of the perspectives supporting the idea of the mass society, see E. V. Walter, "'Mass Society': The Late Stages of an Idea," *Social Research, 31* (December 1964), pp. 391–410.

25. William Kornhauser, *The Politics of Mass Society* (New York: Free Press, 1959), pp. 21, 39.

26. Maurice R. Stein, *The Eclipse of the Community: An Interpretation of American Studies* (New York: Harper & Row, 1960).

27. Arthur Vidich and Joseph Bensman, *Small Town in Mass Society* (Princeton, NJ: Princeton University Press, 1958).

28. Herbert Marcuse, *One-Dimensional Man*.

29. Vance Packard, *The Hidden Persuaders* (New York: David McKay, 1957); Richard Severo, "Vance Packard, 82, Challenger of Consumerism, Dies," *The New York Times* (13 December 1996), p. B16.

30. Betty Friedan, *The Feminine Mystique* (New York: Dell, 1964).

31. As quoted in Neil Postman, *Teaching as a Conserving Activity* (New York: Dell, 1979), p. 81.

32. C. Wright Mills, *The Power Elite* (New York: Oxford University Press, 1956), p. 300.

33. Mills, *The Power Elite*, pp. 298–324.

34. C. Wright Mills, "Mass Society and Liberal Education," in *Power, Politics and People: The Collected Essays of C. Wright Mills,* edited by Irving Louis Horowitz (New York: Oxford University Press, 1963), pp. 353–373. It is interesting to note that Mills used the term *technological illiteracy* instead of *psychological illiteracy* in this earlier essay, perhaps wanting to emphasize the impact of communication technologies.

35. For an insightful discussion of Mills and the concept of alienation, see Ernest Becker, "Mills' Social Psychology and the Great Historical Convergence on the Problem of Alienation," in *The New Sociology: Essays in Social Science and Social Theory in Honor of C. Wright Mills,* edited by Irving Louis Horowitz (New York: Oxford University Press, 1964), pp. 108–133.

36. Mills, *The Power Elite*, p. 304.

37. Ibid., pp. 299, 314.

38. Ibid., pp. 302–304.

39. Ibid., p. 314.

40. Ibid., p. 313.

41. Ibid., p. 312.

42. Ibid., p. 318.

43. Ibid., pp. 314–315.

44. Ibid., p. 319.

45. Ibid., p. 313.

46. C. Wright Mills, *The Sociological Imagination* (New York: Oxford University Press, 1959), p. 143.

47. William W. Biddle, "Who Is Qualified to Teach Citizenship," *The Journal of Teacher Education, 2* (September 1951), p. 219.

48. These "Annual Reports," 1948 through 1960, were published as part of the *Earlham College Bulletin* and are available from Earlham College.

49. Paul Goodman, "Utopian Thinking," in *Utopian Thinking and Practical Proposals* (New York: Random House, 1962), pp. 18–19.

50. One exception to this, of course, is John F. Galliher and James M. Galliher's excellent book, *Marginality and Dissent in Twentieth-Century American Sociology: The Case of Elizabeth Briant Lee and Alfred McClung Lee* (Albany: State University of New York Press, 1995).

51. I am indebted to Prof. William Fuson, retired sociologist from Earlham College, for important insight into the circumstances of Biddle's tenure at Earlham. E-mail correspondence from William Fuson, March 14, 1997.

52. As one might expect, the PCD was run on a "shoestring" budget. Apparently, the yearly PCD budget (including salaries, travel expenses, publications, etc.) never exceeded $15,000. Records indicate that in most years the budget was approximately $10,000 or less. See William W. Biddle Papers, Box 19, File: "Budget," Western Historical Manuscript Collection, 23 Ellis Library, University of Missouri at Columbia.

53. William W. Biddle, *The Cultivation of Community Leaders: Up From the Grass Roots* (New York: Harper Brothers, 1953), p. 90.

54. William W. Biddle, "First Annual Report—Program of Community Studies and Dynamics," *Earlham College Bulletin* (Summer 1948), p. 1.

55. Historically, of course, there has been a great range of educational ideas and practices that fall under the term *liberal arts* education, and some of these ideas and practices would be

fundamentally antagonistic to the kind of progressive ideas that Biddle had in mind. For a discussion of some of these traditions, see Bruce A. Kimball, *Orators and Philosophers: The History of the Idea of Liberal Education* (New York: Teachers College Press, 1986).

56. William W. Biddle, "First Annual Report—Program of Community Studies and Dynamics," *Earlham College Bulletin* (Summer 1948), p. 1.

57. William W. Biddle, "Second Annual Report—Program of Community Dynamics," *Earlham College Bulletin* (Summer 1949), p. 2.

58. William W. Biddle, *The Cultivation of Community Leaders: Up From the Grass Roots* (New York: Harper Brothers, 1953), p. 13.

59. In 1953 he wrote:
If these [small, liberal arts] institutions are to find a unique purpose, they must call upon their faculties to work together to discover and to pursue some central themes. Professors will find it necessary to abandon the effort to operate each academic department as though it were a separate college of a university. They may find it necessary to revise their teaching methods, type of research and relationships to each other, to students, and to citizens of nearby communities. Such unique purposes can be found only as faculties are willing to hammer out such objectives cooperatively. The cannot be imposed by administrative fiat.
William W. Biddle, "Sixth Annual Report—Program of Community Dynamics," *Earlham College Bulletin* (Fall 1953), p. 3.

60. William W. Biddle, "First Annual Report—Program of Community Studies and Dynamics," *Earlham College Bulletin* (Summer 1948), pp. 2–3.

61. William W. Biddle, "Second Annual Report—Program of Community Dynamics," *Earlham College Bulletin* (Summer 1949), p. 2.

62. Ibid., p. 3.

63. William W. Biddle, *The Cultivation of Community Leaders: Up From the Grass Roots* (New York: Harper Brothers, 1953), p. 136.

64. As he wrote in 1957:
Those who lack faith in people are antagonistic to or weak in support of democratic processes. Such opposition is not limited to outright dictators; it is found also in authoritarian persons who use all manner of devices to gain citizen acquiescence to decisions already made. A community educator uses as much skill to awaken citizen desire for improvement of community and of people. He finds support for his faith in persons out of experience with the way in which they grow when adequately stimulated. He needs enough faith in the ultimate competence of citizens to induce and sustain a self-choosing process of growth.
William W. Biddle, "Adult Development: Some Guidelines for Community Educators," *Earlham College Bulletin* (Fall 1957), p. 9.

65. William W. Biddle, "The Citizen in Training: Seventh Annual Report—Program of Community Dynamics," *Earlham College Bulletin* (Fall 1954), p. 19.

66. "Earlham Inspires Civic Pride," *The Indianapolis Star Magazine* (4 June 1950), pp. 4–8. The article is located in with William W. Biddle Papers, Box 19, File: "Community Dynamics of Earlham College," Western Historical Manuscript Collection, 23 Ellis Library, University of Missouri at Columbia.

67. Biddle summarized these various projects in his final annual report. See William W. Biddle, "The Community Dynamics Experiment: An Interpretation of a Social Process," Program of Community Dynamics—Twelfth Annual Report, *Earlham College Bulletin* (Winter 1960).

68. For an in-depth analysis of the Tanama, Puerto Rico, project, see William W. Biddle, "A Pattern of Fundamental Education," *Earlham College Bulletin* (Winter 1955–56), pp. 9–21.

69. William W. Biddle, "The Community Dynamics Experiment: An Interpretation of a Social Process," Program of Community Dynamics—Twelfth Annual Report, *Earlham College Bulletin* (Winter 1960), p. 30.

70. William W. Biddle, *Growth Toward Freedom: A Challenge for Campus and Community* (New York: Harper & Brothers, 1957), p. 105.

71. See William W. Biddle Papers, "Proposal For Evaluation of the Program of Community Dynamics—4/10/54" Box 19, File: "Community Dynamics of Earlham College," Western Historical Manuscript Collection, 23 Ellis Library, University of Missouri at Columbia.

72. William W. Biddle, The Community Dynamics Experiment: An Interpretation of a Social Process," Program of Community Dynamics, Twelfth Annual Report, *Earlham College Bulletin* (Winter 1960), p. 38. In one interesting 1958 exchange, Biddle reviewed a proposal for a possible PCD project in Kenya, apparently anonymously submitted by Bolling. Biddle did not mince words in his evaluation of the proposal, calling it "unimaginative" and stating that "the writer of the proposal gives no indication of understanding present trends in adult education." Bolling admitted several days later that he was the author of the proposal. It is not clear whether Biddle knew this all along. See "Letter to Landrum Bolling May 21, 1958" and "Letter to William W. Biddle, May 26, 1958," William W. Biddle Papers, Box 19, File: "Interdepartmental Correspondence," Western Historical Manuscript Collection, 23 Ellis Library, University of Missouri at Columbia.

73. Hannah Arendt, "Society and Culture," *Daedalus, 89* (Spring 1960), p. 278.

CHAPTER SEVEN

Conclusion

"TV is a problem only if you've forgotten how to look and listen,"
Murray said. "My students and I discuss this all the time. They're
beginning to feel they ought to turn against the medium, exactly as
an earlier generation turned against their parents and their country.
I tell them they have to learn to look as children again.
Root out content. Find the codes and messages. . . ."
 —Don DeLillo, *White Noise*, 1984[1]

BY THE EARLY 1950s, television had begun to make deep inroads into all facets of U.S. life, changing political discourse, leisure patterns, and social behavior in ways that could not have been fully predicted. Although most people in the United States came quickly and uncritically to accept this new communications device as simply one of among many new technological innovations available for their enjoyment, other more thoughtful citizens realized that television represented nothing less than "the most important instrument for cultural change developed in the last half-century,"[2] capable of exerting tremendous influence on the very formation of human consciousness. As early as 1951, *The New York Times* reported that "one thought receiving wide expression" about the effects of television "was that the politician of tomorrow must become an 'actor' and that a premium might be placed on personality rather than competence."[3] That same year, *The New York Times* attributed a sharp decline in attendance at local community meetings around the country to the growth of television.[4] Parents and educators were worried about the effects of television on learning and literacy, as well as the role violent television shows played in creating youngsters who were emotionally disturbed and aggressive. Many people were alarmed to discover in the early 1950s that, in some parts of the country where sufficient programming existed, "children in households owning TV *spend as much time looking at video as they do in school*"[5] (emphasis in the original). Still other people were worried about the passivity, conformity, and consumerism that the medium seemed to engender. Despite the rapid growth of television during the 1950s, there existed significant concern about the larger social, cultural, educational, and political effects of television.

The criticism of television in the 1950s in many ways paralleled the criticism of radio and motion pictures that took place between the two world wars, except for two highly important and closely related historical circumstances. First, largely absent from the general public's criticism of television at mid-century was the concern over television as a means of propaganda. The critical ability to recognize television as a vehicle for propaganda, as radio and film had been recognized a generation earlier, seemed to be lost on many people during the 1950s (with some notable exceptions, as mentioned in chap. 6). According to one writer, Maurice B. Mitchell, in 1957, the average person "was not conscious of the growing army of people who were learning to use these media to motivate him, influence him, change his way of living, change his attitudes, his thinking, his cultural level, his beliefs and indeed his very personality."[6] The propaganda debate of the 1920s and 1930s had died due to factors relating to World War II, and although the term *propaganda* continued to conjure up images of nefarious activity, the people of the 1950s seemed less able to recognize and deal with it. Invoking comparisons that may have seemed extreme in 1957 but are quite appropriate 40 years later, Mitchell wrote:

> The average person had a vague understanding of what propaganda was and how it might be employed but, in the United States at least, he was under the general impression that this was something usually used by dictators on captive populations and that it was nothing he had to worry about. It did not occur to him that these instruments of communication might constitute a force far more powerful than any atom bomb or any other physical instrument that man could envision.[7]

This inability to see television as a propaganda vehicle was in part the result of the common belief that television possessed some special properties that made it immune to being used as a tool of deception. This was John Steinbeck's view, for instance, when he argued that Senator Joseph McCarthy's exposure on television was an important contributing factor in his eventual demise.[8] But this inability to recognize television as a propaganda device was closely related to the second important historical circumstance that differentiated the criticism of television in the 1950s from the criticism of the other mass media between the two world wars. This was, of course, the institutionalization of communication study on university campuses at mid-century, and the concomitant rise of the mass communications "expert" who appeared to possess the talents by which to judge and evaluate the "effects" of various mass media. As we have seen, the development of mass communications research was closely tied to the semantic transformation of the term *propaganda*. Out of the propaganda debate of the 1920s and 1930s emerged the view—among propagandists and social scientists who both viewed propaganda as necessary and who provided the propagandist with scientific insight—that the term *propaganda* had come to possess such negative implications that it was rendered unusable as a description for their vocation. Although continuing to engage in the same activity of mass persuasion, propagandists and the social scientists who assisted them opted for a series of more neutral-sounding terms to describe their work, the most common being *mass communications*. This semantic shift from *propaganda* to *mass communications* successfully shielded the growing army of mass communications researchers from the criticisms of such attempts at mass persuasion that were rife throughout U.S. society during the first part of the 20th century.

Although the belief in the functional necessity of propaganda existed in the culture before World War II, the war seemed to legitimize the work of these mass communications researchers. On the domestic scene, the conduct of a large-scale, modern, technological war required that great masses of people willingly accept the policy decisions of their leaders. On the foreign front, the war demanded the careful creation and coordination of mass opinion against both enemy and allied nations. In either case, it was this growing army of mass communications researchers who provided the technical knowledge needed for these operations. In addition to legitimizing the ideology of social control that undergirded their work, the construction of propaganda organizations during World War II provided an important training ground for mass communications researchers, as well as facilitated personal contacts among like-minded researchers. When the war ended and the extended period of Cold War began, it became clear that the expertise of these mass communications researchers was equally important in the conduct of this highly ideological Cold War. Mass communications research units were established on university campuses throughout the United States during this period, and these units greatly profited from the needs of the national security apparatus to control and shape opinions about foreign and domestic policy.

The individuals who led in the founding of mass communications research came from varied disciplinary backgrounds: Schramm, the literary humanist; Lazarsfeld, the mathematician; Berelson, the librarian; Dodd, the intelligence tester; and Cantril, Hovland, and Stanton, the psychologists. Nevertheless, as they coalesced around the field certain shared views could be discerned. Without exception, these researchers were interested in the mass media in terms of how they could be utilized most effectively in shaping the opinions of the mass society. Although World War II and the Cold War provided the climate in which their research could thrive, these researchers brought with them prior ideological commitments that fit comfortably with this type of research. The seeds of Lazarsfeld's interest in propaganda could be seen in his early attempt in Vienna to create effective propaganda for the socialist cause; Schramm's interest in propaganda could be seen in his early adherence to neohumanism with its elitist orientation and emphasis on persuasion. And although the researchers brought varying degrees of commitment to the Cold War—Schramm, for instance, was certainly a more committed Cold War warrior than was Lazarsfeld—these researchers shared a common vision about the importance of keeping the subjects of their research unaware of the objectives behind the research. This was true whether one considered the false reasons Stanton gave for the device he attached to radio receivers during his dissertation project, or Lazarsfeld and Cantril's attempts to develop surreptitious methods of interviewing people, or Schramm's plans to establish and run secret experiments through "community laboratories." Although one rationale for this secrecy was that subject foreknowledge would invalidate research results, another rationale for it was based on the realization that many people would not participate in such studies if they were aware of the research objectives. In either case, a view of human beings as objects to be manipulated emerges, one that does not treat human beings as capable of deciding things for themselves. Also, it should be noted that such a methodological emphasis on secrecy dovetailed nicely with the needs for secrecy of the growing national security apparatus for which these mass communications researchers increasingly worked.

It might seem surprising, then, that these mass communications researchers could be seen as legitimate experts on the social, political, cultural, and educational effects of television by the 1950s. They certainly had no particular insight into such larger issues of the effects of the mass media, and in fact had worked to perfect these mass media as a means of social control. And yet, these mass communications researchers, having been established on university campuses in the postwar period, were seen as experts who could speak with authority on the larger issues relating to television. Lazarsfeld, for instance, was called before the Hendrickson-Kefauver Congressional subcommittee investigating juvenile delinquency in 1955, to speak about the effects that television violence had on children. In 1961, Schramm headed what was to that date the largest study of television's effects on children. Tantamount to having the fox guard the chicken coop, Lazarsfeld and Schramm successfully deflected much of the criticism of television that was taking shape in the 1950s and early 1960s. Lazarsfeld explained to the Hendrickson-Kefauver subcommittee that television violence might indeed have a cumulative effect on children, but that research was not available to either prove or disprove this claim. However, he used the opportunity before the Congressional subcommittee to make his argument for greater national funding of research on television's effect on children:

> I do not want to make an invidious comparison, but we certainly would not have an atomic bomb today if the development had been merely left to Ph.D. dissertations. I don't think we exactly need a Los Alamos Laboratory to study the effects of television, but we need, if it is an urgent social problem, then some central planning and central organization, and some pressure; some priority has to be put on it.[9]

Lazarsfeld urged the subcommittee to consider making National Science Foundation funds, or perhaps a White House conference, available for extensive research on the effects of television on children. It should be obvious that Lazarsfeld and his peer mass communications researchers would be the ones to profit from such arrangements, as Willard J. Rowland pointed out in his book *The Politics of TV Violence.* "The subcommittee was apparently heavily influenced by Lazarsfeld's testimony," Rowland wrote, "and it adopted these recommendations as part of its interim report."[10] Yet, Lazarsfeld's testimony went beyond simply helping to provide another source of revenue for mass communications researchers; it also helped to make it appear that questions concerning television were so complex that they were better left to experts. The testimony implied that it was not parents and educators who should be the ones to decide whether television was a negative or positive influence on children, but instead experts, with their advanced statistical and sampling techniques. That Lazarsfeld had spent his career attempting to develop advertising techniques for industry, and propaganda techniques for the national security apparatus, apparently did not bother the Hendrickson-Kefauver subcommittee.

Schramm went further still in defending television against the criticism of parents and educators in the early 1960s, who were concerned about the negative influence television was having on children. Through his massive study of television's effects on children, *Television in the Lives of Our Children* (which was funded by the Ford Foundation), Schramm was able to effectively quiet much of the criticism of television. If his conclusions were a bit ambiguous they must have permitted many parents and educators to put their worst nightmares about television to rest: "For some children, under some conditions, some television is harmful. For other children under the same conditions, or for the same children under other conditions, it may be beneficial. For most children, under most conditions, most television is probably neither harmful nor particularly beneficial."[11]

The casual reader of this report would most likely not have been aware of the ideological perspective concerning the role of the mass media that was informing Schramm's work concerning television's effects on children or, for that matter, in his extensive work in advocating for the benefits of programmed instruction.[12] Nor would they have been aware of the close ties Schramm had developed with the national security apparatus, which possessed a vested interest in seeing that the mass media were utilized and understood in particular ways. Schramm, like Lazarsfeld and their other colleagues in mass communications research, had as his primary concern the development of ways in which the mass media could be utilized to effect changes in opinions and behaviors.

At the precise historical moment when a critical perspective on television was *most* needed, those individuals who came to speak with *most* authority on the subject were those mass communications researchers who were *most* interested in using it as a propaganda device. It is little wonder why they chose to defuse criticism of the medium, and thus ensured that people kept watching. This is one important legacy of the institutionalization of mass communications research at mid-century. People still remain largely unable to hold the medium of television up for adequate inspection, or to understand the powerful ways in which it is used to shape and control their thinking.

Another important legacy concerns the way in which mass communications research was used to call into question the critical notion of an emerging mass society, which many scholars were describing during this period. If the notion of a mass society represented a prevalent conceptualization during this period, it was also a highly contested idea, particularly among those Cold War intellectuals who saw as one of their primary tasks the defense of U.S. society and "way of life" from any significant criticism. Writing for the CIA's Congress for Cultural Freedom, Daniel Bell scoffed at the idea: "The theory [of a mass society] is central to the thinking of the principal aristocratic, Catholic, or Existentialist critics of modern society. These critics . . . have been concerned less with the general conditions of freedom in society than with the freedom of the *person* and with the possibility, for some few persons of achieving a sense of individual self in our mechanized society."[13] Bell went on to explain that the theory of the mass society was premised on romanticized and idealized view of the past and that it "overlooks the human capacity for adaptiveness and creativeness, for ingenuity in shaping new social forms."[14] "The theory of the mass society," Bell concluded, "no longer serves as a description of Western society but as an ideology of romantic protest against contemporary life."[15]

Edward Shils, also heavily involved in the CIA's Congress for Cultural Freedom, was even more vocal in his condemnation of the view, calling it "an untruthful picture of Western society of recent decades," a view that "has cognitive and ethical overtones which are repugnant to me."[16] Shils argued that increased educational attainment and modern communication technologies, including radio and television, had "spread the culture which was once confined to a narrow circle at the center over a far greater radius."[17] Contrary to the claims made by the critics of the mass society, Shils maintained that there is:

> within the mass society, more of a sense of attachment to the society as a whole, more sense of affinity with one's fellows, more openness to understanding, and more reaching out of understanding among men, than in any earlier society of our Western history or in any of the great Oriental societies of the past. The mass society is not the most peaceful or "orderly" society that has ever existed; but it is the most consensual.[18]

Shils had stressed a key point about the mass society in this essay, an essay that Lewis Mumford pointed out "flatly contradicts" his own view; the mass society was, indeed, understood to be a society characterized by a high degree of consensus.[19] From Dewey to Mills to Biddle, however, it was precisely this notion of consensus that remained problematic to those who envisioned an emerging mass society, and it sat squarely at the center of their critique of U.S. society at mid-century. How was one to regard the nature of consensus that prevailed? On what basis and in whose interests was consensus achieved? On what basis was this consent being given, and what conditions must be present in order to legitimate this consent? These were, of course, the traditional philosophical questions about the nature of consent in a democratic society, although these were the very questions that the Cold War intellectuals refrained from posing. Instead, as media historian Daniel J. Czitrom pointed out, these Cold War intellectuals sought to debunk the notion of mass society by providing "empirical evidence" gleaned from the newly instituted field of mass communications research.[20] Ironically, as we have seen, much of this mass communications research was itself the by-product of propaganda and psychological warfare work conducted for the U.S. national security apparatus.

At the center of the critique of the notion of an emerging mass society was the famed "dominant paradigm" in mass communications research, the conceptualization of the "two-step flow of mass communications." Although one can locate expressions of this conceptualization as early as the 1930s, it is generally understood that in Paul Lazarsfeld and Elihu Katz's 1955 text *Personal Influence*, the "two-step flow" was given its most extensive academic articulation.[21] As was noted in chapter 4 (this volume), the conceptualization of the "two-step flow of mass communications," or the dominant paradigm of "personal influence," refers to an approach to propaganda and mass persuasion that aims to identify and target "opinion leaders" in various communities, who then more or less unwittingly influence other people by whom they are respected. The consequence or "effect" of the propaganda is considered to be indirect—the larger society becomes persuaded through the personal influence of the opinion leaders and not directly by the propaganda. Because of their social status, educational attainment, or personality traits, opinion leaders are able to exert influence in those social contexts where their perspective and opinion is highly regarded. The goal of the propagandist, given this view, is to develop effective ways to both identify and persuade these opinion leaders. The opinion leaders are regarded as the central conduit by which social conformity and consensus might be achieved. The two-step flow is essentially a practical technique to be used by the propagandist to create uniformity in thinking and behaving; it is not a theoretical understanding about the social and individual impact of the mass media as such.

C. Wright Mills had a particularly advantageous position to observe the development of and rationale for the two-step flow conceptualization. While at Columbia University in the 1950s, he crossed paths with Paul Lazarsfeld, the founder and director of the Bureau of Applied Social Research (BASR) and the chair of the sociology department. As a young sociologist, Mills actually conducted some of the field work for Lazarsfeld's *Personal Influence* during the early 1950s.[22] But Mills became increasingly critical of Lazarsfeld and the bureau's activities by the time he wrote *The Power Elite*. The mass media of communications were "among the most important of these increased means of power now at the disposal of elites of wealth and power," he wrote. "Some of the higher agents of these media are themselves either among the elites or very important among their servants." Without mentioning Lazarsfeld explicitly, Mills went on: "Alongside or just below the elite, there is the propagandist, the publicity expert, the public relations man, who would control the very formation of public opinion in order to be able to include it as one more pacified item in the calculation of effective power, increased prestige, more secure wealth."[23] After discussing how the propagandist had had to change his approach to meet the growing distrust of the population, Mills implicated Lazarsfeld's *Personal Influence* as a book central to the work of propagandists, but again did not mention Lazarsfeld's name. Mills understood, perhaps more clearly than anyone else, the objectives behind the two-step flow of communications—the conceptualization of personal influence—on which Lazarsfeld worked so diligently to perfect. The propagandists, Mills wrote, had learned "to accept the principle of social context."

> To change opinion and activity, they say to one another, we must pay close attention to the full context and lives of the people to be managed. Along with mass persuasion, we must somehow use *personal influence;* we must reach people in their life context and through other people, their daily associates, those whom they trust: we must get at them by some kind of 'personal' persuasion. We must not show our hand directly; rather than merely advise or command, we must manipulate. (emphasis added)[24]

Mills' position at Columbia gave him an insider's view of the kind of work that was being conducted within the bureau. It is unfortunate that Mills did not name Lazarsfeld directly, because much subsequent confusion about the nature of Lazarsfeld's work, and about the field of mass communications research generally, might have been avoided. Still, Mills' observation that propagandists had become concerned with personal persuasion and personal influence in a social context was a clear allusion to Lazarsfeld's *Personal Influence*.

And yet, it is only a secret to historians of mass communications research that Lazarsfeld and Katz's 1955 text *Personal Influence* was essentially an attempt to refine the means by which propaganda could be aimed at opinion leaders; these historians continue to argue that *Personal Influence* represented an attempt to understand the larger social effects of the mass media.[25] Nevertheless, the evidence is overwhelmingly against this view. Propagandist (and Freud's nephew) Edward L. Bernays thought that Lazarsfeld had stolen the idea of the opinion leader from him, although Lazarsfeld argued that he had given this notion a new twist by maintaining that opinion leaders could be found in all social strata and not just within the educated class, as Bernays had maintained.[26] Lazarsfeld himself spoke freely of the commercial and ideological applications of the two-step flow of communications research.[27] And the United States Information Agency, among other organizations, noted the idea's practical utility and trained USIA officers how to locate these opinion leaders and devise ways to influence them.[28] Like other work Lazarsfeld and the bureau conducted for commercial and governmental organizations, the dominant paradigm of personal influence had its origins and reason for existence in the applied needs of the propagandist.

There can be no doubt about the value of the two-step flow of communications conceptualization to the applied needs of the propagandists. But Cold War intellectuals also used the conceptualization of the two-step flow of communications to argue that those who envisioned an emerging mass society had placed too much emphasis on the power of the mass media. If, as the two-step flow conceptualization suggests, mass media influence is not direct, then claims about the mass media's influence are overwrought. In addition, if social context remains a central variable in determining how mass media messages are interpreted and received, then the claims of about the degradation of the community and the individual are also overstated. In 1961, Leon Bramson, a chief exponent of this view, defended the mass media as follows:

> Now to the extent that mass communications research has revealed the existence and the importance of intermediary groups between the media and the "masses," it has also undermined this concept of manipulatability as following from the atomization and isolation of the individuals who compose the mass. So that evidence which contradicts the one image will also contradict the other. . . . Where previously there had been a widespread belief in the omnipotence of the media, now several studies and even some "armchair" research indicated that this was misleading.[29]

Similarly, Alice and Raymond Bauer, in an essay that made wide use of the "evidence" suggested by the two-step flow conceptualization, wrote in 1960 that:

> The accumulated evidence of communication research challenges sharply three premises that underlie, either implicitly or explicitly, the model of communications still held by the "critics of the mass society" and which have been abandoned by the researchers: (1) that informal communications play a minor role, if any, in modern society; (2) that the audience of mass communication is a "mass" in the sense of being socially "atomized"; (3) that content and effect can be equated.[30]

Now it is true, as Daniel Czitrom claimed, that the view of the "theory of a mass society" presented by Bramson, Bell, the Bauers, and others, was something of an "intellectual strawman"—"an artificial and spurious construct."[31] "Only the most stark and grotesque version of the mass society argument would claim that primary relationships disappear," wrote Brandeis University sociologist E. V. Walter. "The important question is not whether primary groups exist or whether they flourish in mass society, but rather what their orientation and function tend to be; whether they are autonomous or dependent; whether they provide conditions of freedom or become auxiliary engines for the forces of mass society."[32] Today this remains an especially important question to raise about the function and orientation of schools and other subordinate institutions. Beyond these concerns, however, an examination of the Cold War intellectuals' critique of the mass society argument provides a glimpse at the multiply deceptive ways mass communications research has been used to sustain a dominant view of communications in our society—a view in which a propaganda technique itself is used to explain the larger social impact of the mass media, and the propagandist is regarded as the expert on how the mass media are to be understood. An analysis of this situation, therefore, goes a long way in understanding the paradox observed by Todd Gitlin in 1978: "Since the Second World War, as mass media in the United States have become more concentrated in ownership, more centralized in operations, more national in reach, more pervasive in presence, sociological study of the media has been dominated by the theme of the relative powerlessness of the broadcasters."[33]

It is within this Cold War context that the various critical perspectives on the mass media and the mass society were marginalized. C. Wright Mills, for instance, found it increasingly difficult to obtain sources of research funding after he published *The Power Elite* in 1956.[34] In a letter to Lazarsfeld on May 6, 1959, Mills wrote: "The N.S.F [National Science Foundation] has turned down my research proposal. . . . So has the Ford Foundation, the Health Department, and Columbia's own Council of Social Research. The N.S.F. rejection is going to make it tough on half time pay for the sabbatical year but I think I can manage that somehow."[35]

Mills went on to ask Lazarsfeld if he knew where he might find "two or three thousand dollars to hire a part-time secretary." Lazarsfeld's response to Mills does not remain in Lazarsfeld's papers. Nevertheless, it appears that Lazarsfeld, despite having easy access to large research funds, did not go out of his way to help Mills. On July 9, 1959, Mills wrote a second, highly sarcastic letter to Lazarsfeld: "Thanks, anyway for helping me with the money-bags. Never mind, I'll write books in long-hand. And anyway, why the hell *should* you help—what's in it for you?"[36]

The ideological and methodological differences between Mills and Lazarsfeld were well known; yet one suspects that the differences between Mills and Lazarsfeld went well beyond the criticism of Lazarsfeld's "abstracted empiricism" that appeared in Mills' *The Sociological Imagination.* Lazarsfeld could accept this kind of criticism, and in fact he encouraged it by reprinting Mills' methodological critique in an anthology he published several years after Mills' death.[37] What Lazarsfeld may not have been able to accept, however, was criticism that held the very nature of his work up for moral scrutiny, and this is precisely what occurred in Mills' *The Power Elite.* After all, the upshot of Mills' thinly veiled commentary on Lazarsfeld's book *Personal Influence* was that Lazarsfeld's research into propaganda facilitated the development of psychological illiteracy within the context of an emerging mass society.

One might consider Mills an exemplar of the kind of knowledgeable person in a community of publics about whom he wrote, attempting to translate his personal troubles into social issues—to understand the relationship between his personal milieu and the larger social structure. Of course, Mills' milieu was unique and it gave him rare insight into the power elite and mainstream U.S. sociology and communication studies, and the growing relationship between them during this period of the Cold War. Mills' personal biography intersects with the history of the United States during a period of enormous social and technological change, and he wrote with great sensitivity about the consequences of many of these changes. Yet, he was marginalized for doing so. A study of his marginalization may tell us much about the social and academic worlds we have inherited.

This kind of study would necessarily raise additional questions and issues, some of which may provide important and fruitful directions for future research. One such question concerns the larger impact that Schramm, Lazarsfeld, and other mass communications researchers had on popular conceptions of democracy and education in the postwar period. For instance, Berelson's conceptualization of the necessity of an apathetic citizenry for the efficient functioning of a democracy might be understood in light of the educational model, associated with mass communications research, that equates learning with mere exposure to information and its simple recall. Furthermore, the development of educational broadcasting at mid-century —in which Schramm, Lazarsfeld, and other researchers played a decisive role—might be understood, in the context of the perceived ideological needs of the Cold War, as a practical application of the dominant paradigm of the two-step flow of communications. Finally, we might seriously revisit the critical notion of an emerging mass society, which Mills and others saw as central, and raise questions about the relevance of this marginalized idea to our current social predicament. What might a reconsideration of the modernist notion of the mass society offer in terms of how we might approach educational matters?[38] A few tentative observations may be ventured, although one suspects that the implications here are quite limitless.

First, an historical analysis indicates a deep foreboding among educators and other social observers in the 1920s and 1930s about the social and educational consequences of propaganda. Curricular materials that sought to teach students to understand and resist propaganda were created during this interwar period; and although this antipropaganda movement dissolved with the onset of World War II, it might be beneficial to resurrect the temper and perspective that shaped it. It might be advantageous to situate the study of propaganda and advertising as a central focus in schools. Students might be taught to question the accuracy and legitimacy of the messages they hear, read, and see, and to evaluate whether their own best interests coincide with the powerful interests of those who create and distribute these messages. Furthermore, students might be encouraged to raise critical questions as to why some events and some forms of experience are considered mass mediaworthy (whether in news or entertainment or curricula) whereas others are not. Students might be taught to recognize the techniques of the propagandist by studying how they were developed and used in the past.

Existing and emerging communication technology might be held up for legitimate and close scrutiny as to their impact on community and individual consciousness. In 1956, C. Wright Mills pointed out that the social and psychological changes brought about by the mass media were so extensive and subtle that they could not be fully understood by the methods of social research then available. But it was clear to Mills, as it was to many of his contemporaries, that the mass media had not served to democratize the public sphere, did not aid in the fuller development of human beings, and would not, as they were then constituted, enlarge the range of experience and discourse. If the full implications of the mass media were not at that time entirely discernible, the stark general nature of their effects were comprehensible, and serious inquiry and discussion concerning the mass media's likely impact was demanded. Today, these social research methods remain largely underdeveloped and still inadequate to the task of creating an understanding of the social, educational, and psychological implications of the various mass media. Far outpacing the development of this understanding, however, has been the creation of ever-more sophisticated means to persuade, manipulate, and otherwise control the population—get them to buy, vote, and think in ways that others deem necessary. This is entirely to be expected given the pervasive preoccupation with the need for conformity during the Cold War, because the nation's chief intellectual resources in the new field of communication studies were used to that end. An examination of the origins of communication research reveals the way ideological commitments and perceived historical necessity, coupled with extensive funding provided by the national security apparatus, helped to create and sustain narrow and restrictive views of what Wilbur Schramm once accurately called "the fundamental social process."[39] Moreover, the central purpose for this new field of communications consisted essentially of devising techniques of social control.

In addition to asking questions about the differences among print, oral, and visual media, we might ask how mass communications technology could be utilized to advance genuine forms of community life, or whether the one-directionality and inaccessibility of some of this technology actually thwarts the possibility of such a community. If the latter is the case—and if, as Dewey, Mills, Biddle, and others argued, authentic community life was a necessary requisite to individuality and the solving of real problems—how might we act to curtail the tendencies of these mass communications technologies to degrade community and that foster a situation in which systemic social problems are allowed to go unaddressed? Recalling Dewey, Mills, Biddle, and others, we might place special emphasis on the capacity to draw connections between one's individual circumstances and the larger social structure—between one's personal problems and what should be the larger social issues of the day. How might the boredom, apathy, and thoughtlessness of our own age be related to our inability to draw these connections? How might we, by looking through the lenses provided by the critics of the mass society, begin to think of knowledge as both personally and socially relevant and meaningful?

We might well apply the mass society argument to discussions about educational policy, school reform, and the work of teachers. To what degree have educational institutions come to function merely as "auxiliary engines for the forces of mass society," or to what degree have they come to function autonomously and in opposition to the demands of the mass society? Where do the dominant educational issues of the day originate and for what reasons, and how do these educational issues relate to the personal troubles and problems encountered by classroom teachers? How are teachers and schooling portrayed in the mass media, and whose interests are served by this portrayal? How does the notion of the mass society relate to the despair that accompanies almost any discussion of public school reform (except, perhaps, among the naive and those looking to cash in on the reform)? How is the notion of a mass society reflected in the continued centrality of standardized achievement, intelligence, and psychological tests; the dominance of behavior modification techniques in classroom practice; and the prevalence of schools without any clearly discernible educational philosophy or purpose beyond their own efficient administration?

The repercussions of the loss of genuine community life, described by the mass society theorists, are still widely felt even if they are not widely understood. Recent discussion in the mass media has turned to plans to increase community service requirements for students in both secondary schools and colleges, and to emphasize the so-called "civil education."[40] Yet, if this practice is to mean something more than merely requiring students to volunteer their labor to shore up a largely gutted social service infrastructure (if it is to mean something more than a form of punishment, as in being sentenced to so many hours of "community service"), it will need to be rooted in some type of meaningful pedagogical approach. The Program of Community Dynamics, developed by William Biddle 50 years ago to respond to the social and psychological ramifications of a mass society, may still have relevance for us today.

Finally, being centrally an historical "ideal type" or conceptualization, the idea of a mass society would seem to provide countless opportunities for historians to demonstrate that history should be (in Mills' words) "the shank of social study." As an ideal type, the notion of the mass society offers a conceptual mechanism to critically address the relationship between social structure and personal psychology, between historical epoch and individual biography. It was also a widely held idea, the development of which can be situated historically. Although the idea of the mass society was partly an outgrowth of conditions relating to the Cold War, it was also an idea that was significantly contested by the dominant forces waging this war. An historical analysis of the mass society concept, therefore, would compel educational historians to a critical examination of the way in which Cold War forces shaped academic and popular knowledge during this period. In addition to revealing that radically different visions for our social order once existed, such an historical examination would force us to confront the legacy of the Cold War institutions with which we remain saddled.

NOTES

1. Don DeLillo, *White Noise* (New York: Viking-Penguin, 1984), p. 50.

2. Bruce Bliven, "Politics and TV," *Harper's Magazine, 205* (November 1952), p. 27.

3. Jack Gould, "What TV Is Doing to Us," reprinted booklet from *The New York Times* (24 June 1951–30 June 1951), p. 4.

4. Ibid., p. 9.

5. John Houseman, "Battle of Television," *Harper's Magazine, 200* (May 1950), p. 52.

6. Maurice B. Mitchell, "A Forward Look at Communications," in *Britannica Book of the Year 1958,* edited by Walter Yust (Chicago: Encyclopedia Britannica, 1958), p. 52.

7. Ibid., p. 52.

8. John Steinbeck, "How to Tell Good Guys from Bad Guys," *The Reporter, 12* (10 March 1955), pp. 42–45.

9. As quoted in Willard J. Rowland, *The Politics of TV Violence* (Beverly Hills, CA: Sage, 1983), pp. 104–105.

10. Ibid., p. 105.

11. Wilbur Schramm, Jack Lyle, and Edwin B. Parker, *Television in the Lives of Our Children* (Palo Alto, CA: Stanford University Press, 1961), p. 1.

12. See, for instance, Wilbur Schramm, *Programed Instruction: Today and Tomorrow* (New York: The Fund for the Advancement of Education, 1962); Wilbur Schramm, *What is Programed*

Instruction? An Introduction for the Layman (Palo Alto, CA: Stanford University, Institute for Communication Research, 1964); Godwin C. Chu and Wilbur Schramm, *Learning From Television: What the Research Says* (Washington, DC: National Association of Educational Broadcasters, 1967).

13. Daniel Bell, "America as a Mass Society: A Critique," in *The End of Ideology: On the Exhaustion of Political Ideas in the Fifties* (Glencoe, IL: Free Press, 1964), p. 21. For a discussion of the CIA's role in the activities of the Congress for Cultural Freedom, see Christopher Lasch, "The Cultural Cold War: A Short History of the Congress for Cultural Freedom," in *Towards a New Past: Dissenting Essays in American History*, edited by Barton J. Bernstein (New York: Pantheon, Random House, 1968), pp. 322–359.

14. Bell, "America as a Mass Society," p. 27.

15. Ibid., p. 36.

16. Edward Shils, "The Theory of a Mass Society," *Diogenes* (Fall 1962), p. 47. For a sympathetic treatment of the Congress, see Peter G. Coleman, *The Liberal Conspiracy: The Congress for Cultural Freedom and the Struggle for the Mind of Postwar Europe* (New York: Free Press, 1989). For a brief comment on Shils' work with the Congress, see also Philip G. Altbach, "Introduction," to Edward Shils, *Order of Learning: Essays on the Contemporary University*, edited by Philip G. Altbach (New Brunswick, NJ: Transaction, 1997).

17. Edward Shils, "The Theory of a Mass Society," p. 50.

18. Ibid., p. 53.

19. Lewis Mumford, *The Myth of the Machine: The Pentagon of Power* (New York: Harcourt Brace Jovanovich, 1970), p. 463.

20. Daniel J. Czitrom, *Media and the American Mind: From Morse to McLuhan* (Chapel Hill: University of North Carolina Press, 1982).

21. Elihu Katz and Paul F. Lazarsfeld, *Personal Influence: The Part Played by People in the Flow of Mass Communications* (Glencoe, IL: Free Press, 1955).

22. Todd Gitlin, "Media Sociology: The Dominant Paradigm," *Theory and Society, 6* (September 1978), pp. 237–239.

23. C. Wright Mills, *The Power Elite* (New York: Oxford University Press, 1956), p. 315.

24. Ibid., p. 316.

25. See, for instance, Jeffery L. Bineham, "A Historical Account of the Hypodermic Model in Mass Communication," *Communication Monographs, 55* (September 1988), pp. 230–246; Jesse G. Delia "Communication Research: A History," in *Handbook of Communication Science*, edited by Charles R. Berger and Steven Chaffee (Newbury Park, CA: Sage, 1987), pp. 20–98; and most recently, Everett M. Rogers, *A History of Communication Study: A Biographical Approach* (New York: Free Press, Macmillan, 1994).

26. Paul F. Lazarsfeld Oral History Project, Columbia University, The William E. Wiener Oral History Library of the American Jewish Committee (21 February 1975–19 April 1975), pp. 123–124.

27. See, for instance, Paul F. Lazarsfeld, "Some New Advances in the Behavioral Sciences, November 28, 1956," Paul F. Lazarsfeld Papers, Columbia University Archives, Box 20: Subject File L, Folder: Subject File—Lectures (Speeches, Interviews, etc.), #4.

28. See United States Information Agency, "Prestige, Personnel Influence, and Opinion," in *The Process and Effects of Mass Communications,* edited by Wilbur Schramm (Urbana: University of Illinois Press, 1954), pp. 402–410.

29. Leon Bramson, *The Political Context of Sociology* (Princeton, NJ: Princeton University Press, 1961), pp. 108–109.

30. Raymond A. Bauer and Alice H. Bauer, "America, 'Mass Society' and 'Mass Media,'" *The Journal of Social Issues, 26* (1960), p. 13.

31. Czitrom, *Media and the American Mind*, p. 136.

32. E. V. Walter, "'Mass Society': The Late Stages of An Idea," *Social Research, 31* (December 1964), p. 404.

33. Todd Gitlin, "Media Sociology: The Dominant Paradigm," *Theory and Society, 6* (September 1978), p. 205.

34. Barbara Chasin, "C. Wright Mills, Pessimistic Radical," *Sociological Inquiry, 60* (Fall 1990), pp. 337–351.

35. "C. Wright Mills to Dr. Paul F. Lazarsfeld, May 6, 1959," Paul F. Lazarsfeld Papers, Columbia University Archives, Box 15, Subject File: BSS-CH—Columbia University (1), Folder: Departmental.

36. "CWM to Paul, July 9, 1959," Paul F. Lazarsfeld Papers, Columbia University Archives, Box 15, Subject File: BSS-CH—Columbia University (1), Folder: Departmental.

37. C. Wright Mills, "Abstracted Empiricism," in *Qualitative Analysis: Historical and Critical Essays,* edited by Paul F. Lazarsfeld (Boston: Allyn & Bacon, 1972), pp. 428–440.

38. It is important to keep in mind that if the Cold War historical context circumvented the development of more critical perspectives on communication and the mass media, it also oversaw a shift in the very ground where these critical perspectives were traditionally rooted. Mills, for one, was decisively opposed to those social and technological and intellectual currents leading to what he referred to derisively as a "postmodern" world. That we accept and frequently celebrate this postmodernism may tell us much about our lack of historical imagination, and our difficulty in apprehending the possible alternatives that Mills and other critics of the mass society envisioned. Mills also referred to this postmodern period as "The Fourth Epoch," which could be distinguished from the modern world because of the ambiguity surrounding the values of freedom and reason. In this postmodern "Fourth Epoch, increased rationality may not be assumed to make for increased freedom." See C. Wright Mills, *The Sociological Imagination* (New York: Oxford University Press, 1959), p. 167.

39. As quoted in Everett M. Rogers, *A History of Communication Study: A Biographical Approach* (New York: Free Press, 1994), p. 1.

40. See "Plan Adds 'Civil Education' To the Basics of Schooling," *The New York Times* (14 April 1997), p. B8.

Bibliography

Altbach, Philip G. "Introduction." In Edward Shils, *The Order of Learning: Essays on the Contemporary University,* edited by Philip G. Altbach. New Brunswick, NJ: Transaction, 1997.

"The American Fascists." *The New Republic, 98* (8 March 1939), pp. 117–118.

Anderson, Sherwood. *Winesburg, Ohio.* New York: Penguin, 1976.

"Announcement." *Propaganda Analysis: A Bulletin to Help the Intelligent Citizen Detect and Analyze Propaganda,* 1 (October 1937), pp. 1–4.

Arendt, Hannah. *The Origins of Totalitarianism.* New York: Harcourt, Brace, 1951.

———. "Society and Culture." *Daedalus,* 89 (Spring 1960), pp. 278–287.

Aronson, James. *The Press and the Cold War.* New York: Bobbs-Merrill, 1970.

Bagdikian, Ben. *The Media Monopoly.* Boston: Beacon, 1987.

Babbitt, Irving. *Literature and the American College.* New York: Kelley, 1972.

Barnouw, Erik. *A Tower of Babel: A History of Broadcasting in the United States, Volume I—1933.* New York: Oxford University Press, 1966.

———. *The Golden Web: A History of Broadcasting in the United States, Volume II—1933 to 1953.* New York: Oxford University Press, 1968.

———. *The Image Empire: A History of Broadcasting in the United States, Volume III—From 1953.* New York: Oxford University Press, 1970.

Barton, Allen H. "Paul Lazarsfeld and the Invention of the University Institute for Applied Social Research." In *Organizing for Social Research,* edited by Burkart Holzner and Jiri Nehnevajsa, pp. 17–83. Cambridge, MA: Shenkman, 1982.

Barton, Judith S. *Guide to the Bureau of Applied Social Research.* New York: Clearwater, 1984.

Bauer, Raymond A., and Alice H. Bauer. "America, 'Mass Society' and Mass Media," *The Journal of Social Issues, 26* (1960), pp. 3–77.

Beck, Frederick A. G. *Greek Education: 450–350 B.C.* New York: Barnes and Nobel, 1964.

Becker, Ernest. "Mills' Social Psychology and the Great Historical Convergence on the Problem of Alienation." In *The New Sociology: Essays in Social Science and Social Theory in Honor of C. Wright Mills,* edited by Irving Louis Horowitz, pp. 108–133. New York: Oxford University Press, 1964.

———. *Beyond Alienation: A Philosophy of Education for the Crisis of Democracy.* New York: Braziller, 1967.

Beineke, John A. "The Investigation of John Dewey by the FBI." *Educational Theory, 37* (Winter 1987), pp. 43–52.

Bell, Daniel. *The End of Ideology: On the Exhaustion of Political Ideas in the Fifties.* Glencoe, IL: Free Press, 1964.

Berelson, Bernard. *Content Emphasis, Recognition, and Agreement: An Analysis of the Role of Communications in Determining Public Opinion.* Ph.D. Dissertation, University of Chicago, 1941.

———. "The Effects of Print Upon Public Opinion." In *Print, Radio, and Film in a Democracy,* edited by Douglas Waples, pp. 41–65. Chicago: University of Chicago Press, 1942.

220 *Bibliography*

————. *The Library's Public.* New York: Columbia University Press, 1949.

Berelson, Bernard, and Morris Janowitz, editors, *Public Opinion and Communication.* Glencoe, IL: Free Press, 1950.

Berelson, Bernard. *Content Analysis in Communication Research.* Glencoe, IL: Free Press, 1952.

Berelson, Bernard R., Paul F. Lazarsfeld, and William N. McPhee. *Voting: A Study of Opinion Formation in a Presidential Campaign.* Chicago: University of Chicago Press, 1954.

Berelson, Bernard. "The State of Communication Research." *Public Opinion Quarterly, 28* (Spring 1959), pp. 1–17.

Bernays, Edward L. *Propaganda.* Port Washington, NY: Kennikat, 1928.

Beyers, Bob. "Media Pro Wilbur Schramm Dead at 80." *The Stanford University Campus Report, 6* (January 1988), p. 3.

Biddle, William W. "A Psychological Definition of Propaganda." *The Journal of Abnormal and Social Psychology, 26* (October–December 1931), pp. 283–295.

————. *Propaganda and Education.* New York: Bureau of Publications, Teachers College, Columbia University, 1932.

————. "Who Is Qualified to Teach Citizenship." *The Journal of Teacher Education, 2* (September 1951), pp. 219–222.

————. *The Cultivation of Community Leaders: Up From the Grass Roots.* New York: Harper & Brothers, 1953.

————. *Growth Toward Freedom: A Challenge for Campus and Community.* New York: Harper & Brothers, 1957.

————. *The Community Development Process: The Rediscovery of Local Initiative.* New York: Holt, Rinehart & Winston, 1965.

————. Annual Reports of the Program of Community Dynamics, 1–12. *Earlham College Bulletin* (1948–1960). Earlham College, Richmond, IN.

Biddle, William W., and Loureide J. Biddle. *Encouraging Community Development: A Training Guide for Local Workers.* New York: Holt, Rinehart & Winston, 1968.

"Biddle, William Wishart." *Contemporary Authors—Permanent Series.* Edited by Christine Nasso, Vol. 2. Detroit: Gale, 1978.

Biddle, William W. Papers. Western Historical Manuscript Collection—Columbia. University of Missouri/State Historical Society of Missouri.

Biderman, Albert A. *March To Calumny: The Story of American POW's in the Korean War.* New York: Macmillan, 1963.

Bineham, Jeffery L. "A Historical Account of the Hypodermic Model in Mass Communication." *Communication Monographs, 55* (September 1988), pp. 230–246.

Blakely, Robert J. *To Serve the Public Interest: Educational Television in the United States.* Syracuse, NY: Syracuse University Press, 1974.

Bliven, Bruce. "Politics and TV." *Harper's Magazine, 205* (November 1952), p. 27.

Blum, William. *The CIA: A Forgotten History—Global Interventions Since World War 2.* London: Zed, 1986.

Boehm, Eric H. "The 'Free Germans' in Soviet Psychological Warfare." In *A Psychological Warfare Casebook,* edited by William E. Daugherty and Morris Janowitz, pp. 812–821. Baltimore: Johns Hopkins University Press, 1960.

Bowers, Raymond V. "The Military Establishment." In *The Uses of Sociology,* edited by Paul F. Lazarsfeld, William H. Sewell, and Harold L. Wilensky, pp. 234–274. New York: Basic, 1967.

Bramson, Leon. *The Political Context of Sociology.* Princeton, NJ: Princeton University Press, 1961.

Brinkley, Alan. "World War II and American Liberalism." In *The War in American Culture: Society and Consciousness During World War II,* edited by Lewis A. Erenberg and Susan Hirsch, pp. 313–330. Chicago: The University of Chicago Press, 1996.

Brookeman, Christopher. *American Culture and Society Since the 1930s.* New York: Schocken, 1984.

Brown, Roscoe C. E. "The Menace to Journalism." *The North American Review, 214* (November 1921), pp. 610–618.

Calmer, Charles. "The Many Sides of Wilbur Schramm." *Playbill, 66* (April 1987), pp. 18–20.

Cantril, Hadley, and Gordon W. Allport. *The Psychology of Radio.* New York: Harper & Brothers, 1935.

Cantril, Hadley. *The Invasion From Mars.* Princeton, NJ: Princeton University Press, 1947.

———. *The Cantril Report on Plausible Appeals in Psychological Warfare.* Princeton, NJ: The Office of Public Opinion Research, Princeton University, 1952.

———. *The Human Dimension: Experiences in Policy Research.* New Brunswick, NJ: Rutgers University Press, 1967.

———. *Psychology, Humanism, and Scientific Inquiry: The Selected Essays of Hadley Cantril,* edited by Albert H. Cantril. New Brunswick, NJ: Transaction, 1988.

Carey, James W. "The Mass Media and Critical Theory: An American View." In *Communication Yearbook 6,* edited by Michael Burgoon, pp. 18–33. Beverly Hills, CA: Sage, 1982.

"Carl Iver Hovland." *The National Cyclopedia of American Biography.* pp. 263–264. New York: James T. White, 1970.

Carmen, H. J. "Review of Merle Curti's *The Social Ideas of American Educators,*" *Survey, 71* (October 1935), p. 315.

Cartier, Jacqueline Marie. *Wilbur Schramm and the Beginnings of American Communication Theory: A History of Ideas.* Ph.D. Dissertation, University of Iowa, 1988.

Catlin, George E. Gordon. "Propaganda as a Function of Democratic Government." In *Propaganda and Dictatorship: A Collection of Papers,* edited by Harwood Lawrence Childs, pp. 125–145. Princeton, NJ: Princeton University Press, 1936.

"Catlin, George Edward Gordon." *Contemporary Authors—First Revision,* Vol. 13–16, edited by Clare D. Kinsman, pp. 147–148. Detroit: Gale, 1975.

Catton, Jr., William A. "Stuart C. Dodd." In *International Encyclopedia of the Social Sciences,* pp. 147–150. New York: Macmillan–Free Press, 1980.

Chaffee, Steven H., editor. *Contributions of Wilbur Schramm to Mass Communication Research.* Lexington, KY: Association for Education in Journalism, 1974.

Chaffee, Steven H., and Everett M. Rogers. "The Establishment of Communication Study in America." In Wilbur Schramm, *The Beginnings of Communication Study in America: A Personal Memoir,* edited by Steven H. Chaffe and Everett Rogers. Thousand Oaks, CA: Sage, 1997.

Chasin, Barbara. "C. Wright Mills, Pessimistic Radical." *Sociological Inquiry, 60* (Fall 1990), pp. 337–351.

Chomsky, Noam. "A Dialogue with Noam Chomsky." *Harvard Educational Review, 65* (Summer 1995), pp. 127–144.

Chu, Godwin C., and Wilbur Schramm. *Learning from Television: What the Research Says.* Washington, DC: National Association of Educational Broadcasters, 1967.

"CIA Secret Financing of Private Groups Disclosed." *Congressional Quarterly Almanac,* 90th Cong., 1st Sess. 23. Washington, DC: Congressional Quarterly Service, 1967.

CIA v. Sims 108 S.Ct. 1881 (1985).

Clark, Carrol D. "News and Social Control." *American Sociological Society Papers, 29* (August 1935), pp. 128–140.

Cogley, John. *Report on Blacklisting I. —Movies.* New York: Fund for the Republic, 1956.

———. *Report on Blacklisting II. —Radio and Television.* New York: Fund for the Republic, 1956.

Coleman, James S. "Lazarsfeld, Paul Felix." In *Encyclopedia of American Biography,* edited by John A. K. Garraty, pp. 646–647. New York: Harper & Row, 1974.

———. "Paul F. Lazarsfeld: The Substance and Style of His Work." In *Sociological Traditions From Generation to Generation: Glimpses of the American Experience,* edited by Robert K. Merton and Matilda White Riley, pp. 153–174. Norwood, NJ: Ablex, 1980.

Coleman, Peter. *The Liberal Conspiracy: The Congress for Cultural Freedom and the Struggle for Postwar Europe.* New York: Free Press, 1989.

Cremin, Lawrence A. *Popular Education and Its Discontents.* New York: Harper & Row, 1989.

Curti, Merle. *The Social Ideas of American Educators.* Paterson, NJ: Littlefield, Adams, 1963. Originally published in 1935.

Czitrom, Daniel J. *Media and the American Mind: From Morse to McLuhan.* Chapel Hill: University of North Carolina Press, 1982.

Darley, John G. "Psychology and the Office of Naval Research: A Decade of Development." *The American Psychologist, 12* (June 1957), pp. 305–323.

Daugherty, William E., and Morris Janowitz, editors. *A Psychological Warfare Casebook.* Baltimore: Johns Hopkins University Press, 1958.

Daugherty, William E. "Post-World War II Developments." In *A Psychological Warfare Casebook,* edited by William E. Daugherty and Morris Janowitz, pp. 135–145. Baltimore: Johns Hopkins University Press, 1958.

Davis, Elmer. "Report to the President." *Journalism Monograph, 7,* edited by Ronald T. Farrar (August 1968).

DeFleur, Melvin L., and Otto N. Larsen. *The Flow of Information.* New York: Harper & Brothers, 1948.

———. *The Flow of Information: An Experiment in Mass Communications.* New Brunswick, NJ: Transaction, 1987.

DeFleur, Melvin L., and Sandra Ball-Rokeach. *Theories of Mass Communication.* New York: Longman, 1975.

Delia, Jesse G. "Communication Research: A History." In *Handbook of Communication Science,* edited by Charles R. Berger and Steven Chaffee, pp. 20–98. Newbury Park, CA: Sage, 1987.

DeLillo, Don. *White Noise.* New York: Viking/Penguin, 1984.

DeLuca, Tom. *The Two Faces of Political Apathy.* Philadelphia: Temple University Press, 1995.

Dewey, John. "The New Paternalism." *The New Republic, 17* (21 December 1918), pp. 216–217.

———. "Public Opinion." *The New Republic, 30* (3 May 1922), pp. 286–288.

———. *Individualism Old and New.* New York: Capricorn, 1962. Originally published in 1929.

Diamond, Sigmund. *Compromised Campus: The Collaboration of Universities with the Intelligence Community, 1945–1955.* New York: Oxford University Press, 1992.

Dodd, Stuart C. *International Group Mental Tests.* Ph.D. Dissertation, Princeton University, 1926.

———. *Dimensions of Society: A Quantitative Systematics for the Social Sciences.* New York: Macmillan, 1942.

———. "The Religion of the Social Scientist." *Educational Theory, 1* (August 1951), pp. 87–96.

———. "Historic Ideals Operationally Defined." *Public Opinion Quarterly, 15* (Fall 1951), pp. 547–556.

———. "Can the Social Scientist Serve Two Masters?—An Answer Through Experimental Sociology." *Research Studies of the State College of Washington, 21* (September 1953), pp. 195–213.

———. "An Alphabet of Meanings for the Oncoming Revolution in Man's Thinking." *Educational Theory, 9* (July 1959), pp. 174–192.

Dodge, Raymond. "The Psychology of Propaganda." *Religious Education, 15* (October 1920), pp. 241–252.

Doob, Leonard W. *Propaganda: Its Psychology and Technique.* New York: Henry Holt, 1935.

———. "The Utilization of Social Scientists in the Overseas Branch of the Office of War Information." *The American Political Science Review, 41* (August 1947), pp. 649–667.

Dreher, Carl. *Sarnoff: An American Success.* New York: Quadrangle/New York Times Book Company, 1977.

"Earlham Inspires Civic Pride." *The Indianapolis Star Magazine* (4 June 1950), pp. 4–8.

"Edward Barrett Named to Succeed George Allen as Assistant Secretary for Secretary for Public Affairs." *UNESCO National Commission News, 3* (February 1950), pp. 1, 6.

Edwards, Violet. *Group Leader's Guide to Propaganda Analysis.* New York: Institute for Propaganda Analysis, 1938.

Ellis, Elmer, editor. *Education Against Propaganda: Developing Skill in the Use of the Sources of Information about Public Affairs,* Seventh Yearbook. Philadelphia, PA: National Council for the Social Studies, 1937.

Ellul, Jacques. *The Technological Society.* New York: Knopf, 1967.

———. *Propaganda: The Formation of Men's Attitude.* New York: Knopf, 1971.

Englembrecht, H. C., and F. C. Hanighen. *Merchants of Death: A Study of the International Armament Industry.* New York: Dodd, Mead, 1934.

Ewen, Stuart. *PR!: The Social History of Spin.* New York: Basic, 1996.

Fine, Benjamin. "Propaganda Study Instills Skepticism in 1,000,000 Pupils," *The New York Times* (21 February 1991), p. 1A.

Fiske, Marjorie, and Paul F. Lazarsfeld. "The Office of Radio Research: A Division of the Bureau of Applied Social Research, Columbia University." In *How to Conduct Consumer and Opinion Research,* edited by Albert B. Blankenship, pp. 141–146. New York: Harper & Brothers, 1946.

Foerster, Norman. *The American Scholar.* Port Washington, NY: Kennikat, 1929.

———, editor. *American Poetry and Prose.* Boston: Houghton Mifflin, 1934.

———. "A University Prepared for Victory." In *The Humanities After the War,* edited by Norman Foerster, pp. 26–31. Freeport, NY: Books for Libraries Press, 1944.

Foerster, Norman, John C. McGalliard, Rene Wellek, Austin Warren, and Wilbur Schramm, editors. *Literary Scholarship: Its Aims and Methods.* Chapel Hill: University of North Carolina Press, 1941.

Foerster, Norman. Papers. University of Iowa Archives. Iowa City.

Ford, Guy Stanton. "A New Educational Agency." *Addresses and Proceedings of the National Educational Association, 56* (1918), pp. 207–210.

———. "The Schools As They Have Affected Government Activities." *Addresses and Proceedings of the National Educational Association, 57* (1919), pp. 538–541.

———. *On and Off Campus.* Minneapolis: The University of Minnesota Press, 1938.

"Forward." *The Public Opinion Quarterly, 1* (January 1937), pp. 3–5.

"Frank Stanton." In *Political Profiles—The Kennedy Years,* edited by Nelson Lichtenstein, p. 483. New York: Facts on File, 1976.

Friedan, Betty. *The Feminine Mystique.* New York: Dell, 1964.

Fromm, Erich. *The Sane Society.* New York: Holt, Rinehart & Winston, 1955.

Galliher, John F., and James H. Galliher. *Marginality and Dissent in Twentieth Century American Sociology: The Case of Elizabeth Briant Lee and Alfred McClung Lee.* Albany, NY: State University of New York Press, 1995.

Garber, William. "Propaganda Analysis—To What Ends?" *American Journal of Sociology, 48* (September 1942), pp. 240–245.

Gitlin, Todd. "Media Sociology: The Dominant Paradigm." *Theory and Society, 6* (September 1978), pp. 205–253.

Glander, Timothy. "The Battle for the Minds of Men: Wilbur Schramm at the University of Illinois, 1947–1953." Urbana: Archibald O. Anderson Library, University of Illinois, 1988.

Goodman, Paul. *Growing Up Absurd.* New York: Vintage, 1960.

———. "Utopian Thinking." In *Utopian Thinking and Practical Proposals.* New York: Random House, 1962.

———. "Don't Disturb the Children." *The New Republic, 148* (March 16, 1963), pp. 28–30.

———. "Sick Beside the Screen." *The New Republic, 148* (8 June 1963), pp. 28–30.

———. "The Universe of Discourse in Which They Grow Up." In *Compulsory Mis-education and the Community of Scholars.* New York: Vintage, 1964.

———. *New Reformation: Notes of a Neolithic Conservative.* New York: Random House, 1970.

———. *Speaking and Language: Defence of Poetry.* London: Willwood, 1971.

————. "The Present Plight of a Man of Letters." In *Criticism and Culture: Papers of the Midwest Modern Language Association,* edited by Sherman Paul. Iowa City: Midwest Modern Language Association, 1972.

Gould, Jack. "What TV Is Doing to Us." Reprinted booklet from *The New York Times* (24–30 June 1951).

Greenfield, Patricia. "CIA's Behavior Caper." *American Psychological Association Monitor,* 8 (December 1977), pp. 1, 10–11.

Gruber, Carol S. *Mars and Minerva: World War I and the Uses of the Higher Learning in America.* Baton Rouge, LA: Louisiana State University Press, 1975.

Guetzkow, Harold, editor. *Groups, Leadership and Men: Research in Human Relations.* Pittsburgh: Carnegie Press, 1951.

Hamlin, C. H. *The War Myth in the United States History.* New York: Vanguard, 1927.

Harrell, Thomas W., Donald E. Brown, and Wilbur Schramm. "Memory in Radio Listening." *Journal of Applied Psychology, 33* (June 1949), pp. 265–273.

Heilbut, Anthony. *Exiled in Paradise: German Refugee Artists and Intellectuals in America from the 1930's to the Present.* Boston: Beacon, 1983.

Henry, Jules. *Culture Against Man.* New York: Vintage, 1963.

Hitler, Adolf. *Mein Kampf.* Translated by Ralph Manheim. Cambridge, MA: Riverside Press, 1943.

Hoeveler, Jr., J. David. *The New Humanism: A Critique of Modern America 1900–1940.* Charlottesville: University of Virginia, 1977.

Hojem, Phyllis Meadows. *A Study of Propaganda and of the Analyses of the Institute for Propaganda Analysis, Incorporated.* Unpublished Masters Thesis, University of Colorado, 1950.

Honey, Maureen. *Creating Rosie the Riveter: Class, Gender, and Propaganda During World War II.* Amherst: University of Massachusetts Press, 1984.

Houseman, John. "Battle of Television." *Harper's Magazine, 200* (May 1950), pp. 51–59.

Hovland, Carl I., Arthur A. Lumsdaine, and Fred D. Sheffield. *Experiments on Mass Communication.* Princeton, NJ: Princeton University Press, 1949.

Hovland, Carl I., Irving L. Janis, and Harold H. Kelly. *Communication and Persuasion: Psychological Studies of Opinion Change.* New Haven: Yale University Press, 1953.

"How to Detect Propaganda." *Propaganda Analysis, 1* (November 1937), pp. 5–8.

Hubbert, Erin, and Herbert H. Rosenberg. *Opportunities for Federally Sponsored Social Science Research.* Syracuse, NY: The Maxwell Graduate School of Citizenship and Public Affairs, Syracuse University, 1951.

Hudson, Robert B. "The Illinois Years." In *Communication Research—A Half-Century Appraisal,* edited by Daniel Lerner and Lyle M. Nelson, pp. 311–316. Honolulu: University of Hawaii Press, 1977.

Huthmacher, J. Joseph. *Trial by War and Depression: 1917–1941.* Boston: Allyn & Bacon, 1973.

Institute of Communications Research. Files of the Director. University of Illinois Archives, Urbana.

Irwin, Will. *Propaganda and the News: Or What Makes You Think So?* New York: McGraw-Hill, 1936.

Ittelson, William H. "Cantril, Hadley." *International Encyclopedia of the Social Sciences,* Vol. 18, pp. 99–100. New York: Free Press, 1979.

Jahoda, Marie, Paul F. Lazarsfeld, and Hans Zeisel. *Marienthal: The Sociography of an Unemployed Community.* Chicago: Aldine-Atherton, 1971.

Jowett, Garth S., Ian C. Jarvie, and Kathryn H. Fuller. *Children and the Movies: Media Influence and the Payne Fund Controversy.* New York: Cambridge University Press, 1996.

Karier, Clarence J. *Individual, Society and Education: A History of American Educational Ideas.* Urbana: University of Illinois Press, 1986.

Karier, Clarence J., Paul C. Violas, and Joel Spring, editors. *Roots of Crisis: American Education in the Twentieth Century.* Chicago: Rand McNally, 1973.

Katz, Elihu, and Paul F. Lazarsfeld. *Personal Influence: The Part Played by People in the Flow of Mass Communications.* Glencoe, IL: Free Press, 1955.

Kimball, Bruce A. *Orators and Philosophers: The History of the Idea of Liberal Education.* New York: Teachers College Press, 1986.

Koppes, Clayton R., and Gregory D. Black. *Hollywood Goes to Goes to War: How Politics, Profits, and Propaganda Shaped World War II Movies.* New York: Free Press, 1987.

Kornhauser, William. *The Politics of Mass Society.* New York: Free Press, 1959.

Krug, Edward A. *The Shaping of the American High School, 1880–1920.* Madison: University of Wisconsin Press, 1969.

Langer, William L. "Scholarship and the Intelligence Problem." *Proceedings of the American Philosophical Society, 92* (March 1948), pp. 43–45.

Larsen, Otto N. "In Memoriam: Stuart Carter Dodd, 1900–1975." *Public Opinion Quarterly, 40* (Fall 1976), pp. 411–412.

Lasch, Christopher. "The Cultural Cold War: A Short History of the Congress for Cultural Freedom." In *Towards a New Past: Dissenting Essays in American History,* edited by Barton J. Bernstein, pp. 322–359. New York: Pantheon Books, Random House, 1968.

Lasswell, Harold D. *Propaganda Technique in the World War.* New York: Knopf, 1927.

Lasswell, Harold D., Ralph D. Casey, and Bruce Lannes Smith. *Propaganda and Promotional Activities: An Annotated Bibliography.* Minneapolis: University of Minnesota Press, 1935.

Lasswell, Harold D. *Democracy Through Public Opinion.* Menasha, WI: George Banta, 1941.

Lavine, Harold, and James Wechsler. *War Propaganda and the United States.* New Haven: Yale University Press, 1940.

Lazarsfeld, Paul F. "Radio Research and Applied Psychology." *The Journal of Applied Psychology, 23* (Spring 1939), pp. 1–7.

———. *Radio and the Printed Page.* New York: Duell Sloan and Pearce, 1940.

Lazarsfeld, Paul, and Frank Stanton, editors. *Radio Research 1941.* New York: Duell, Sloan and Pearce, 1941.

Lazarsfeld, Paul F. *Radio Research 1942–1943.* New York: Duell, Sloan and Pearce, 1944.

Lazarsfeld, Paul F., Bernard Berelson, and Hazel Gaudet. *The People's Choice: How the Voter Makes Up His Mind in a Presidential Campaign.* New York: Duell, Sloan and Pearce, 1944.

Lazarsfeld, Paul F. "Radio and International Co-operation as a Problem for Psychological Research." *Journal of Consulting Psychology, 10* (January–February 1946), pp. 51–56.

Lazarsfeld, Paul, and Frank Stanton, editors. *Communication Research 1948–1949.* New York: Duell, Sloan and Pearce, 1949.

Lazarsfeld, Paul F., and Robert Merton. "Studies in Radio and Film Propaganda." In *Social Theory and Social Structure: Toward a Codification of Theory and Research,* edited by Robert Merton, pp. 265–285. Glencoe, IL: Free Press, 1949.

Lazarsfeld, Paul F., and Genevieve Knupfer. "Communications Research and International Co-operation." in *The Science of Man in World Crisis,* edited by Ralph Linton, pp. 465–95. New York: Farrar, Straus, & Giroux, 1980.

"Lazarsfeld, Paul Felix." *The Cyclopedia of American Biography,* Vol. 59, pp. 331–332. Clifton, NJ: James T. White, 1980.

Lazarsfeld, Paul F. "An Episode in the History of Social Research: A Memoir." In *The Varied Sociology of Paul F. Lazarsfeld,* edited by Patricia Kendall, pp. 11–73. New York: Columbia University Press, 1982.

Lazarsfeld, Paul F. Papers. Columbia University Archives. New York.

Lee, Alfred McClung, and Elizabeth Briant Lee, editors. *The Fine Art of Propaganda: A Study of Father Coughlin's Speeches.* New York: Harcourt, Brace, 1939.

Lee, Alfred McClung. "Book Department." *Annals of the American Academy of Political and Social Science, 265* (September 1949), p. 174.

Lee, Alfred McClung, and Elizabeth Briant Lee. "An Influential Ghost: The Institute for Propaganda Analysis, 1936–1942." *Propaganda Review* (Winter 1988).

Leighton, Alexander H. *The Governing of Men: General Principles and Recommendations Based on Experience at a Japanese Relocation Camp.* Princeton, NJ: Princeton University Press, 1945.

———. "Personnel Utilization in Strategic Psywar Evaluation." In *A Psychological Warfare Casebook,* edited by William E. Daugherty and Morris Janowitz, pp. 214–224. Baltimore: Johns Hopkins University Press, 1958.

Lens, Sidney. *The Military Industrial Complex.* Philadelphia: Pilgrim Press and The National Catholic Reporter, 1970.

Lerner, Daniel. *Psychological Warfare Against Nazi Germany: The Sykewar Campaign, D-Day to VE-Day.* Cambridge, MA: MIT Press, 1949.

———. *The Passing of Traditional Society: Modernizing the Middle East.* Glencoe, IL: Free Press, 1958.

Lerner, Daniel, and Lyle M. Nelson, editors. *Communication Research—A Half Century Appraisal.* Honolulu: University of Hawaii Press, 1977.

Leslie, Stuart W. *The Cold War and American Science: The Military–Industrial Academic Complex at MIT and Stanford.* New York: Columbia University Press, 1993.

Lippmann, Walter. *Public Opinion* New York: Macmillan, 1927. Originally published in 1922.

Lowenthal, Leo. *An Unmastered Past: The Autobiographical Reflections of Leo Lowenthal.* Edited by Martin Jay. Berkeley, CA: University of California Press, 1987.

"Lowenthal, Leo, 1900– ." *Contemporary Authors: New Revision Series,* Vol. 5, p. 336. Detroit: Galesburg Research, 1982.

Lowery, Shearon A., and Melvin L. DeFleur. *Milestones in Mass Communication Research.* New York: Longman, 1988.

Lumley, Frederick. *The Propaganda Menace.* New York: Century, 1933.

Lynd, Robert S. *Knowledge for What? The Place of Social Science in American Culture.* Princeton, NJ: Princeton University Press, 1939.

———. "The Science of Inhuman Relations." *The New Republic* (29 August 1949), p. 22.

Lyons, Gene M. *The Uneasy Partnership: Social Science and the Federal Government in the Twentieth Century.* New York: Russell Sage, 1969.

MacDonald, Dwight. *Against the American Grain: Essays on the Effects of Mass Culture.* New York: Random House, 1962.

Marcuse, Herbert. *One Dimensional Man: Studies in the Ideology of Advanced Industrial Society.* Boston: Beacon, 1964.

Marks, Barry Allen. *The Idea of Propaganda in America.* Unpublished Ph.D. Dissertation, University of Minnesota, 1957.

Marks, John. *The Search for the "Manchurian Candidate": The CIA and Mind Control.* New York: New York Times Books, 1979.

Marquis, Donald W. "Research Planning at the Frontier of Science." *The American Psychologist, 3* (October 1948), pp. 430–438.

Martin, Everett Dean. *The Meaning of a Liberal Education.* New York: Norton, 1926.

———. "Are We Victims of Propaganda: A Debate." *The Forum, 81* (March 1929), pp. 142–145.

McDonald, J. Fred. *Television and the Red Menace: The Video Road to Vietnam.* New York: Praeger, 1985.

McDonald, John. "The War of Wits." *Fortune, 43* (March 1951), pp. 99–158.

Mead, Margaret. "Thinking Ahead." *Harvard Business Review, 36* (November/December 1958), p. 24.

Merton, Robert K. *Mass Persuasion: The Social Psychology of a War Bond Drive.* New York: Harper & Brothers, 1946.

Merton, Robert K., James S. Coleman, and Peter H. Rossi, editors. *Qualitative and Quantitative Social Research: Papers in Honor of Paul F. Lazarsfeld.* New York: Free Press, Macmillan, 1979.

Metz, Robert. *CBS: Reflections in a Bloodshot Eye.* Chicago: Playboy, 1975.

Miller, Clyde R. "Preface." *Propaganda Analysis, 1* (October 1938), pp. iii–v.

Miller, Martha. "Writers' Workshop Founder Dies at 80." *The Iowa City Press Citizen, 30* (December 1987), p. 12.

Mills, C. Wright. *The Power Elite.* New York: Oxford University Press, 1956.

———. *The Sociological Imagination.* New York: Oxford University Press, 1959.

———. "Mass Society and Liberal Education." In *Power, Politics and People: The Collected Essays of C. Wright Mills,* edited by Irving Louis Horowitz, pp. 353–373. New York: Oxford University Press, 1963.

———. "Abstracted Empiricism." In *Qualitative Analysis: Historical and Critical Essays.* Edited by Paul F. Lazarsfeld, pp. 428–440. Boston: Allyn & Bacon, 1972.

Mitchell, Maurice B. "A Forward Look at Communications." In *Britannica Book of the Year 1958,* edited by Walter Yust, pp. 49–64. Chicago: Encyclopedia Britannica, 1958.

Mitgang, Herbert. *Dangerous Dossiers: Exposing the Secret War Against America's Greatest Writers.* New York: Fine, 1988.

Mock, James R., and Cedric Larson. *Words That Won the War: The Story of the Committee on Public Information, 1917–1919.* Princeton, NJ: Princeton University Press, 1939.

Molnar, Thomas. *The Decline of the Intellectual.* Cleveland: World, 1961.

Morrison, David E. "Kultur and Culture: The Case of Theodor W. Adorno and Paul F. Lazarsfeld." *Social Research, 45* (Summer 1978), pp. 331–355.

———. "The Beginning of Modern Mass Communication Research." *European Journal of Sociology, 19* (1978), pp. 347–359.

Mumford, Lewis. *The Conduct of Life.* New York: Harcourt, Brace, 1951.

———. *The Myth of the Machine: The Pentagon of Power.* New York: Harcourt Brace Jovanovich, 1970.

Mundt, Karl E. "Need for a National Freedom Academy." In *Propaganda and the Cold War,* edited by John Boardman Whitton, pp. 75–84. Washington, DC: Public Affairs Press, 1963.

National Education Association. *Report of the Committee on Propaganda in the Schools,* presented at the Atlanta Meeting of the National Education Association, July 1929.

Nelson, Lyle M. "The Stanford Years." In *Communication Research—A Half Century Appraisal,* edited by Daniel Lerner and Lyle M. Nelson, pp. 317–324. Honolulu: University of Hawaii Press, 1977.

Odegard, Peter. "Review of *Education Against Propaganda,* edited by Elmer Ellis." *Public Opinion Quarterly, 1* (October 1937), pp. 144–146.

Office of War Information. Bureau of Special Services and Bureau of Intelligence. University of Illinois Main Library. Urbana.

Ogden, August Raymond. *The Dies Committee: A Study of the Special House Committee For the Investigation of Un-American Activities, 1938–1944.* Washington, DC: The Catholic University Press, 1945.

Olson, Philip, editor. *America as a Mass Society: Changing Community and Identity.* New York: Free Press of Glencoe, 1963.

Packard, Vance. *The Hidden Persuaders.* New York: McKay, 1957.

Paisley, William. "Communication in the Communication Sciences." In *Progress in Communication Sciences,* Vol. 5, edited by Brenda Dervin and Melvin J. Voight, pp. 1–43. Norwood, NJ: Ablex, 1984.

Peters, John Durham. *Reconstructing Mass Communication Theory.* Ph.D. Dissertation, Stanford University, 1986.

Phenix, Philip H. "Education and Mass Communications." *Phi Delta Kappan, 43* (October 1961), pp. 15–19.

"Plan Adds 'Civil Education' to the Basics of Schooling." *The New York Times* (14 April 1997), p. B8.

Pollard, John A. "Words Are Cheaper Than Blood." *Public Opinion Quarterly, 9* (Fall 1945), pp. 283–312.

Ponsonby, Arthur. *Falsehoods in War-Time.* New York: Dutton, 1928.

"Postcards From Heaven." *Newsweek, 38* (13 August 1951), pp. 20–21.

Postman, Neil. *Teaching as a Conserving Activity.* New York: Dell, 1979.

Preston, Jr., William. *Aliens and Dissenters: Federal Suppression of Radicals, 1903–1933.* New York: Harper & Row, 1963.

Propaganda: How to Recognize It and Deal With It. New York: Institute For Propaganda Analysis, 1938.

"Reading List on Propaganda." *The World Tomorrow, 10* (April 1927), p. 183.

Repplier, Agnes. "A Good Word Gone Wrong." *The Independent and the Weekly Review, 107* (7 October 1921), p. 5.

Riegel, O. W. *Mobilization for Chaos: The Story of the New Propaganda.* New Haven: Yale University Press.

Riesman, David. "Introduction." In *The Passing of Traditional Society,* by David Lerner, pp. 1–15. Glencoe, IL: Free Press, 1958.

Riley, John W., and Wilbur Schramm. *The Reds Take a City: The Communist Occupation of Seoul.* New Brunswick, NJ: Rutgers University Press, 1951.

———. "Communication in the Sovietized State, as Demonstrated in Korea." *American Sociological Review, 16* (December 1951), pp. 757–766.

Riley, J. W., Wilbur Schramm, and F. W. Williams. "Flight from Communism: A Report on Korean Refugees." *Public Opinion Quarterly, 15* (Summer 1951), pp. 274–284.

Robbins, Natalie. *Alien Ink: The FBI's War on Freedom of Expression.* New Brunswick, NJ: Rutgers University Press, 1992.

Rockefeller Foundation. Documents Re. A Study of Mass Communication. State Historical Society Archives of Wisconsin. Division of Manuscripts, Madison.

Rogers, Everett M. Foreword to *Milestones in Mass Communication Research,* by Shearon A. Lowery and Melvin L. DeFleur, pp. vii–xv. New York: Longman, 1988.

Rogers, Everett M. *A History of Communication Study: A Biographical Approach.* New York: Free Press, 1994.

Roosevelt, Kermit. *War Report of the O.S.S.* New York: Walker, 1976.

Rosenberg, Bernard, and David Manning White, editors. *Mass Culture: The Popular Arts in America.* Glencoe, IL: Free Press, 1957.

Rosenberg, Howard L. *Atomic Soldiers: American Victims of Nuclear Experiments.* Boston: Beacon, 1980.

Roth, Lois W., and Richard T. Arndt. "Information, Culture, and Public Diplomacy: Searching for an American Style of Propaganda." In *The Press and the State: Sociohistorical and Contemporary Studies,* edited by Walter M. Brasch and Dana R. Ulloth, pp. 723–745. New York: University Press of America, 1986.

Rowland, Willard J. *The Politics of TV Violence: The Policy Uses of Communication Research.* Beverly Hills, CA: Sage, 1983.

Saintsbury, E. T. "Memoirs of a Four-Minute Man." *The American Mercury, 10* (March 1927), pp. 284–291.

Salmon, Lucy Maynard. *The Newspaper and Authority.* New York: Oxford University Press, 1923.

Sargent, Porter. *Between Two Wars: The Failure of Education, 1920–1940.* Boston: Porter Sargent, 1945.

Saxon, Wolfgang. "O. W. Riegel, 94, Early Expert on Propaganda." *The New York Times* (26 August 1997), p. D21.

Schiller, Herbert I. *Mass Communications and the American Empire.* Boston: Beacon, 1971.

———. *Culture, Inc.: The Corporate Takeover of Public Expression.* New York: Oxford University Press, 1989.

Schramm, Elizabeth. "Early Years." In *Communication Research: A Half Century Appraisal,* edited by Daniel Lerner and Lyle M. Nelson, pp. 297–301. Honolulu: University of Hawaii Press, 1977.

Schramm, Wilbur L. *Studies in the Longer Narrative Verse of America, 1775–1860.* Ph.D. Dissertation, University of Iowa, 1932.

———. *Approaches to a Science of English Verse.* Iowa City: University of Iowa, 1935.

———. *The Story Workshop.* Boston: Little, Brown, 1938.

———. "Imaginative Writing." In *Literary Scholarship: Its Aims and Methods,* edited by Norman Foerster, John C. McGalliard, Rene Wellek, Austin Warren, and Wilbur Schramm, pp. 177–213. Chapel Hill: University of North Carolina Press, 1941.

———. *Windwagon Smith and Other Yarns.* New York: Harcourt, Brace, 1947.

———, editor. *Mass Communications.* Urbana: University of Illinois Press, 1949.

———, editor. *The Process and Effects of Mass Communications.* Urbana: University of Illinois Press, 1954.

Schramm, Wilbur, and Hideya Kumata. *Four Working Papers on Propaganda Theory.* Urbana: Institute of Communications Research, University of Illinois, 1955.

Schramm, Wilbur, editor. *The Impact of Educational Television.* Urbana: University of Illinois Press, 1960.

Schramm, Wilbur, Jack Lyle, and Edwin B. Parker. *Television in the Lives of Our Children.* Palo Alto, CA: Stanford University Press, 1961.

Schramm, Wilbur, editor. *Educational Television: The Next Ten Years.* Stanford, CA: Institute for Communications Research, Stanford University, 1962.

———. *Programed Instruction: Today and Tomorrow.* Fund for the Advancement of Education, 1962.

———. *What Is Programed Instruction? An Introduction for the Layman.* Palo Alto, CA: Institute for Communication Research, Stanford University, 1964.

———. *The Audiences of Educational Television: A Report to NET.* Stanford, CA: Institute for Communications Research, Stanford University, 1967.

Schramm, Wilbur, and Lyle M. Nelson. *The Financing of Public Television.* Aspen, CO: Institute for Humanistic Studies and the Academy for Educational Development, 1972.

Schramm, Wilbur. "The Unique Perspective of Communication: A Retrospective View." *Journal of Communications, 33* (Summer 1983), pp. 6–17.

———. "The Beginnings of Communication Study in the United States." In *The Media Revolution in America and in Western Europe,* edited by Everett M. Rogers and Francis Balle, pp. 200–211. Norwood, NJ: Ablex, 1985.

———. *The Beginnings of Communication Study in America: A Personal Memoir,* edited by Steven H. Chaffe and Everett Rogers. Thousand Oaks, CA: Sage, 1997.

Schramm, Wilbur. Vertical File. University of Iowa Archives, Iowa City.

Schramm, Wilbur. Papers. National Archives. Record Group 208. OWI, OFF. Subject File, 1942. E-7. Suitland, MD.

Schrecker, Ellen. "Academic Freedom and the Cold War." *The Antioch Review, 38* (Summer 1980), pp. 313–327.

Scott, John. "Non-Governmental Agencies Engaged in Cold War Propaganda Operations." In *A Psychological Warfare Casebook,* edited by William E. Daugherty and Morris Janowitz, pp. 153–157. Baltimore: Johns Hopkins University Press, 1958.

Severo, Richard. "Vance Packard, 82, Challenger of Consumerism, Dies." *The New York Times* (13 December 1996), p. B16.

Shils, Edward. "The Theory of a Mass Society." *Diogenes* (Fall 1962), pp. 45–66.

Sills, David L. "Bernard Berelson: Behavioral Scientist." *Journal of the History of the Behavioral Sciences, 17* (July 1981), pp. 305–311.

Sills, David. "Paul F. Lazarsfeld." *International Encyclopedia of the Social Sciences,* Vol. 18, pp. 411–427. New York: Free Press, 1979.

Simpson, Christopher. *Blowback: America's Recruitment of Nazis and Its Effects on the Cold War.* New York: Weidenfeld and Nicolson, 1988.

———. *Science of Coercion: Communication Research & Psychological Warfare, 1945–1960.* New York: Oxford University Press, 1994.

Soley, Lawrence C. *Radio Warfare: OSS and CIA Subversive Propaganda.* New York: Praeger, 1989.

Sorenson, Gail Paulus. "Indoctrination and the Purposes of American Education: A 1930's Debate." *Issues in Education, 3* (Fall 1985), pp. 79–98.

Spiegleman, Bob. "A Tale of Two Memos." *Covert Action Information Bulletin, 31* (Winter 1989), pp. 71–74.

Spring, Joel. *Images of American Life: A History of Ideological Management in Schools, Movies, Radio, and Television.* Albany: State University of New York Press, 1992.

Sproule, J. Michael. "The Institute for Propaganda Analysis: Public Education in Argumentation, 1937–1942." In *Argument in Transition: Proceedings of the Third Summer Conference on Argumentation,* edited by David Zarefsky, Malcolm O. Sillars, and Jack Rhodes, pp. 486–499. Annandale, VA: Speech Communication Association, 1983.

———. "Propaganda Studies in American Social Science: The Rise and Fall of the Critical Paradigm." *Quarterly Journal of Speech, 73* (1987), pp. 60–78.

———. "Progressive Critics and the Magic Bullet Myth." *Critical Studies in Mass Communications, 6* (1989), pp. 225–246.

———. "Propaganda and American Ideological Critique." *Communication Yearbook, 4* (1991), pp. 211–238.

Stanton, Frank Nicholas. *A Critique of Present Methods and a New Plan for Studying Radio Listening Behavior.* Ph.D. Dissertation, Ohio State University, 1935.

Stauber, John, and Sheldon Rampton. *Toxic Sludge Is Good For You: Lies, Damn Lies, and the Public Relations Industry.* Monroe, ME: Common Courage Press, 1995.

Steel, Ronald. *Walter Lippmann and the American Century.* Boston: Little, Brown, 1980.

Steele, Richard W. "Preparing the Public for War: Efforts to Establish a National Propaganda Agency, 1940–1941." *The American Historical Review, 75* (October 1970), pp. 1640–1653.

Stein, Maurice R. *The Eclipse of the Community: An Interpretation of American Studies.* New York: Harper & Row, 1960.

Stein, Maurice R., Arthur J. Vidich, and David Manning White, editors. *Identity and Anxiety: Survival of the Person in Mass Society.* Glencoe, IL: Free Press, 1960.

Steinbeck, John. "How to Tell Good Guys from Bad Guys." *The Reporter, 12* (10 March 1955), pp. 42–45.

Steiner, Gary A. *The People Look At Television: A Study of Attitudes.* New York: Knopf, 1963.

Stern, Sol. "A Short Account of International Student Politics & the Cold War with Particular Reference to the NSA, CIA, Etc." *Ramparts, 5* (March 1967), pp. 29–39.

Stoddard, George D. *The Pursuit of Education: An Autobiography.* New York: Vantage, 1981.

Stoehr, Taylor. *Format and Anxiety: Paul Goodman Critiques the Mass Media.* Brooklyn, NY: Autonomedia, 1995.

Stone, Charles. "UI Wouldn't Have Objected to CIA-Sponsored Projects." *The Daily Illini* (11 November 1977), p. 3.

Strong, Jr., Edward K. "Control of Propaganda as a Psychological Problem." *The Scientific Monthly, 14* (March 1922), pp. 234–252.

Towers, Wayne M. "Lazarsfeld and Adorno in the United States: A Case Study in Theoretical Orientations." In *Communication Yearbook I,* edited by Brent D. Ruben, pp. 1933–1945. New Brunswick, NJ: Transaction, 1977.

United States Information Agency. "Prestige, Personnel Influence, and Opinion." In *The Process and Effects of Mass Communications,* edited by Wilbur Schramm, pp. 402–410. Urbana: University of Illinois Press, 1954.

U.S. Bureau of the Census. *Historical Statistics of the United States: Colonial Times to 1970—Part I.* Washington, DC: U.S. Government Printing Office, 1975.

U.S. Bureau of the Census. *Historical Statistics of the United States: Colonial Times to 1970—Part II.* Washington, DC: U.S. Government Printing Office, 1975.

U.S. Congress, House Committee on Foreign Affairs. *United States Information and Educational Exchange Act of 1947.* 80th Cong. Washington, DC: U.S. Government Printing Office, 1947.

U.S. Congress. *National Security Act of 1947—Public Law 253.* 80th Cong. Washington, DC: U.S. Government Printing Office, 1966.

U.S. Congress, Senate Select Committee to Study Governmental Operations with Respect to Intelligence Activities. *Foreign and Military Intelligence—Book I.* 94th Cong. Washington, DC: U.S. Government Printing Office, 1976.

U.S. Congress, Senate Select Committee to Study Governmental Operations with Respect to Intelligence Activities. *Supplementary Reports on Intelligence Activities, Book VI.* 94th Cong. Washington, DC: U.S. Government Printing Office, 1976.

U.S. Congress, Senate Joint Hearing Before the Select Committee on Intelligence and the Subcommittee on Health and Scientific Research of the Committee on Human Resources. *Project MKULTRA, The CIA's Program of Research in Behavioral Modification.* 95th Cong., 1st session (3 August 1977). Washington, DC: U.S. Government Printing Office, 1977.

University of Illinois. Registrar's Report Comparative Summary of Students: Year 1939–1940 and Year 1940–41. University of Illinois Archives, Urbana.

University of Illinois. *Transactions of the Board of Trustees.* Urbana: University of Illinois Press, 1954.

Van Nostrand, A. D. *Fundable Knowledge: The Marketing of Defense Technology.* Mahwah, NJ: Lawrence Erlbaum Associates, 1997.

Vaughn, Stephen. *Holding Fast the Inner Lines: Democracy, Nationalism, and the Committee on Public Information.* Chapel Hill: University of North Carolina Press, 1980.

Vidich, Arthur, and Joseph Bensman, *Small Town in Mass Society.* Princeton, NJ: Princeton University Press, 1958.

Viereck, George Sylvester. *Spreading Germs of Hate.* New York: Horace Liveright, Inc., 1930.

Violas, Paul C. "The Indoctrination Debate and the Great Depression." In *Roots of Crisis: American Education in the Twentieth Century,* edited by Clarence J. Karier, Paul C. Violas, and Joel Spring (pp. 148–162). Chicago: Rand McNally, 1973.

Walter, E. V. "Mass Society: The Late Stages of an Idea." *Social Research, 31* (December 1964), pp. 391–410.

Weinberg, Sydney Stahl. *Wartime Propaganda in a Democracy: America's Twentieth-Century Information Agencies.* Ph.D. Dissertation, Columbia University, 1969.

Weinstein, Harvey. *Psychiatry and the CIA: Victims of Mind Control.* Washington, DC: American Psychiatric Press, 1990.

Wilbers, Steve. *The Iowa Writers' Workshop: Origins, Emergence & Growth.* Iowa City: University of Iowa Press, 1980.

"Wilbur Schramm." *Illiniweek, 7* (January 1988), p. 5.

"Wilbur Schramm, Wrote Many Works on Communications." *The New York Times* (1 January 1988), p. 10.

Willey, Malcolm M. "Communication Agencies and the Volume of Propaganda." *The Annals of the American Academy of Political and Social Science, 179* (May 1935), pp. 194–200.

Winkler, Allan M. *The Politics of Propaganda: The Office of War Information, 1942–1945.* New Haven: Yale University Press, 1978.

Winks, Robin W. *Cloak and Gown: Scholars in the Secret War, 1939–1961.* New York: Quill William Morrow, 1987.

Wisconsin Teachers Association. *Report of the Committee on Propaganda in Schools,* 1929 and 1930.

Workshop Correspondence with Steve Wilbers. University of Iowa Archives, Iowa City.

"Worldwide Propaganda Network Built by the CIA." *The New York Times* (26 December 1977), pp. 1, 37.

Young, Kimball, and Raymond D. Lawrence. "Bibliography on Censorship and Propaganda." *Journalism Series,* Vol 1. Eugene: University of Oregon Publications, 1928.

Zeisel, Hans. "The Vienna Years." In *Qualitative and Quantitative Social Research: Papers in Honor of Paul F. Lazarsfeld,* edited by Robert K. Merton, James S. Coleman, and Peter H. Rossi, pp. 10–15. New York: Free Press, Macmillan, 1979.

Zinn, Howard. *A People's History of the United States.* New York: Harper & Row, 1980.

Index